NEW DIRECTIONS IN POST-KEYNESIAN ECONOMICS

NEW DIRECTIONS IN MODERN ECONOMICS SERIES
Series Editor: Malcolm C. Sawyer, Professor of Economics,
University of York

New Directions in Modern Economics presents a challenge to
orthodox economic thinking. It focuses on new ideas
emanating from radical traditions including post-Keynesian,
Kaleckian, neo-Ricardian and Marxian. The books in the
series do not adhere rigidly to any single school of thought but
share in common an attempt to present a positive alternative
to the conventional wisdom.

The main emphasis of the series is on the development and
application of new ideas to current problems in economic
theory and economic policy. It will include new original
contributions to theory, overviews of work in the radical
tradition and the evaluation of alternative economic policies.
Some books will be monographs whilst others will be suitable
for adoption as texts. The series will highlight theoretical and
policy issues common to all modern economies and is designed
to appeal to economists throughout the world regardless of
their country of origin.

NEW DIRECTIONS IN POST-KEYNESIAN ECONOMICS

Edited by
JOHN PHEBY
Professor of Economics
Department of Financial Services
Birmingham Polytechnic

EDWARD ELGAR

Published by
Edward Elgar Publishing Limited
Gower House
Croft Road
Aldershot
Hants GU11 3HR
England

Gower Publishing Company
Old Post Road
Brookfield
Vermont 05036
USA

ISBN 1 85278 013 4

Printed and bound in Great Britain at
The Camelot Press Ltd, Southampton

Contents

List of Contributors

Stephan Böhm, Lecturer in Economics, University of Graz, Austria.

Alexander Dow, Professor and Head of Economics Department, Glasgow College of Technology.

Sheila Dow, Reader in Economics, University of Stirling.

Peter Earl, Senior Lecturer in Economics, University of Tasmania, Australia.

John Foster, Senior Lecturer in Economics, University of Glasgow.

Omar Hamouda, Associate Professor of Economics, York University, Toronto.

Geoff Harcourt, Fellow in Economics, Jesus College, University of Cambridge.

Geoff Hodgson, Reader in Economics, Newcastle upon Tyne Polytechnic.

Neil Kay, Professor of Economics, Strathclyde University.

John Pheby, Professor of Economics, Birmingham Polytechnic.

G. L. S. Shackle, Emeritus Professor of Economics, University of Liverpool.

John Smithin, Associate Professor of Economics, York University, Toronto.

Lorie Tarshis, Professor of Economics, York University, Toronto.

Acknowledgements

I would like to thank Basil Blackwell Limited for allowing me to reprint Chapter 1 of this collection and also the individual authors who were extremely helpful in the preparation of the manuscript. Finally a special word of thanks is due to Edward Elgar whose advice, and cajoling, proved invaluable.

J.P.

Introduction

The papers in this book were originally presented at the New Directions in Post-Keynesian Economics conference which took place at Great Malvern in August 1987. The conference brought together a group of economists to consider the past achievements and future prospects of post-Keynesianism.

The first three chapters are written by Geoff Harcourt, G. L. S. Shackle and Lorie Tarshis, all prominent post-Keynesians. Collectively, they provide us with a clear indication of many of the traditional concerns of post-Keynesians.

The first chapter by Omar Hamouda and Geoff Harcourt is an excellent overview. It considers the different strands of post-Keynesianism and questions whether an integrated and coherent research tradition can emerge. After clarifying what post-Keynesianism means to different groups, the authors conclude that attempts to integrate the three identifiable strands are doomed to failure.

The next two chapters are contributed by Lorie Tarshis and G. L. S. Shackle. Tarshis provides an interesting consideration of Keynes's notion of the entrepreneurial economy and the co-operative economy. Some intriguing issues are raised. For example, Tarshis notes similarities between Keynes's views and those in Weitzmann's *Share Economy*. G. L. S. Shackle's chapter is a particularly helpful reminder of his distinctive interpretation of Keynes's masterpiece. He emphasizes the methodological and epistemological underpinning of Keynes's views. This proves very appropriate as his perspective serves as the basis for many of the chapters that follow.

Stephan Böhm's chapter investigates the subjectivist elements in Austrian and post-Keynesian thinking. This is an original and scholarly chapter that does much to clarify the notion of subjectivism. Böhm indicates the usefulness, for post-Keynesians of adopting subjectivism. He points out how Shackle and Lachmann perceived a strain of subjectivism in Keynes's own methodological writings. However, in terms of policy prescriptions Böhm argues that post-Keynesians will differ from that other noted group of subjectivists – the Austrians.

Geoff Hodgson's contribution also explicitly considers how post-Keynesians can benefit from linkages with other research traditions. He critically surveys some of the post-Keynesian strands and finds them wanting in certain respects. He argues that some, but by no means all, of these difficulties could be aided by incorporating a more explicitly institutionalist framework. Although the emphasis of Shackle and other post-Keynesians on uncertainty and indeterminacy is a useful aspect of their work it can leave them open to the charge of nihilism. However, by taking on board notions such as habits and routines this charge can be met more convincingly.

John Foster's chapter continues in an institutionalist vein. He argues convincingly that Keynes's *General Theory* is not incompatible with modern non-Darwinian concepts of evolutionary change. Such modern interpretations place more emphasis on creativity as a motive force for evolutionary development. The problem with the *General Theory* is that it was cast in the short run. Consequently its potential for being considered in an evolutionary context is easily missed. The chapter by Shackle is cited as being particularly helpful in this respect.

The chapter by Alexander and Sheila Dow starts from the familiar theme of endogeneity of the money supply. They argue that Keynes's notion of liquidity preference has been relatively neglected. Their central contention is that without explicitly considering the notion of liquidity preference 'it is hard to understand the financial developments which so powerfully dominate cyclical acitvity'. Indeed the detailed analysis undertaken in this chapter persuasively argues that Keynes's notion of liquidity preference, suitably modified and extended, forms an integral and useful part in rendering post-Keynesian monetary theory a more robust vehicle for analysis. Peter Earl's contribution also seeks to extend post-Keynesian monetary theory. He considers psychological and behavioural economics literature to be particularly relevant in an era of deregulation of money markets in which the role of information technology has become more important. He also believes that the charge of nihilism levelled at Shackle can be countered by adopting the appropriate behavioural assumptions.

The contribution by Neil Kay seeks linkages with the work of Herbert Simon in the context of industrial economics. The role of bounded rationality is considered as a means of making decisions under conditions of uncertainty. Kay finds that certain post-Keynesian concerns, although primarily macroeconomic, are, reflected in the new industrial economics.

Finally, John Smithin provides us with a welcome addition to the increasing number of scholars who have taken issue with so-called Keynesian fine-tuning fiscal policy as being an accurate reflection of Keynes's actual views on macroeonomic policy. Smithin illustrates clearly how Keynes was careful to distinguish between the consumption and investment aspects of public expenditure. From this, interesting interpretational and policy implications are drawn.

One of the directions in which post-Keynesians may wish to travel has been highlighted in this volume. It has become increasingly doubtful whether post-Keynesianism alone can cope with the increasing diversity and challenge of contemporary theoretical and policy issues. Consequently a desire and willingness to draw upon the insights provided by alternative perspectives is a route that is as necessary to take as it is worthwhile.

John Pheby
January 1989

1. Post-Keynesianism: From Criticism to Coherence?

O. F. Hamouda and G. C. Harcourt

INTRODUCTION

There have been several review and/or interpretative articles written on post-Keynesianism and post-Keynesian economics in the last dozen years or so: Harris (1975), Eichner and Kregel (1975), Shapiro (1977), Davidson (1980, 1981), Rowthorn (1974, 1981), Harcourt (1982c), Cohen and Cohen (1983), Groenewegen (1986), Amedeo and Dutt (1986). The American Economic Association devoted a session to the topic at its 1979 meeting in Atlanta, Georgia (see Tarshis, 1980; Yellen, 1980; Crotty, 1980; Kenyon, 1980; and Harcourt, 1980). There have also been several volumes: Kregel's *Reconstruction of Political Economy*, Kregel (1973, 1975); Harris (1978); Eichner (1979) (which reprints a series of articles on aspects of post-Keynesianism from *Challenge*); Nell (1980); Walsh and Gram (1980); Blatt (1983); Broome (1983); Lichtenstein (1983); Mainwaring (1983); Arestis and Skouras (1985) (which reprints a number of the *Thames Papers in Political Economy* that are concerned with post-Keynesian economics); and Eichner (1985) (which previews a much longer work on post-Keynesians and institutionalists which Eichner is preparing). Marglin recently published a major book (Marglin, 1984b) which attempts to synthesize some important strands in post-Keynesian and Marxian theory in so far as they relate to the problems of growth, distribution and prices (see also Bhadhuri, 1986, which synthesizes major macroeconomic

1

strands in Marx, Keynes and Kalecki; and Jarsulic, 1987). But, judging from the ongoing reactions in the profession (see, for example, Hahn, 1982, 1984; Solow, 1984, pp. 137–8) *exactly* what post-Keynesianism is about is still unclear in the minds of many. Post-Keynesians have not succeeded in getting their message through, partly because of the difficult and controversial economic issues upon which they have embarked, partly because of the diversity of theories which they have generated and partly because of the ideological suspicions of much of the profession today. Sometimes also the proposed theories conflict with one another (see, for example, Eatwell, 1983, and Kregel, 1983b, in the special Joan Robinson memorial issue of the *Cambridge Journal of Economics*.

Post-Keynesian economics is thus a portmanteau term which contains the work of a heterogeneous group of economists who nevertheless are united not only by their dislike of mainstream neoclassical theory and the IS/LM general equilibrium versions of 'Keynesian' theory but also by their attempts to provide coherent alternative approaches to economic analysis. (They are not too fond either of the developments of Keynesian theory associated with Clower and Leijonhufvud, on the one hand (see, for example, Chick, 1978) and the disequilibrium theories of the French economists on the other.) We say 'approaches' because we may identify several strands which differ from each other both with regard to method and with regard to the characteristics of the economy which are included in their models. To understand these differences it is helpful, first, to examine the different routes that came out of (or were discerned as coming out of) classical political economy.

ROUTES FROM CLASSICAL POLITICAL ECONOMY[2]

The first route leads to Marshall, who directly influenced Keynes and those post-Keynesians who start from the *Treatise* and the *General Theory*. Sidney Weintraub, Paul Davidson and (to a lesser extent) Kregel and Minsky. The second route leads to Marx. It contains the approach that was revived by Sraffa to which Keynes's contribution of effective demand recently has been added, principally in the work of Garegnani[3] (1976; 1978, 1979; 1983a, 1983b), Krishna Bharadwaj (1978a, 1978b, 1983), Eatwell (1979, 1983), Milgate (1982, 1983) and Pasinetti (1962, 1974, 1981). Dobb and Meek, who played uniquely important roles in keeping Marxian economics afloat in the UK from the 1920s to the 1950s, were equally important in the task of relating Sraffa's contributions to classical and Marxian political economy in the 1960s and 1970s (see Dobb, 1970; 1973, and Meek, 1961, 1967; 1973, 1977). The third route also goes through Marx and then comes through Kalecki's adaptation of Marx's reproduction schemes in order to tackle the realization problem, to Joan Robinson and her followers. (Towards the end of her life, Joan Robinson became sceptical of any attempt to provide an alternative 'complete theory'. She considered this 'would be only another box of tricks' (Robinson, 1979, vol. 5, p. 119). [4]

As well as these major groups there are some outstanding individual figures, who defy classification within any one group or strand. The most notable is Kaldor. He made immense contributions (see Kaldor, 1960, 1961, 1978), through his so-called Keynesian theory of distribution (Kaldor, 1955–6, 1957, 1959, 1961), in which the different values of the saving propensities of profit-receivers and wage-earners play a vital role; through his theories of growth; through his models of the development of the world economy, in which he emphasizes Allyn Young's insights concerning dynamic increasing returns and cumulative causation; and through his imaginative and innovative contributions to policy debates, often as an advisor to governments. (His critique of Keynes's system with regard to the endogeneity of money (see, for example, Kaldor, 1983, Kaldor and Trevithick, 1981), whereby the causal arrow of the quantity theory of money is reversed so that 'the money supply is seen as a function of nominal income rather than the other way around' (Rousseas, 1986, p. ix), has found a sympathetic hearer in Basil Moore (1979) in the USA (see also Weintraub, 1978b, ch. 1, Rousseas, 1986, and, for reasons for the surprising neglect of money in much Cambridge macroeconomics after Keynes, Kregel, 1985a). Next, there are the contributions of Goodwin and Pasinetti. These span at least two of the three strands. G.L.S. Shackle also is an important influence on both strand one and strand three (see, for example, Shackle, 1973; Hamouda, 1987; and Harcourt 1981b). Finally, Godley and his colleagues in the Department of Applied Economics at Cambridge are in the tradition of Keynes's theory of effective demand but they depart from Keynes's emphasis on flow equilibrium in order to emphasize stock equilibrium (see Godley and Cripps, 1983, and Godley 1983).

FROM CLASSICAL POLITICAL ECONOMY THROUGH MARSHALL TO KEYNES

The core of classical economics, that which is now called the surplus approach (see Garegnani, 1984), implies that theories of value and distribution need to be related to the ability of the economy to produce a surplus over and above the necessities of production used up in the periodic process of production. How the surplus is created, extracted, distributed and used in the capitalist system as analyzed by the classical political economists, and especially by Marx, derives from the ability of the capitalist class to make the wage-earning class work longer than they need in order to produce their own necessaries. A theory of value was required to measure the surplus so that its distribution and composition could be analyzed at a point in time and its size compared over time. A separate theory was needed to explain the level of the wage (or alternatively, of the rate of profits), so that a given value could be introduced into the 'core' in order to determine the pattern of relative prices and the other distributive variable in a system of free competition. The prices themselves – classical natural prices or Marxian prices of production – were associated with the capacity of the system to reproduce itself. The principal object of economic analysis was to explain the characteristics of the long-period position of the economy, the natural prices of commodities and the natural rates of wages, profits and rents, as determined by dominant, persistent forces.

Natural prices are regarded as centres of gravitation; it is argued that they are determined by forces which are largely separate from the demand and supply factors which determine market prices; and that market prices, whenever their values depart from the values of natural prices, tend to revert to the latter or, at least, to fluctuate around them. The classical economists devoted many passages to the analysis of these processes. However, only in recent years have modern scholars returned to these questions and analyzed the conditions under which convergence is likely to occur or not[5] (see, for example, Medio, 1978; Steedman, 1984; Semmler, 1984).

The general price level was then 'explained' by the quantity theory of money.[6] Crises and cycles were thought of as short-run, on the whole monetary deviations around the central long-period position. Theories of value and distribution, on the one hand, and of money, cycles and crisis, on the other, belonged in separate volumes. Money was a veil over the real workings of the economy in which, usually, Say's law implied that a general glut of commodities could not occur in the long-period position. There was not, therefore, any need for a separate theory of the *overall* level of output. Garegnani (1985; 1986) has argued recently that for the classical economists other than Say and his followers, far from it being the case that supply creates its own demand it was the other way around, as far as labour and capital are concerned: the supply of labour and of capital tends to respond over time to the demand for them. And while free competition as understood by the classical political economists tends to determine the level of the natural wage, this would only occur within an upper and lower limit which were themselves determined by a complex set of social forces (see, also, Schefold, 1985, for an elaboration of these themes and of why the classical system of prices and distribution, as set forth, for example, in Sraffa, 1960, may not be subsumed as a special case of neoclassical general equilibrium theory as Hahn, 1982, for example, claimed).

Marshall preserved the dichotomy between value and distribution on the one hand and money on the other, but emasculated value theory by explaining long-period normal prices in terms of the forces of supply and demand (see Bharadwaj, 1978).[7] Though in the text of the *Principles* he used only partial equilibrium analysis, in the appendices he explicitly sketched a general equilibrium model in which *all* prices *and* quantities were determined simultaneously. The normal position of the economy exhibited Say's law, and the theories of money, of the general price level, and of fluctuations and crises were also to be in the second volume. There, had it ever been fully written out (see Keynes, 1972, vol. X, pp. 191–5), we would find an account of causes of deviations from normal positions and of how money management could be used to minimize deviations from a given position and to guide the economy with a minimum of disruption from one long-period position to another, when tastes and/or technical conditions changed. The classical concept of the surplus disappeared, prices no longer reflected reproduction but became indices of scarcity which reflected the subjective factors that underlay supply and demand functions.[8] Prices *and* quantities were determined together, the general price level was explained by the quantity of money.

Keynes inherited this way of seeing and modelling the world and used it to good effect in the *Tract* and, he thought, in the *Treatise*. But in setting up his fundamental equations in the *Treatise* he inadvertently provided a rival theory to the quantity theory, one of sectorial price levels, in which the money-wage level (strictly speaking, normal earnings per unit of output) and the profit margin (as reflected in windfall profits per unit of output) were the main determinants of price levels. The realization that he had emancipated himself from the quantity theory liberated him to write the *General Theory* (see Kahn, 1984). There, he also refuted the main tenet of neoclassical economics (as it had come down to him from Marshall), Say's Law – the *sine qua non* for the quantity theory to hold. In the *General Theory* itself, however, he retained the Marshallian supply and demand theory of prices. Nevertheless his concepts of aggregate demand and supply, his dichotomy whereby investment, unlike consumption, is not constrained by current income and is predominantly determined by expected profitability, allowed him to develop a theory of underemployment equilibrium. The labour market could remain uncleared when the product market cleared because the unemployed had no effective means to signal entrepreneurs that it would be profitable to employ them. Indeed, even if they could signal, it still would not be possible to employ them because there was no mechanism (such as there was thought to be in neoclassical theory, through the rate of interest) to ensure that investment could be such as to absorb full employment saving.

STRAND 1

The implications of the *Treatise* and the *General Theory* were the base on which the American post-Keynesians built. They stressed uncertainty, the necessary integration of money from the start of analysis of the workings of the economy, the central position of the money-wage as both the major determinant of the price level and of the stability (or instability) of the economy, and the stock-flow interrelationship of the process of capital accumulation. Thus Weintraub (see, for example, Weintraub, 1958) took what we would now call the microeconomic foundations of the aggregate supply function as his base (see Kregel, 1985b) and developed a macro theory of distribution as well as of output and employment.

Lorie Tarshis was independently developing a macro theory of distribution to integrate with the theory of effective demand of the *General Theory* and the microeconomic foundations emanating from both Richard Kahn's work on 'The Economics of the Short Period' (Kahn, 1929) and Joan Robinson's *Economics of Imperfect Competition* (Robinson, 1933). Tarshis started this work as a doctoral dissertation, 'The Determination of Labour Income' (Tarshis, 1939), in Cambridge in the mid-1930s. It was essentially an independently discovered version of Kalecki's macro theory of distribution and it contained considerably more empirical work. Tarshis was influenced by Gardiner Means and others then working on mark-up pricing. He included these ideas in his theoretical framework, looking to the relationship between average and marginal labour costs and the gap between price and cost as the clues to distribution. Tarshis has considerably developed this particular framework over his working life (see, for example, Tarshis, 1947, 1948). His mature work is well represented in his masterly paper on the aggregate supply function in the Scitovsky *Festschrift* (Tarshis, 1979a), and in the appendix to Tarshis (1984) (see also Tarshis, 1979b, 1980, 1985). Like Weintraub and his pupils, Davidson and Smolensky, and their common master, Keynes, Tarshis considers the aggregate supply function to be as important as the aggregate demand function. Tarshis and Weintraub both argued that its relative neglect has been a major mistake of modern Keynesian theory – and did so in the 1940s and 1950s when virtually no one else did. They start their exposition of the basic core of the *General Theory* with the aggregate supply function. Weintraub's typical starting point is a Marshallian short-period supply function in an individual industry (see Weintraub, 1977). Business people are assumed to have price expectations which imply certain desired output levels and therefore 'proceeds' which justify offering certain levels of employment – there is an implicit assumption of marginal cost pricing. The proceeds of individual industries are aggregated to give a particular point on the aggregate supply function.[9] By contrast, Tarshis (1979a) starts from an explicitly imperfectly competitive micro foundation so that individual business people have definite sales expectations at any moment of time (in his model the outcome of expected marginal revenues equalling marginal costs). Aggregation of these amounts leads to the determination of employment, output and income which through the aggregate demand function determines whether the business people's short-period sales expectations were correct or not. According to Kregel (1976), Keynes often used a model in which it was 'as if' short period expectations were fulfilled so that the process just described would coincide with the economy immediately finding itself at the point of effective demand for given conditions. Much of Tarshis's and Weintraub's work, however, and also Keynes's again, (see Kregel, 1976), is concerned with how entrepreneurs would

react if short-period expectations are *not* immediately fulfilled. These issues have also been discussed by Asimakopulos
(1982) and Parinello (1980), amongst others.

Weintraub pioneered anti-inflation schemes (commonly
called tax-based incomes policy, TIP) which awarded penal-
ties and incentives to decision-makers, especially with regard
to money-wages, in order to achieve an acceptable overall
outcome with respect to changes in the general price level. In
this particular venture he was joined by Abba Lerner. Both
designed institutional arrangements which achieve their
desired results not by coercion but by appeal to individuals'
self-interest. In Weintraub's case, we have Marshallian-
Pigouvian carrot and stick incentives provided through the tax
system. Individuals are penalized by an excess profits tax if
they take actions which raise prices at rates which are greater
than are thought to be socially desirable. They are rewarded by
tax concessions if they take the opposite actions. Lerner's
solution was to achieve full employment and a stable overall
price level by creating a market in the right to buy or sell
permits to increase or decrease prices (see Lerner and Colander, 1979, 1983). Thus, the libertarians could not complain,
as they had of TIP, that a wedge had been driven between
social and private benefits.

Davidson too uses the Marshallian framework of the *Treatise* and the *General Theory* to analyze the development of a
monetary production economy operating in an uncertain
environment in which Marshall's 'reasonable' people do the
best they can. In his theory of accumulation he relates current
flows of investment spending to existing stocks, using Keynes's theory of spot and future markets to connect the two
(see, for example, Davidson, 1965, 1967, 1978, 1980a, 1980b,
1982). The same contrast between spot and future markets
(and their respective prices) is used by Davidson and Kregel
(1980) (see also Kregel, 1982, 1983a, 1983b, 1983c), to illuminate the analysis of Chapter 17 of the *General Theory* where
the real forces associated with accumulation and the monetary
forces determining the rate of interest come together. The vital
clue is the peculiar and essential properties of money-liquidity.
Underemployment equilibrium is possible because switching

demand from goods to money does not necessarily create employment opportunities, due to the latter's negligible elasticities of production and distribution. The details of this complex argument, both as it is to be found in the *General Theory* itself and as it has been developed by Kregel, Davidson and others, constitutes a central source of disagreement between this particular strand of post-Keynesianism and the second strand (see pp. 11–15). In particular, the Marshallian foundations of Keynes's argument, whereby Keynes assumes that the demand and supply curves for various assets are 'well-behaved' are argued by the latter to be faulty.

Minsky's financial instability hypothesis, which he locates in the *General Theory* (Minsky, 1975), concerns an endogenous theory of cyclical fluctuations resulting from the interaction of real and monetary factors. Non-realization of expected cash flows creates exaggerated real movements (in the sense of having greater amplitude than otherwise would be the case) as firms respond to the implications of financial commitments into which they entered on the basis of their initial expectations. The essence of the process is as follows (see, for example, Minsky, 1974, 1975, 1977, 1978, 1982): production and investment decisions have to be made in advance of their eventual outcomes. This often requires that finance be raised; this commits individual firms to certain patterns of repayment of interest and principal. When actual cash flows turn out to be different from those which were initially anticipated, firms find that their liquidity positions are either unexpectedly enhanced, relative to the known prior claims on them, if the outcomes are more favourable than expected; or they are unexpectedly diminished if the outcomes are disappointing. Re-evaluations of real production, employment and investment decisions are likely to be undertaken. These create changes in activity that are additional to the real rhythms associated with, say, the well-known multiplier-acceleration mechanism. Victoria Chick (1984, p. 291) put this view succinctly:

The interactions amongst key behavioural relations share with the financial aspect responsibility for the asymmetry between the precipitous downturn and gradual upturn. The financial and real aspects are fully integrated.

Minsky argues (see, for example, Minsky, 1978), that these movements are not cumulative in nature but instead contain within them the genesis of an inherent cyclical pattern.

We have . . . a model in which the path of income, depends crucially upon two phenomena: the determination of total investment demand and the external financing of investment through monetary changes. Thus, it is the views of businessmen and bankers about the appropriate financial relations that call the tune for aggregate demand and employment. These views are volatile, responding to the past of the economy, and they change as the economy transits among the various types of behaviour (boom, crisis, debt–deflation, stagnation, and relatively steady expansion) which characterise the performance of capitalism. (Minsky, 1975, p. 136)

Like, Marx, Kalecki, Goodwin, Kaldor, Pasinetti and Joan Robinson, Minsky draws out the significance of the different constraints on the expenditure decisions of the two main classes in the capitalist economy. Wage-earners are fundamentally constrained in their expenditure decisions (which are principally concerned with consumption goods) by their incomes, while business people are constrained in their decisions in regard to accumulation by the conditions under which short and long-term finance are available (Minsky, 1978, 1982). The latter are basically determined by the banking and financial institutions. This particular dichotomy has become the hallmark of much post-Keynesian cycle and growth theory (see, for a recent example, Marglin, 1984a, 1984b, and for a fine example of the extension of these ideas to an open economy, Shelia Dow, 1986–7).

THE SECOND STRAND

The second strand, usually known as the neo-Ricardians, takes on Keynes's theory of effective demand in that desired saving is equalized to desired investment through changes in the level of income. They argue, however, that it is, or it should be, a theory of a *long-period* level of income and employment (in the sense of the ultimate outcome of persistent forces) that should be placed alongside the classical theories of value and distribution in the core (see also Groenewegen, 1986, p. 11).

We digress now briefly to remind the reader of Sraffa's contributions (see also Harcourt, 1982a, 1983, 1986, Essay 5; Kurz, 1985; Roncaglia, 1978). The relatively little which Sraffa published in a long lifetime has had a profound impact on economic theory (see Harcourt, 1982a; 1983, p. 117; 1986, p. 76). He was Ricardian without accepting Say's law, Marxian while rarely referring explicitly to Marx's theory. He attempted to re-establish the surplus approach to economic analysis that had been lost – 'submerged and forgotten' – with the emergence of the marginal school, the 'marginal' method and the accompanying dominance of the subjective theory of value, itself brought to its most refined form in neoclassical general equilibrium theory.[10]

Sraffa attacked on two fronts; the object on the first was to overthrow the marginal theory of value and distribution, including the theory of value as it was presented to the English-speaking world in Marshall's work in particular. His 1925 and 1926 articles were specifically directed against Marshall's theory (see also Sraffa, 1930).

Both the introductions to the Ricardo volumes, Sraffa with Dobb (1951–5), and *Production of Commodities . . .* itself were directed against the neoclassical theory of value and distribution which invoked supply and demand, in the sense that the fundamental idea was that the relative prices of 'capital' and 'labour', and their relative shares were what they were because of relative scarcities – the rate of profits, for example, was high or low depending upon whether or not the economy in question had a 'little' or a 'lot' of 'capital' in relation to its supplies of 'labour'. This notion, together with 'the dynamical principle of "substitution" . . . seen ever at work' (Marshall, 1890, p. xv), were the principal clues to the levels of normal profits and wages in a competitive economy (see Sraffa, 1961, 1962).

Sraffa had exacting standards concerning measurement, theory and the criteria which they should meet. He stated his views succinctly at the Corfu Conference on capital theory in the late 1950s, distinguishing between two types of measurement:

First, there was the one in which the statisticians were mainly interested. Second, there was measurement in theory. The statisticians' measures were only approximate. . . . The theoretical measures required absolute precision. Any imperfections in these theoretical measures were not merely upsetting, but knocked down the whole theoretical basis . . . The work of J. B. Clark, Böhm-Bawerk and others was intended to produce pure definitions of capital, as required by their theories. . . . If we found contradictions, then these pointed to defects in the theory, and an inability to define measures of capital accurately. It was on this – the chief failing of capital theory – that we should concentrate. (Sraffa, 1961, pp. 305–6)

Sraffa found orthodox theory wanting by these standards. He himself merely stated the results: reswitching (Sraffa, 1960, Part III), the famous passage in parenthesis in the 'Reduction to Dated Labour' chapter (p. 38), and the 'remarkable effect' in the chapter on fixed capital (p. 70). There Sraffa considered

a complete range of n similar machines, each being one year older than the preceding one, and thus forming a group such as we might find in a self-replacing system. The requirement that the life-sum of the depreciation quotas should be constant and independent of the rate of profits is now embodied in the fact that . . . such a group is maintained simply by bringing in a new machine every year. But the redistribution over the various ages of this constant life-sum has the remarkable effect that with any rise in the rate of profits the value of the group as a whole *rises* relative to the original value of a new machine.

It has been left to his younger colleagues, especially Krishna Bharadwaj, Eatwell, Garegnani, Pasinetti, Steedman, to spell them out, and for Roncaglia (1978) to document the story in so far as it applies to Sraffa himself. The upshot of the discussions was to argue that the supply and demand theory of the rate of profits in the economy as a whole was incoherent.[11]

The second front from which he attacked contained his positive contributions. This was to give coherence to the core concept of the surplus in the rebuilding in modern times of classical analysis. The structure itself is described by, for example, Walsh and Gram (1980) (see also Dutt, 1986). Sraffa himself directed attention to some unsolved problems in Ricardo and Marx; for example, the invariant standard of value and the transformation problem respectively. He showed that once alterations in methods of production were allowed, it was not possible coherently to define an invariant standard of value. He also provided a neat solution to the transformation problem in a circulating commodity model as Meek (1961, 1967) noted in his review. Garegnani (1984), following on from Sraffa's contributions, set out the analytical structure of the surplus approach both as it is to be found in classical political economy and Marx, and as it may be set out more appropriately for modern use.

Combining the long-period theory of effective demand with the surplus approach involves rejecting supply and demand determination of prices (distribution and quantities) and the vestiges of neoclassicism in Keynes's analysis of investment – the downward-sloping marginal efficiency of capital (and investment) schedules, the demand schedules for assets discussed in Chapter 17 of the *General Theory*. These constructions are said to be inconsistent with the findings of the capital theory debates with regard to reswitching and capital-reversing (see, for example, Harcourt, 1969, 1986, Essay 7; 1972; 1982b, Essays 16–19), for example, that there is no presumption that either the mec or the mei schedule *should* be downward sloping. It follows, Garegnani (1983b) argues, that outside a corn model of the economy, it is not possible to derive a coherent supply and demand determination of prices, distribution and quantities, in the sense that a stable long-period equilibrium of supply and demand may not be shown to exist. But if the mei concerns capital *widening* not capital *deepening*, it is problematic as to whether Garegnani's argument goes through.[12] Moreover, the use of the liquidity preference theory of the rate of interest in the argument of Chapter 17 whereby the money rate of interest rules the roost is regarded as an example of the use of 'imperfections', a use which is inadmissable in long-period theory. By contrast they argue that getting the long-period theory of output and employment correct clears the way for a coherent theory of accumulation with which to replace the neoclassical theory that is built on a Fisherian (or a Walrasian or a Clarkian) base.[13]

The capital theory results also affect other areas. Steedman, often in the company of Metcalfe, has reworked much international trade theory to see how the results of orthodox theory stand up to the critique, especially that aspect which brings out the implications of commodities being produced by commodities. Not surprisingly, the answer is that many results do not (Steedman, 1979). (David Evans, 1975, 1976, 1984, 1986, has applied the Marxian-Sraffian critique to international trade theory within the context of theories of trade and development.) Secondly, Steedman (1977) has argued that most Marxian insights may be gained by starting from the Sraffian production system rather than from labour values which many modern economists find objectionable.

Needless to say, Steedman's arguments have not been accepted by all interested parties. The reaction has revolved around whether the labour theory of value is needed or not, in particular about what exactly is meant by it, and whether or not all propositions in a coherent economic theory have to be expressed in a precise form, usually akin to a series of mathematical arguments, or whether theoretical reasoning in a social science may be carried out in many dimensions, of which the mathematical form is only one (see, for example, Harcourt, 1979b, 1982b, Essay 14). Thirdly, Steedman and Schefold (1971, 1976) have investigated problems of joint production and technical change, considerably extending Sraffa's results in these and other areas.

THE THIRD STRAND

The third strand also starts from classical and Marxian economics. The social relationships of the sphere of production, together with technical structure of production, determine the potential surplus available at any moment of time. That is, at any moment, the real wage is historically determined by the state of the class war (amongst other factors), and it determines in turn the *maximum* rate of profits available. Whether what is *potentially* there is realized *in fact* as a rate of profits and a rate of accumulation depends upon the forces of effective demand. These are summarized in the interplay between the accumulation function, Joan Robinson's 'animal spirits' function, in which the planned rate of accumulation is dependent on the expected rate of profits, on the one hand, and a saving function, in which the distribution of income plays a pivotol role (because of differing saving propensities as between classes), on the other. Kalecki (1938, 1943, 1954, 1971) is the pioneering figure. (For a thorough survey of Kalecki's contributions, see, for example, Sawyer, 1985.)

Kalecki, like Keynes, analyzed the idea of effective demand but began from a different starting point, Marx's reproduction schemes. He based his theory on Marx's idea that the dynamic of a capitalist economy is one result of class struggle. Social relations, therefore, should be considered when the dynamic process is analyzed. Kalecki seems never to have declared himself in print as to where he stood in relation to the labour theory of value. He assumed that prices were fixed by firms according to their unit costs of production to which margins or mark-ups were added to secure certain levels of profit. Kalecki then tried to study from observed facts how mark-ups were related to the degrees of monopoly of the firms.

As we mentioned above, Kalecki regarded Marx's theory of exploitation as determining what the limits of the real wage rate and the overall rate of profits could be at any moment of time. Within those constraints, his theory of effective demand, together with his theory of pricing and distribution determined what the rate of profits, the real wage and overall activity would be in fact. As with Keynes, investment spending is the *causa causans*. In Kalecki's theory, while expected profits provide a major incentive for investment, actual investment (together with capitalists' consumption) is the principal creator of actual profits, which in turn are a major determinant of the ability to invest. Both equilibrium activity and distribution are determined by the equality of saving and investment.

Investment, the driving force in Kalecki's model, takes time to plan, realize and bring into operation. In between decisions various things can happen, and adjustments take place continuously. The theory of investment behaviour that Kalecki tried all his working life to develop was intended to be an endogenous theory of accumulation, the key to the cyclical growth pattern of capitalism in which 'the long-run trend (would be) but a slowly changing component of a chain of short-period situations . . . (not an) independent entity.' (Kalecki, 1971, p. 165). Moreover, on average, there would not be full employment of either labour or the stock of capital goods. Josef Steindl (1952, 1981), a former colleague of Kalecki, makes a unique contribution at this juncture with his theories of cycles and stagnation within the context of modern monopoly capitalism.

Kalecki was already aware of the central importance of this approach to the theory of investment when he wrote his review of Keynes's *General Theory* in 1936. He gave Keynes full marks for his theory of the determination of the level of employment, *if* the level of investment could be taken as given – and then advanced reasons why Keynes's analysis of investment was faulty. The following passage from Targetti and Kinda-Hass's 1982 translation of Kalecki's review sets out his arguments:

Therefore it is difficult to consider Keynes' solution of the investment problem to be satisfactory. The reason for this failure lies in an approach which is basically static to a matter which is by its nature dynamic. Keynes takes as given the state of the expectations of returns and from this he deduces a certain determined level of investment, overlooking the effects that investment will have in turn on expectations. It is here that one can see a [sketch] (sic) of the road one must follow in order to build a realistic theory of investment. Its starting point should be the solution of the problem of investment decisions, of *ex ante* investment. Let us suppose there to be at a given moment of time a certain state of expectations as to future incomes, a given price level of investment goods and finally a given rate of interest. How great then will be the investment that entrepreneurs intend to undertake in a unit of time? Let us suppose that this problem has been solved (despite the fact that it seems impossible to us to do this without introducing some special hypothesis about the psychology of the entrepreneurs or even, an hypothesis about money market imperfections). A further development of the theory of investment could be as follows. The decisions concerning investment, corresponding to the initial state, will not generally be equal to the actual level of investment. Therefore in the next period the size of investment will generally be different and the short-period equilibrium will change together with it. Therefore we should now deal with a state of expectations that in general will be different from that of the initial period, different prices of investment goods and a different rate of interest. From these a new level of investment decisions will result and so on. (p. 252)

Apart from Kalecki and Steindl, these theories have been principally developed by Joan Robinson (five volumes, 1959–79, 1956, 1962) and her followers (especially Asimakopulos, 1969, 1970, 1975, 1977, 1980–81, 1982, 1983) – witness her famous banana diagram (Robinson, 1962, p. 48). It illuminates the two-sided relationship between accumulation and profitability – expected profitability induces accumulation, while realized accumulation itself creates the profitability which makes accumulation possible, partly through the supply of internal funds.

If we assume a link between achieved profitability and expected profitability (for expositional purposes, make it one-to-one; i.e., what has happened will be expected to happen again), we obtain the relationships shown in Figure 1.1 for given states of long-term expectations and financial conditions. $g^* = g^*(r^*)$ is the first relationship, where g^* is the planned rate of accumulation and r^* is expected profitability. $r = r(g)$ is the second relationship, where r is the realized rate of profit and g is the realized rate of accumulation. (This is derived from the famous 'Cambridge' relationship for the overall rate of profits, $r = g/s_c$, where s_c is the saving propensity of the capitalist class.)

If the actual rate of accumulation were g_1, realised profita-

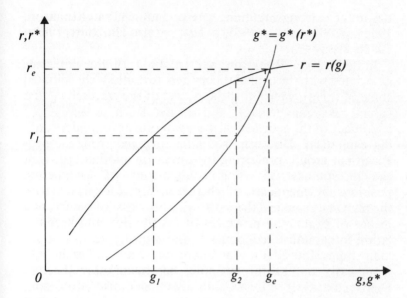

Figure 1.1.

bility would be r_1. This implies expected profitability of r_1 which induces a rate of accumulation of g_2. If the two functions are stable – one of Joan Robinson's major points is that there is little reason to suppose that they should be – and provided that the $g^* = g^*(r^*)$ relationship is fairly inelastic, an iterative process takes the economy to the intersection point, g_e, r_e. But, even here, we have not 'solved' Harrod's or Domar's problem, for there is no reason why g_e should coincide with the natural rate of growth, g_n. Nor are there any mechanisms in the model to cause it to seek a path to g_n. Moreover, even if the economy does attain the point, g_e, r_e, there is nothing to ensure that it will not be driven away from it at future points in time.

This mode of analysis also reflects her later views on method: 'The short period is here and now, with concrete stocks of the means of production in existence. Incompatibilities in the situation will determine what happens next. Long-period equilibrium is not at some date in the future: it is an imaginary state of affairs in which there are no incompatibilities in the existing situation, here and now' (Joan Robinson, 1962a, p. 690; vol. III, 1965, p. 101; see also Harcourt, 1981a, 1982b, Essay 15).

Initially Joan Robinson went along with the criticisms associated with the capital theory debate (indeed, she initiated some of them), welcoming the results of the reswitching and capital-reversing debates, and always loath to accept the legitimacy of the neoclassical theory of profits for understanding capitalism. However, she later diverged from the neo-Ricardian group, preferring to emphasize another criticism, the illegitimacy of using comparisons of long-period positions, independently of whether they were associated with the revival of classical theory or with neoclassical theory, as a means of examining processes of distribution and accumulation in capitalist economies.[14] She returned to this theme many times. Indeed it was an important strand of her thought from early on, as for example, her remarkable 'Lecture Delivered at Oxford by a Cambridge Economist' (Robinson, 1953; reprinted in vol. IV, 1973). Perhaps the most succinct account is her 1974 paper, *History versus Equilibrium* (reprinted in vol. V, 1979), the title of which sums up her objections to the method. She concluded this essay, the conciseness of the arguments of which defy summary, as follows:

The lack of a comprehensible treatment of historical time, and failure to specify the rules of the game in the type of economy under discussion, make the theoretical apparatus offered in neo-classical text-books useless for the analysis of contemporary problems, both in the micro and macro spheres. (Vol. V, p. 58)

For good measure, she added in a later paper (Robinson, 1980, p. 128), 'What role does Garegnani's long period play in the kind of analysis which aims to help us to understand the world that we are living in?'[15]

PRICES

In the Kaleckian tradition, therefore, the stress is on macro theories of activity *and* distribution. The macro relationships in turn have micro foundations in the decisions of firms with regard to pricing. This usually is set in oligopolistic price-making environments. In Kalecki's work this is associated with his 'degree of monopoly' theory. (The most comprehensive account of the development of Kalecki's ideas on pricing and their link with distribution is Kriesler, 1987.)

Joan Robinson (1977, pp. 7–17) provided an illuminating exposition of Kalecki's system, on which generations of Cambridge undergraduates have been brought up. Consider the simplest case of no consumption by rentiers, no saving by workers and no overseas or government sectors. Then, with these assumptions, profits (π) must be exactly equal to investment (I). Kalecki (1971, pp. 78–9) argued that 'capitalists may decide to . . . invest more in a given period than in a preceding one, but they cannot decide to earn more . . . therefore, their investment . . . decisions . . . determine profits, . . . not vice versa', that is, causation runs: $I \rightarrow \pi$

Now consider Figure 1.2, in which costs and prices are measured on the vertical axis, and employment in the consumption and investment goods sectors on the horizontal axis. We assume that the marginal product of direct labour in the short period is constant up to capacity in the consumption goods trades (the reverse L-shaped marginal cost curve), that investment (in real terms) is given for the period we are considering and requires AB of the available work force. Because of our assumption of constant marginal costs, if we measure all real amounts in terms of the amount of labour that is needed to produce one unit of the consumption good, price and cost, on the one hand, and price per unit of labour and the wage rate itself, on the other, may all be measured on the vertical axis.

The consumption spending of the investment good trades wage-earners constitutes the total profits of the consumption goods trades. Whatever the employment in the latter, they get their costs (the wage costs for the sector as a whole) back from the spending of the consumption goods trades wage-earners. $\pi\pi$ is a rectangular hyperbola which subtends the area w.AB, where w is the money-wage, and is the profits of the consumption goods trades. If there were competitive forces in price

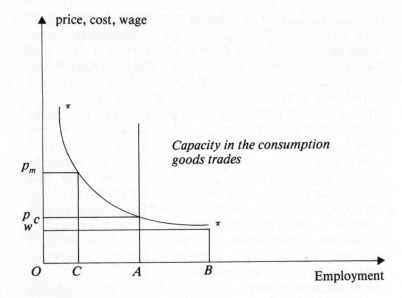

Figure 1.2.

setting, a price of Op_c would tend to be set with accompanying full employment of the existing stock of capital goods in the consumption goods trades, OA employment of the work force and profit per unit of employment of wp_c. However, if there is administered pricing in the consumption goods trades, so that a higher price of Op_m is set, there will be unemployment of CA, basically because the real wage of the workers is *lower* than in the first situation. The money-wage is the same but the price is higher; total profits are the same but profit per unit of output, wp_m, is higher in the second situation.

The prices of the investment goods and the profits of the investment goods trades are not explicitly determined in the model. However, as investment expenditure in real terms is fixed, whatever process determines the mark-up in the investment goods trades will ensure that the money expenditure on investment goods will cover the wage costs and the total profits implied by the size of the mark-up.

Kalecki's degree of monopoly theory subsequently has been

refined and modified by various mark-up theories, some of which are associated with the normal cost pricing hypothesis of Steindl (1952), Sylos-Labini (1962), Neild (1963), Godley and Nordhaus (1972), Coutts, Godley and Nordhaus (1978), and many others. In other versions the finance of investment is linked to the ability of firms to set prices which raise their financial requirements, directly through retention of profits and indirectly through the effects on their ability to raise external funds (see, for example, Sylos-Labini, 1962, 1974, 1979; Ball, 1964; Cowling, 1981, 1982; Eichner, 1973, 1976; Harcourt and Kenyon, 1976; Harris, 1974; Wood, 1975, 1978; Sylos-Labini, 1962, 1974, 1979). Sardoni (1984) links with insight Sraffa's influence on Kalecki with regard to the theory of the firm, of investment (and its finance) and of the distribution of income, on the one hand, and the theory of effective demand, on the other (see also Sardoni, 1986, 1987).

A feature that is common to these latter models is that they attempt to provide an endogenous theory of the determination of the mark-up while relating the size of the mark-up itself to traditional investment theory – how much and what sort of investment to do, and how to finance it. Ball, Eichner and Wood's theories are long-period equilibrium theories, while the models of Steindl, Sylos-Labini and of Harcourt and Kenyon are more in the spirit of Joan Robinson's analysis. Harcourt and Kenyon also incorporate aspects of Salter's analysis of vintage models and the choice of technique (see Salter, 1960, 1966).

Sometimes the sizes of the mark-ups are related to an underlying Sraffian theory of prices of production. The long-run nature of the factors which determine prices is stressed, as opposed to the short-run nature of price setting in markets for raw materials where Marshallian supply and demand factors are held to hold sway (a dichotomy which Kalecki (1938) was amongst the first to make). Mainwaring (1977) and Bhaduri and Joan Robinson (1980) make this link, while Kaldor's model of the operation of the world economy is built around two different pricing behaviours, one for industrial goods, one for primary products. Finally, we mention Sylos-Labini, whose contributions predate most of the others. They have been admirably summarized by Groenewegen (1986, p. 10; see also p. 30):

With the addition of some Schumpeterian and Robertsonian dynamics and history, [what we call the third strand] includes Sylos-Labini, though in many respects he is a class in himself. . . . his combination of Kalecki's short term considerations with the dynamics of the classics, suitably modified by his emphasis on the different form of competition induced by greater concentration of industry (as first identified by Marx) and developed in his theory of oligopoly and technical progress embodies much of what is valued in this part of the post Keynesian tradition.

KALDOR'S CONTRIBUTIONS

Kaldor (1985) combined his views on pricing with the view that dynamic economies of scale are more to be found in the industrialized countries producing industrial products, while the less developed countries depend more on the production of primary products, either food or raw materials for the industrialized countries. In recent years Hicks (1976) has used a similar distinction to good effect in his analyses of world inflation and the problems of growth.

It is too restricting to comment on Kaldor's general influence on post-Keynesian economics by discussing his views on pricing in isolation, for, by the breadth of his interests both in theory and in policy, Kaldor resembled Keynes more than any other twentieth-century economist, even to the extent of belonging to the House of Lords. We really should start with his postwar views on method (see, for example, Kaldor, 1966, 1972, 1985). Kaldor proceeded from empirical regularities – his 'stylized facts' – which are true in the broad majority of observed cases, certainly often enough to warrant explanation, to explanations that themselves should be the most reasonable ways capable 'of accounting for the "facts" independently of whether they fit into the general framework of received theory or not' (Kaldor, 1985, p. 8). Kaldor wanted us to escape from the strait-jacket of always having to fit issues and problems within received theory so that we beg questions about the actual situations we examine. Instead, we should construct a different kind of abstract model to the general equilibrium one. The latter, he argued, 'has created a serious brake on the development of economic thought' (Kaldor, 1985, p. 57), so much so that modern theorists' views of the world have become so distorted as to make them fit their images to the theory rather than the other way round. We need a model 'that recognises . . . that time is a continuing and irreversible process; that it is impossible to assume the constancy of anything *over* time' (Kaldor, 1985, p. 57). It is no accident that, for much of the postwar period, he attacked, first, 'the standard price-cleared auction market model of the economy' and, secondly, the idea of equilibrium economics itself (see, for example, Kaldor, 1972, 1975). He wished to put in its place a theory of cumulative causation, of dynamic increasing returns (see, for example, Thirlwall, *et al*, 1983; Thirlwall, 1986, for an evaluation and interpretation of this aspect of his contributions).

Another Kaldorian theme is the importance of the existence of established norms for the attainment of stability in economic systems. Before the Second World War Kaldor wrote a most perceptive article on the link between speculation and stability within the context of Keynes's theory of effective demand (Kaldor, 1939). In his first Okun Lecture, Kaldor (1985) discussed the role of the normal price in commodity markets, those markets which were thought to be the nearest real world counterparts to what Walras had in mind in his general equilibrium theory. Kaldor attributed the great increase in the volatility of the fluctuations of those prices in the postwar period, and especially since the 1970s, to the lack of 'norms'. Without them, speculation leads to enhanced rather than to dampened fluctuations. Finally, we should note that Kaldor's views on method coincided broadly with those of Joan Robinson in the postwar period (allowing for differences in temperaments – Kaldor remained the perpetual optimist, Joan Robinson became increasingly despondent), and that in recent years, John Hicks (1976, 1977, 1979, 1985) has been expressing broadly similar views on method, so distancing himself from his 'uncle' J. R. Hicks of *Value and Capital* (see Hicks, 1975, p. 365). Kaldor's work has influenced Cornwall (1972, 1977, 1983) who studies the processes of growth in modern capitalist economies as the outcome of the interrelationship of demand and supply factors. He blurs the sharp distinction between the two in the Harrod-Keynesian tradition, on the one hand, where g_n is postulated as independent of g_w and g itself, and the stress of neoclassical growth theories on population growth, substitution and technical change, to the neglect of demand as the necessary means of embodiment, on the other.

In recent years, Cornwall has become interested in the causes of stagflation and in the design of policies to overcome its effects. Integral to his package deal of policies have been institutional reforms to allow for the establishment of some form of permanent incomes policy (see Cornwall, 1985). Indeed, it is a feature of virtually all strands of post-Keynesian economics – the neo-Ricardians may be an exception – that their logic leads inescapably to the advocacy of incomes policies because they incorporate the essential Keynesian insight that the level of money-wages is the fulcrum around which both the explanation of the overall price level *and* the stability generally of the economy itself revolves (see, for example, Eichner, 1985, ch. 9; Harcourt, 1982, essays 18 and 20; 1986, essays 9 and 10; Weintraub, 1978b).

GROWTH AND DYNAMICS: JOAN ROBINSON, PASINETTI AND GOODWIN

With the exceptions of Kaldor, Hicks and the neo-Ricardians, the theories so far have been concerned with either the short-period theory of employment and the distribution of income or with cyclical growth. But, of course, in the postwar period the theory of growth has been a principal preoccupation of all these groups. Harrod (1936, 1939, 1948) was the stimulus; Joan Robinson's *The Accumulation of Capital* (Robinson, 1956) is one of the classics of the literature though it is a book which has caused much bewilderment, so much so that the author herself felt it necessary to follow it with at least two

'Child's Guides' (Robinson, 1960, 1962b). Kahn's contributions are also most important, especially for his wise and cautionary views on method and the limitations of analysis (Kahn, 1972, 1984). Perhaps the bewilderment would have been less, if she had included in later editions the following preface, a draft of which was found in her papers. It explains very clearly the four main sorts of issues and questions with which she was concerned. This list also shows why the book was difficult to grasp in its entirety.

Joan Robinson considers a model of an unregulated free enterprise economy in which firms 'within the limits set by their command of finance' determine the rate of capital accumulation, while the members of the public, constrained 'by their command of purchasing power, are free to make the rate of expenditure what they please, . . . [a] model . . . not . . . unrealistic in essential respects'.

The model may be used 'to analyse the chances and changes of the development of an economy as time goes by' by considering 'four distinct groups of questions':

1. We make comparisons of situations, each with its own past, developing into its own future, which are different in some respect (for instance the rate of accumulation going on in each) in order to see what the postulated difference entails.
2. We trace the path which a single economy follows when the technical conditions (including their rate of change) and the propensities to consume and to invest are constant through time.
3. We trace the consequences of a change in any of these conditions for the future development of the economy.
4. We examine the short-period reaction of the economy to unexpected events.

The first group of questions is more naturally handled in terms of comparisons of steady states (including stationary states). The conditions for steady states to be achieved are set out but there is no implication that the unregulated behaviour of the decision-makers will ever bring them about. When discussing the choice of techniques, the relationship between the value of capital and physical capital in the economy as a whole becomes relevant and 'takes up several chapters (Book II Section II) and is difficult out of all proportion to its importance'.

The second set of questions concerns what happens when one of the conditions for steady growth (other than technical conditions and the consumption propensities) is not satisfied. The third set relates to the path which the economy will follow when, having been in a steady state, a basic change occurs, for example, 'an increase in monopoly which causes profit margins to increase'. The fourth set concerns the reactions to current events of the inducement to invest in an uncertain world and relates to the possibility of oscillation in the transition from one state of affairs to another, or even to the generation of a trade cycle by 'mere uncertainty' without any change in basic conditions. In principle, 'this type of analysis enables us to deal with all the possible vicissitudes of a developing economy, and prepares the way for discussions of public policy'.

Pasinetti (1974, 1980, 1981) has probably carried the analysis further and has created a more unified system than anyone else. For thirty years he has been developing a multi-sector growth model which encompasses both classical and Keynesian concerns (see, for example, Pasinetti, 1962, 1966, 1981). It is classical because it is concerned with the origin of profits in the characteristics of the production and distribution systems; Keynesian, because of a preoccupation with effective demand and the conditions necessary for full employment, both at a point in time and over time. His distinctive contributions are not only his work on the rate of profits and the distribution of income within a growing economy in which investment is constrained to be at levels that are needed to maintain full employment growth over time, but also a major extension to take account of changing patterns of demand as income grows because the demands for individual products grow at different rates over their life cycles. He also considers the problems of production interdependence, technical advance, exhaustible resources and international considerations from the point of view of maintaining overall balance over time, deriving an intricate and comprehensive set of conditions.

In his review article of Pasinetti (1981), Harris (1982) points out that in attempting to derive these conditions, Pasinetti is led to

a theory of what might be called 'structural' or 'technological' unemployment considered as an inherent feature of the process of expansion and development of the economy. It is a distance removed from the usual Keynesian explanation of unemployment and must be seen, therefore, as a distinct theory. . . . [T]he full import of Pasinetti's analysis is to suggest that 'the very nature of the process of long-run growth requires a structural dynamics which leads to difficulties in the short run' (p. 243). As such, it falls within the general class of theories of secular stagnation due to 'under-consumption', though within this class it stands by itself because of its own special and unique features. (p. 36)

For Pasinetti, as for most post-Keynesians, relative prices are related not so much to scarcity as to the conditions for reproduction and expansion. In a recent paper (Pasinetti, 1986) he has set out again his views on this distinction, arguing that the exchange-production duality as between the surplus approach on the one hand, and the subjective theory of value on the other, 'can be traced back to a deeper dichotomy in the theories of value' (Baranzini and Scazzieri, 1986, p. 77).[16]

Richard Goodwin's contributions serve in a sense to link aspects of the Kalecki-Robinson approach with Pasinetti's approach. For many years his thoughts evolved along two separate lines – on the one hand, the nature of cyclical processes in aggregative models, on the other, the nature of production interdependence in multi-sector models (Goodwin, 1982, 1983). Goodwin's ideas on the trend and cycle, whereby they should be regarded as 'fused indissolubly' (see Goodwin, 1982, p. 117), evolved considerably over the years. A seminal paper, 'The Problem of Trend and Cycle', was published in the *Yorkshire Bulletin* in 1953 (Essay 9 in Goodwin, 1982). In addition to arguing out this central point, he made good use, in filling in the details of the phases of the cycle, 'of Marshall's famous principle that the short period is very much shorter for expansions than for contractions' (Goodwin, 1982, p. 117), the insight through which Kahn was to influence Keynes as he moved from the *Treatise* to the *General Theory* (see Kahn, 1984, p. 174). Goodwin's ideas came to fruition in his 1967 paper (in the Dobb *Festschrift*: Feinstein, 1967), which, significantly, is entitled 'A Growth Cycle'. There, he took the Volterra prey-predator model whereby the analogy of 'the symbiosis of two populations – partly complementary, partly hostile – is helpful in . . . understanding . . . the dynamical contradictions of capitalism, especially when stated in a . . . Marxian form' (Goodwin, 1982, p. 167). He analyzed the fight over wages and profits and the feedback on real variables – and spawned a literature which is still expanding.

Nevertheless Goodwin was not satisfied. He needed effectively to integrate effective demand into the model. So the two lines of thought have now come together, as an impressive whole, in Goodwin and Punzo (1987). The work is extremely eclectic; the influence of Marx, Schumpeter, Keynes, von Neumann, Joan Robinson, Sraffa and Kalecki may all be discerned (see also Goodwin, 1986). So, too, may the developments of catastrophe theory and the concept of 'bifurcation', together with the older biological analogy drawn from the Volterra prey-predator model. Goodwin concentrates on the nature of evolutionary structures which experience from time to time large jumps and breaks, which he regards as the key to the cyclical development of economies characterized by production interdependencies.

THE CONTRIBUTIONS OF GODLEY AND HIS DAE COLLEAGUES

Finally, we come to Godley and his colleagues who stand apart because their distinctive contribution concerns, in the main, stocks and not flows. The balance sheet and the flow of funds statement, more than the profit and loss account and income and expenditure flows, is the crucial framework in their approach. They take as their theoretical reference point the end, in effect, of a Marshallian long period (applied to the economy as a whole) where stocks as well as flows are in equilibrium. Their object is to see whether the long-period position constitutes a sensible outcome to the flow relationships, when these are constrained by certain key stock-flow relationships, for example, the desired wealth to income ratio (α) (see Cripps and Godley, 1976; Godley and Cripps, 1983). A key result is that the 'mean lag in the response of expenditure behind income is necessarily equal to α: and that this mean lag is entirely independent of the asset adjustment process itself' (Godley, 1983, p. 140).

The approach is akin to that of the neo-Ricardians because the emphasis is on the existence of systematic and persistent forces, the characteristics of long-period positions and the non-permanence of short-period positions because the flows associated with them must by definition soon change the stocks and therefore one of the important sets of determinants of the equilibrium flows themselves. Stocks here relate to the real assets and the financial liabilities of the balance sheet and in particular to the means by which inventories are financed in and out of equilibrium. As Vines (1984) points out, this work links on to the Blinder and Solow literature (see, for example, Blinder and Solow, 1973, 1974, 1976a, 1976b), and Tobin's concern with full portfolio equilibrium relationships (see, for example, Tobin, 1978, 1980, Lecture 4). All are of course thoroughly Keynesian in their outlook; perhaps too much so, it has been argued (see Malinvaud, 1983, and Solow, 1983), in that Godley makes the very strong statement that 'the sustained expansion of real demand is the necessary and sufficient condition for expansion of real output on any scale whatever in the long run' (Godley, 1983, p. 157). (He does add in a footnote that the statement in *this form* 'is vacuous. Is the long run 5 or 2000 years?' (p. 157). In any event, his view of the role of demand would not be unacceptable to, say, Garegnani.)

Godley and Cripps also investigate the nature of the price mechanism which is consistent with what they call inflation neutrality, making an empirical judgement that the world is not too far away from this position most of the time. They derive the conditions by which monetary and fiscal policies may determine real income regardless of what is happening to inflation. As these conditions relate to a number of key relationships, for example, that the wealth-income ratio should be inflation neutral, the determination, measurement and definition of which are sometimes left unclear, these claims too have been criticised (see, for example, Vines, 1984, p. 399).

CONCLUSION

We subtitled this reflective survey essay 'from criticism to coherence', deliberately ending with a question mark. What we have tried to show is that within the various strands that we have discerned and described, there *are* coherent frameworks and approaches to be found, though obviously there remain within each unfinished business and unresolved puzzles. The real difficulty arises when attempts are made to synthesize the strands in order to see whether a coherent whole emerges. Our own view is that this is a misplaced exercise, that to attempt to do so is vainly to search for what Joan Robinson called 'only another box of tricks' to replace the 'complete theory' of mainstream economics which all strands reject. The important perspective to take away is, we believe, that there is no uniform way of tackling all issues in economics and that the various strands in post-Keynesian economics differ from one another, not least because they are concerned with different issues and often different levels of abstraction of analysis.[17]

An important implication of the above conclusion is that the policies which may be rationalized by post-Keynesian analysis are very much geared to concrete situations, the historical experiences and the sociological characteristics of the economies concerned. More generally this approach, which was that, for example, of Keynes, Kalecki, Joan Robinson and Arthur Okun, sometimes and most appropriately, has been dubbed the 'horses for courses' approach.[18]

NOTES

1. We thank but in no way implicate Roger Backhouse, Sheila Dow, Peter Kriesler, Cristina Marcuzza, and Peter Reid for their comments on a draft of the survey.

2. The ordering of the routes and of the strands associated with them is purely for convenience of exposition; it implies neither relative importance nor chronological priority for any one strand.

3. While Garegnani's papers were published in English towards the end of the 1970s they are based on research which he did in the early 1960s following the completion of his PhD Dissertation (Garegnani, 1959) on distribution theory.

4. Carvalho (1984–5) surveyed the three strands from the viewpoint of how they react to and analyze short and long periods. He is more sympathetic to strands one and three than to two. He has an especially soft spot for Shackle's work. (See also Carvalho, 1983–4.)

5. As a result of this re-examination the coherence of the concept of natural prices and their independence from market prices has been called into question; see Harcourt (1981, 1982); Hamouda (1984); Levine (vol. II, 1981); Allaoua (1986).

6. Cristina Marcuzza warns us that this statement smacks of backward reading; that in classical theory, Ricardo, for example, held that though it is true that causality ran from money to prices, nevertheless this did *not* imply a theory of the equilibrium level of prices (or of money).

7. Roger Backhouse writes that the account in the text makes the break appear too sharp, that 'Samuel Bailey . . . a very influential classical economist . . . had a subjective theory of value as early as 1825 [and that] in Mill the surplus approach co-exists with a price theory that has much in common with Marshall's.'

8. David Levine (1986, p. 16) puts the contrast succinctly: 'the classical theory focussed on technology, reproduction and aggregate distribution; the neoclassical theory focussed on scarce factors and individual preferences.'

9. Other aspects of Weintraub's many contributions may be found in, for example, Weintraub (1958, 1961, 1977a, 1977b, 1978a, 1978b, 1980, 1980–1, 1981).

10. Krishna Bharadwaj (1978) called this process the 'rise to dominance of the supply and demand theories'. Sraffa himself (1926, p. 535) referred to the near end-product of the process, 'the almost unanimous agreement at which economists have arrived regarding the theory of competitive value', as '[a] striking feature of the present position of economic science'.

11. For a similar evaluation of Sraffa's contributions and purposes, see Chakravarty (1986). See also Garegnani (1970, 1983a, 1983b, 1984, 1985, 1986).

12. We are indebted to Ernst Maug and Brothwell (1987, p. 5, n. 1) for this point.
13. We should also mention Edward Nell, Adolph Lowe's protégé at the New School for Social Research in New York, whose vigorous, enthusiastic and energetic contributions span all three strands of post Keynesian economics and are especially influenced by Joan Robinson's and Sraffa's contributions (see, for example, Nell, 1967, 1980, 1983).
14. Of course, Joan Robinson often used such comparisons herself to show neoclassical economists what their answers would have been *in their own contexts* and how limited they were for these other purposes.
15. For a sympathetic evaluation of Joan Robinson's contributions over fifty years, see Gram and Walsh (1983).
16. For a stimulating and thought provoking essay on this theme and 'a reconceptualization of classical economics', see Levine (1986).

2. Keynes's Co-operative Economy and the Aggregate Supply Function

Lorie Tarshis

Keynes, by the end of 1931, realized that his attempt to re-do the *Treatise on Money* had acquired its own direction and momentum. He was on to something exciting and new. From then until the end of 1935 drafts of chapters, notes for lectures, tables of contents, letters and memos flew swiftly across his desk, bearing witness to the intensity of his effort to shape the bricks, craft the foundations and construct what became the *General Theory* (Keynes, 1979a).

All materials relating to its preparation and located by 1973 had been published, wonderfully edited by Donald Moggridge 'Keynes, 1973b). With the discovery in the winter 1975–6, of a laundry hamper filled with additional materials, the written record of his work on the General Theory had presumably been completed. These later materials are to be found in *The General Theory: A Supplement* (Keynes, 1979).

I reached Cambridge in October 1932, attended Keynes's lectures for that year and the next three and, luckily, preserved my notes. I saw much of his activity at first hand. The lectures naturally contained a number of high spots, but this is not the time to set them out. Here I intend to discuss only one of them: Keynes's attempt to account for the contrast between the conclusions reached by 'the classicals' – Ricardo, Say, Mill, Marshall, Edgeworth and Pigou – and those implicit in his own, not yet fully worked-out theory. I accepted his picture of

35

the older theory – I had been exposed to it from 1929 when I began my work in the Principles of Economics, reading Marshall – and I recognized the accuracy of Keynes's description. It had no room for involuntary unemployment, once the economy had attained equilibrium – the Panglossian version of the subject. Keynes's theory, by contrast, would show that the economy could – and often *would* – come to rest with unemployment well above zero. To many students in 1932 and 1933 that made sense; and I should add, it still does – at least to me.

He knew better than to search for the roots of this contrast in the stupidity or blindness of his predecessors. He made a beginning in the opening lecture of his new series on 'The Monetary Theory of Production', 10 October 1932. He asked: 'Now suppose that the short-period supply price of labour was just like that of a machine; what would happen then? Prime cost would be next door to zero. . . . Thus there would be no need for unemployment even during severe transitions. . . . Thus, if we assume that the short-period supply price of labour is determined on the same principles as that of machines under free competition . . . it follows that there will be no unemployment. . . . These conditions would be satisfied in . . . any state in which employers were equally responsible for the maintenance of their men as they are for the maintenance of their machines, whether they are employing them or not. . . . It seems to me,' he went on, '*that this is that state of affairs generally postulated in Marshall's Principles of Economics and it is the behaviour of an economic system thus governed which he is discussing*' (Keynes, 1979, pp. 51–2, my italics). I suppose I was puzzled by his linking Marshall's theory to Marshall's treating labour as he would have treated a machine, and its result – no unemployment – and that might explain why I failed to see the significance of Keynes's first attempt.

Next year he devoted several minutes in two lectures, on 23 and 30 October 1933, to develop the theme. This time I was fascinated and remember determining to listen as hard as possible, instead of trying to take notes fast enough to match his very rapid delivery. Forty years later all I had, apart from my memory of the argument, was a fragment of a fossilized wish-bone – my too brief notes – because nothing had yet been found in manuscript on this exciting idea. I had asked Don Moggridge several times after he had become my colleague whether he had not run into any reference to it in going through Keynes's papers. No luck. It was not until he returned from Cambridge in the summer of 1976 that he could report the discovery of the missing papers. They are now available (in Keynes, 1979).

As the title of my chapter suggests, I was especially eager to see what he had said about a Co-operative Economy, about the distinction between it and an Entrepreneur Economy and about the implications of that distinction for the puzzle he had set himself. When I was able to read it, I found he had, not one, but two ways of accounting for the contrast, although in his version they sometimes blurred into one. However, the explanation that I thought the more powerful – the one that relied on the distinction between a co-operative and an entre-preneur economy – was not heard after 1933, either in lectures or in print. The other – the one that rested upon the distinction between the kind of economy to which Say's Law was appli-cable and that to which it was not – survived into the General Theory. Indeed in Chapter 17 of that volume he attempted to get behind the role of money in an effort to distinguish the characteristics of a 'Say's Law (or Neutral) Economy' from those of a 'no-Say's Law-economy'.

As to this latter distinction, a few points deserve attention. First, an economy to which Say's Law applies, and which lacks an active government policy, is unlikely to be operating at capacity. When, to use the common description, 'Supply creates its own Demand', it implies that at each level of output the aggregate proceeds *expected* by suppliers will be precisely equal to the aggregate supply price of that output – or, in other words, to the aggregate expectations of proceeds *required* by suppliers to induce them to produce that output. When sellers expect to receive from the sale of that output the precise amount they must have if they are to produce it, it has to mean that they are content to produce at that level. Now consider what this aggregate output implies for each firm. Since for the economy at large the population of firms indicates by its actions its readiness to produce at the present level, it stands to reason that the typical firm is producing at its most profitable level as determined by the demand for its product and its production costs, and at *its* output, its marginal cost must then equal its marginal revenue. From this fact it is easy to see that any change in its output would cause its profits to fall. Every other firm would be in the same situation, unwilling to change its output. Hence, the equilibrium of each firm, and indeed of the economy in one sense, would be stable.

The economy's equilibrium might have been at an output that left 20 per cent of its labour force out of work. But in a Say's Law world it would also be in equilibrium if its output were raised to bring unemployment to 10 per cent to 5 per cent or even 2 per cent. At each of these outputs – say the largest – sellers would expect their proceeds from the sale of output to equal the expectations that sellers *require as a condition of their producing such an output*. And the same would be true for every other output. Thus, in a Say's Law world, the economy would also be in *neutral* equilibrium, like a perfect ball on an absolutely horizontal table. And for both the economy and the ball, no change in position would occur except as an outside force[1] exerted an influence.

Oddly enough, if the outside force that led all firms *together* to raise their output were withdrawn, their total output would remain at the new equilibrium level – with unemployment at a mere 2 per cent. (But remember, this truth applies to a Say's Law world and not necessarily to any other.)

It seems clear that there is nothing about a Say's Law world that guarantees full employment. Keynes, in discussing such an economy concludes: 'the amount of employment is indeterminate except in so far as the marginal disutility of labour sets an upper limit', so unemployment could be in equilibrium at any level. But he takes his conclusion one step further: 'If this were true, *competition between entrepreneurs* would always lead to an expansion of employment up to the point at which etc. . . . Evidently this amounts to the same thing as full employment' (Keynes, 1973a, my italics, p. 26). Keynes's reliance upon 'competition between entrepreneurs' to bring the economy to full employment has no meaning to me – but it scarcely matters since it is intended to apply to a world without meaning.

Keynes, however, in these lectures of 1933, when, in terms of time he was about half-way through his writing of the General Theory, had an alternative explanation. It rested, as noted above, upon the distinction between a co-operative and an entrepreneur economy. The feature that distinguishes them has to do with the nature of the employment contract. In an entrepreneur economy, labour is hired for a specified period – say a week of 36 hours – at so much – say $15 – an hour. At the end of the period, the employer is free to dismiss any worker or to make him a job offer for a second period. It should be clear that if at the end of the first period he has no use for the worker, he would, by dismissing him, lower costs by $540 a week. And if he anticipated a growth in the market for his product, and were to hire an additional worker, his costs of production would be increased by $540 per week. It should be clear that apart from such modern features as taxes on payrolls, severance pay, etc., such an arrangement is characteristic of the employment contract in today's typical business firm. An economy made up of such firms was termed by Keynes an entrepreneur economy.

Other types of employment contracts are of course possible. Workers, to illustrate, may be hired on a *share basis*: in return for their work, they would then be 'rewarded by dividing up in proportions agreed to beforehand the actual output of their cooperative efforts' (Keynes, 1979, p. 66). Such workers might receive, as their reward, an actual part of their own output; but they could instead receive money. It seems likely that such workers, assuming everything else unchanged, would face with this arrangement an even riskier future than they confront under arrangements common now; to their uncertainty as to whether the work would last, they would have to face an added uncertainty as to how much they would get for their work since they cannot be certain about the market for their own product. And it is easy to imagine that they would press for more security *in terms of tenure* in their job, as their pay-off for exposing themselves to nothing better than an imprecise claim to a share of the employer's sales receipts instead of a fixed sum.

It must not be thought that arrangements, in essence similar to those just described, are rare. In agriculture, to illustrate, there have been at least two rather close examples – sharecropping and the family farm. (Obviously there are real differences between them.) An even more primitive example – the favourite model of earlier economists – would be an economy peopled by a population of Robinson Crusoe's, each with his man Friday. It too would exemplify a co-operative economy.

The return paid to labour hired in this way – whether in kind or in money – should properly be regarded, not as an element of the employer's *costs*, but as a distribution of '*profits*', (which equal its receipts from sales minus (a) the amounts to be paid to other firms for raw materials and supplies used in production, (b) taxes on output, and (c) an allowance for depreciation) or, to use Keynes's term for the sum of the items within the brackets, its 'proceeds'. *We emphasize: in a co-operative economy, the sum to be paid to labour is not a component of the firm's costs of production*; and if it is to be thought of as a cost at all, it would be a *fixed* element, not an element that enters into the firm's variable or prime costs. *That being so, it would not be an element in marginal costs of output.* Thus, when the firm raises its output, while its total costs may well be greater – reflecting its need to use more raw materials – there is nothing to correspond to these additional costs from the side of labour. Thus, its marginal costs will consist only in what Keynes in the General Theory called its marginal *user* costs; its marginal *labour* costs being zero.

This may be put in more concrete terms: since, for the decision period just beginning, the firm has its labour force on hand in very much the same way as it has its capital assets, then whether its output is set at 80 per cent, 90 per cent or 95 per cent of capacity, its total costs, if they rose at all, would rise only slightly. And so its *marginal costs of output*, within a wide range extending up to its present capacity, will be close to zero. However, any further extension of output 'beyond capacity' is likely to impose so much in added costs that its marginal costs into that hyper-range for the same decision period, if shown graphically, would turn a corner and approach the vertical.[2]

If it is supposed that management's objective in a co-operative economy is to maximize the firm's profits, [3] and that each firm pays its workers on the basis of predetermined shares, then there is only one position of equilibrium for each of them: where its output is at capacity.[4] So long as the elasticity of the demand for its product is higher than one, its marginal revenue must be positive. And when firms generally expand their output, assuming that the marginal propensity to consume lies between zero and one, their total proceeds from sales must grow. From that conclusion it follows that for each firm, considered in isolation, a *general* increase in output will cause its aggregate sales receipts to grow too but, up to capacity anyway, an increase in output will entail a negligible increase in costs. Hence, up to capacity, an increase in output will add more to receipts than to costs; consequently it will cause the firm's profit to rise and therefore output will stay close to capacity.

We have already introduced Keynes's Aggregate Supply Function (the ASF). It shows, for each level of total output, the aggregate expectations of proceeds required to induce firms – assuming that each of them begins today's period of decision with its own stock of capital goods and its own labour force – to produce each and every level of aggregate output.

This is not the time to extend an analysis of the ASF. But it seems clear that in a co-operative economy, the ASF which describes the relation between (a) various levels of output, and (b) the aggregate expectations of proceeds required to induce suppliers to produce each of these outputs, after starting at the origin, would rise only slightly faster than output. (The very gradual rise in that function reflects the fact that marginal costs in most firms will be close to zero. However, as more and more firms raise their outputs to capacity, the slope of the function for still higher outputs will become steeper, and when bottlenecks to production become common the ASF will be nearly vertical.)

Keynes summarizes the situation as: 'There could be much more violent changes in relative prices and relative wages

without affecting output' (Keynes, 1979, p. 51). Or later, 'In a
. . . barter (or co-operative economy), only miscalculation or
stupid obstinacy can stand in the way of production' (ibid., p.
67). And finally: 'In a barter and co-operative economy there
is no obstacle in the way of the employment of an additional
unit of labour if this unit will add to the social product . . .
output . . . which is sufficient to balance the disutility of the
additional employment' (ibid., p. 78).

Now for the use Keynes made of these conclusions. In a
Say's Law economy, every level of output is in neutral equilibrium and *assuming the appropriate outside force*, there
would be no obstacle to the economy's attaining full employment. However *in a co-operative economy* the case for full
employment in equilibrium is very much stronger. There are
direct and strong incentives for firms to operate at capacity –
the limit being reached when the marginal disutility of labour
is on the point of exceeding the utility to workers of the real
wage – for at that point, though employers would like to hire
more labour, none not working are willing to work for the
going real wage. In short, any apparent unemployment would
then be *voluntary*.

It has been shown that a co-operative economy, in any of
the senses noted above, establishes a sufficient condition for a
full employment equilibrium. The equilibrium of a Say's Law
– economy is neutral rather than stable. Only if most firms
move together towards full employment will that position be
reached. (The operative word here is *together*.) And it is
difficult to see why they would move together, in the absence
of outside pressure. But while Keynes, in those fifty pages,
sometimes managed to separate these two conditions, he too
often ran them together as a joint condition.

Thus, in Keynes (1979) we find: 'The Classical Economics
presupposes that the factors of production desire and receive
. . . nothing but a predetermined share of the aggregate
output' (p. 78). (This defines a cooperative economy.) And he
continues: 'It is not necessary that the factors should receive
their shares . . . in kind . . . ; – the position is substantially the
same if they are paid in money, *provided they all of them
accept the money as a temporary convenience, with a view to*

spending the whole of it forthwith on purchasing such part of current output as they choose' (p. 77, my italics). This segment in italics implies that Say's Law is valid. Classical Economists, in his view, assumed – though perhaps only implicitly – that their economy acted as though it were a co-operative economy *and also* as though it were a neutral money economy. Often their model for the economy had family firms providing most of the output – as must have been a reasonably accurate assumption for most capitalist economies down to 1860 or later. And Alfred Marshall, even as late as 1920 when the last edition of his Principles was published, wrote:

competition is not thus perfectly efficient. Even where the same price is paid all over the market for the same work with the same machinery, the prosperity of a firm increases the chance of advancement for each of its employees and also his chance of continuous employment when trade is slack, and much-coveted overtime when trade is good.

Thus there is *de facto* some sort of profit-and-loss sharing between almost every business and its employees; . . . but such cases (which call for a solidarity of interests – cordial generosity – true brotherly feelings) "are not very common; and as a rule the relations of employers and employed are raised to a higher plane . . . by the adoption of the system of profit-sharing . . .'. (Marshall, 1920, pp. 520–1)

Now, whether Marshall was realistic in his picture of the economy is not the issue. What this lengthy extract shows is that Marshall thought he saw a strong element of profit-sharing in the British economy. And this is in line with Keynes's belief, that the Panglossian character of the older economics partly derives from the nature of the model of the economy they used; that the economy was co-operative in nature. Is not such a model still accepted by many economists even today?

By the time the General Theory appeared, $2\frac{1}{4}$ years later, Keynes sought to justify his rejection of classical economics by charging that those who had developed it, from Say and Ricardo through Mill to Edgeworth, Marshall and Pigou, had accepted Say's Law as the 'True Law', or at least as a good working hypothesis for the study of contemporary economies. Keynes rejected it and set out the basis of his rejection in Chapter 17. But as has been noted, the applicability of Say's Law is not sufficient to do away with involuntary unemployment. Moreover, as he pointed out (Keynes, 1973a, p. 19 n. 2), its acceptance by Marshall was less than wholehearted.

Despite these qualifications to Keynes's critique of the classical school (and in my judgment they very seriously weaken the force of his position), he never again rested his case upon the readiness of the Classicals to accept a co-operative economy, in any of its possible forms, as a revealing model of a contemporary economy. Why did he not return to that vision? It seems to be more persuasive.

I feel this the more strongly because my upbringing as an economist was at its pre-pubescent stage in 1930 and 1931; at that time I had been persuaded that however complicated the economy had become, nothing would be gained by messing up the model of the firm, and in place of factors of production x, y and z, substituting labour that would in some ill-defined way be hired by entrepreneurs who, through their ownership of the firm, would own its capital assets too. Actually, for me, the firm – before Joan Robinson and Richard Kahn – was rather like the pre-Rutherford atom: a tiny, indivisible object that could not, and need not, be further analyzed. But of course such a view rejected the significance of any distinction between an economy made up of Robinson Crusoe- like firms, family firms, large firms in which the individual labourer was paid a predetermined share of its proceeds, slave-holding firms or firms which hired labour for a definite, and short, period and in return committed itself to pay its workers a fixed sum of money. That was our problem.

Why then did Keynes give up all these insights? One reason might have been that by the end of 1933 he had not clearly seen that an economy in which Say's Law rules is not necessarily a co-operative economy. Add to that his growing impatience to have his book finished and published. A third factor, which can easily be overlooked now, is that Britain in those days seemed to many, including Keynes, to be poised uncertainly between fascism which he hated and communism which he despised; yet unless capitalist Britain could compete with Stalin and Hitler–Mussolini in easing unemployment, she could very easily turn to one of them for salvation. He was confident he had found a better way – indeed, the key to a free lunch. But it had better be served quickly.

A final possible explanation for his abandoning the co-operative – entrepreneur distinction is that his focus on the possibilities of a structural change in capitalism to create a co-operative economy that would rid Britain of the plague of unemployment, might add to the appeal of something far more radical – that is to say, of communism. In that connection, it is worth noting that in 1932 when he was beginning to analyze how a co-operative economy would work, he wrote: 'These conditions would be satisfied in a socialist or a communist state' (Keynes, 1979, p. 52). But by 1933, after a more detailed treatment of the distinction between these two types, he said nothing about how other forms of the economy could also contribute to solving the problems of unemployment. By then, too many of his student friends and young colleagues had seen, as they thought, the light; and the situation had become too tense for easy banter. In any event, whatever the reasons, he dropped the whole subject.

A concluding point: I can imagine that any one who comes across Keynes's writing on the co-operative economy would think that Keynes had borrowed some of his insights from Weitzman's brilliantly written '*The Share Economy*' (Weitzman, 1984). For there is no question: Keynes's co-operative economy (of 1933) is very much like Weitzman's Share Economy of 1984. But there are differences, not so much in the descriptions of the two, but rather in the *purpose* each had in mind in setting out his version and in the analysis each supplied of the functioning of his alternative economy.

Keynes, as noted above, had no intention, when he set out his broad outline of a co-operative economy, of urging a great conversion of Britain's major firms to profit-sharing institutions as a way of solving the problem of unemployment. Such schemes did not appeal to him as politically interesting; and he felt that there were other approaches – approaches that would be obvious to any intelligent reader of his forthcoming book – that were more easily adopted.

It is not surprising that Weitzman, a worker in the School that developed 'the neo-classical synthesis' should not be optimistic about Keynes's policy prescriptions. As a result he has proposed his 'Share Economy' as a practicable solution to today's macroeconomic problems.

And that raises my final point: Keynes, it seems to me, *sees the macroeconomic significance of his co-operative economy in the way it influences his ASF*. (In an economy in which Say's Law is applicable, the *ADF is affected*, as we have seen; but Keynes does not point out any way in which a co-operative economy would have a more favourable effect on the ADF than an entrepreneur economy.)   As for Weitzman and his Share Economy: this question is, to me, still obscure. He has managed to write a book about the macroeconomy without making use of either the ADF or the ASF – not even implicitly. That is probably a neat trick but *I* find it a lack, and it explains why I wish that it had been written by someone who can think in the language of Keynes. His book, as brilliant as it is, reminds me of the little boy who shows off his skill in riding his new bike: 'Look, Mum, no hands!' And a few minutes later: 'Look, Mum; no wheels!' Weitzman attempts to tackle his macroeconomic problem by dismissing, or at least disregarding, Macroeconomic Theory. A neat trick if it works. In general, I believe his conclusion to be correct; but I am less convinced by *his* reasoning than I am by Keynes's analysis, skimpy though that is.

NOTES

1. The kind of outside force we have in mind might consist of a government decision to get each firm to raise its output by a predetermined figure – not necessarily the same for each – with the bait being that the demand for each firm's product would rise by just enough to make each expansion worth while. (The demand would rise as and because aggregate output and income rose too.) If this 'Experiment' seems to be completely unrealistic, it is; but a Say's Law economy is completely unrealistic too! If the government decided in a non-Say's

      Law economy to purchase more output from it, borrowing the additional funds it needed, firms would have an incentive to raise their output, but if Say's Law applied strictly – with the Aggregate Demand Price held precisely equal to the Aggregate Supply price – the incentive to expand further would vanish.

2.   Additional workers may not be available but any firm might manage to use the existing work force more intensively by extending hours of work; then it would have to pay premium rates in overtime. If so, the additions to its labour costs for each addition to output beyond its nominal capacity would be higher and higher.

3.   The output that maximizes the firm's profits, in both the narrow sense (the firm's proceeds minus the amount transferred to labour as its share) and the broader (the firm's proceeds) will be the same. In other words, the firm will seek to maximize its 'proceeds', or the amount to be paid to its owners. The two objectives yield the same result. There would be a manifestation of the conflict between Labour and Capital only when labour's share was to be renegotiated.

4.   This overstates the case. If the demand for the firm's output becomes inelastic, its profit would be maximized – as always – at the output at which marginal revenue equals marginal cost, and the marginal revenue would be *zero* at the output that corresponds to the demand elasticity falling to one. Such a situation may not be rare when the economy is in deep depression. But if many firms continue to produce at capacity even when the demand for their products drops, the relatively high (real) incomes they generate by working to capacity will help maintain the demand for the product of other firms. Because of this built-in protection against depression, the qualification contained in this footnote loses its power.

3. What did the *General Theory* do?

G. L. S. Shackle

SUBJECTIVISM AND LIQUIDITY-PREFERENCE

The human individual process is an intimate two-way relation between what the human being sees taking place and what he imagines as able to take place on condition of his acting in some specific way. By his choice of action he can delimit the imagined possibilities. What takes place may reflect some part of what he supposed himself to be making possible, and suggest fresh possibilities. In such a view there is implicit a view of resources not as sure means to a determinate end, but as the ingredients of an alchemist's experiment. In such a view, therefore, there is implicit a lack of knowledge as an element inseparable from human action. In face of recognized unknowledge, action itself must spring from an impulse of varying force, and it must sometimes occur that the force falls short of what is needed for the adoption of a plan which will make seemingly possible great gains or, instead, great losses. What is the character or quality that resources lose, when once committed to a plan? It is, of course, the freedom of choice that they confer while they still possess *liquidity*.

Before he makes his choice amongst the rival deployments that he has conceived for his resources, the rival plans whose first step is some such deployment, he has a choice to make which is beyond the scope of anything but sheer good fortune, since the choosables present themselves one after another out of the void of time-to-come, the rest at each stage unknowable. This prior decision is that of the moment when choice of action should be made. It should be made, if possible, when the basis of judgements seems, as it were, most clear in its suggestions and most firm in their support. Yet how can he know that the clarity and force of to-day's advice will not be surpassed by to-morrow's? In the politician's language this prior choice is the question how long to 'keep his options open'. In the language of business it is the question whether to seize the apparent moment of opportunity, develop the new invention or exploit the new market, or whether still to be conscious of the unguessable extent of his unknowledge. Shall he keep his assets liquid and miss the golden tide, or embark them and risk the storm?

I do not think the term *liquidity* (or its French counterpart) occurs in Cantillon's *Essai sur la nature du commerce en général*, but Cantillon's grasp of the nature of business as something in which time, and its denial to us of knowledge, is the inescapable conditioner of all our efforts enabled him to make a great fortune, and to write a masterpiece of theoretical and practical insight. Cantillon was a banker and it is, indeed, the banking world which has always needed to be careful that its collections of assets were liquid enough. What, then, is asset or resource *liquidity*? Liquidity is the means of coping with *lack of knowledge of the yet non-existent*. An asset will be liquid if it evades the consequences of such unknowledge. Liquidity of their assets is the resort of business men at times of their keenest awareness of unknowledge. The effects of such *liquidity-preference* in reducing the investment flow is the central theme and the greatest novelty of the *General Theory*.

THE INSTRUMENTATION OF THE *GENERAL THEORY*

The *General Theory* divides productive activity into two kinds. One kind *uses* the existing productive apparatus (mines, farms, factories, transport and communications systems) at a level of output *responding* to consumers' demands. The other kind manifests business men's decisions that the apparatus itself can be profitably augmented or given novelty of form and purpose. This second kind is investment. When such decisions are made, their outcome cannot be known. The decisions themselves, warranted in some degree by the observable movement of affairs in the business man's present are the product none the less of imagination and courage, or, as Keynes says of 'animal spirits'. *Investment*, the aggregate of business men's quarterly or yearly expenditure on augmenting or improving their productive facilities, will be sensitive to forces more unforeseen, erratic and self-reinforcing than those which affect consumers' demand. Employment in the closed society can come only from the society itself. The aggregate of the incomes foreseen by its members will be divided by them between intended consumption expenditure per quarter or year and intended saving per quarter or year, the quantity of the latter being a function of the size of the aggregate. This function, the *propensity to consume*, is subject in the *General Theory* to a very simple rule: the larger the society's foreseen income, the larger in *absolute* amount will be the aggregate of intended saving. But *saved* income does not employ anybody. The gap between intended consumption expenditure and aggregate foreseen income must be filled by planned *investment* expenditure, if the foreseen aggregate of income is to be actualized. How big a gap can be filled, and thus how large an aggregate of expenditure, including both kinds, can be achieved, and thus how much employment can be given, depends on the size of intended *investment* expenditure.

But is not the money-circuit closed? Does not saving go into investment? Whether it does so will depend on how highly savers prize the possession of a reserve of money in the bank, a liquid asset which can be turned, at will, into any purchasable kind of thing. If the rate of interest they charge is so high that business men can see no kind of extra, or improved, or entirely novel, production facilities which would add enough, per unit cost of investing in it, to their clear gain from production to cover the cost of such borrowing, they will eschew investment. Liquidity preference, in one of many detailed ways, will have frustrated in some degree the inducement to invest and reduced the society's foreseen income and also its intended expenditure or consumption. Can the whole sheaf of activities settle down at a relatively low level of employment, production, incomes, consumption and investment? The *General Theory*'s instrumentation in no way precludes such a phase.

THE *GENERAL THEORY'S* NEED FOR EXPRESSION IN *EX-ANTE* TERMS

In thus interpreting the *General Theory*'s basic structure, I have reformed its presentation in one elemental respect. Choice is amongst thoughts. In so far as economics is about choice as a *first cause*, that is the coming into being of decisive thoughts not in all respects to be explained by antecedents, it is *essential* to talk in terms of what is foreseen, expected and intended. Myrdalian *ex ante* language would have saved the *General Theory* from describing the flow of investment and the flow of saving as *identically*, tautologically equal, and within the same discourse, treating their equality as a condition which may, or may not, be fulfilled. If these two time-rates are necessarily equal, is it the savers or the investors whose decisions govern its size? Keynes needed to free himself from such entanglements by asking, not what is equal to what, but what sorts of takings-place engender or suggest what thoughts, and what sorts of takings-place those thoughts, spiced, perhaps by some element of absolute origination, can bring about.

In Jerome Bruner's sense (Bruner, 1986), economics at this level is not logical construction but narrative, though subject, as powerful narrative is, to the need to reflect the nature of man.

INVESTMENT AS THE AUTONOMOUS VARIABLE IN THE THEORY OF EMPLOYMENT

Investment, the aggregate of business men's expenditure per time-unit on augmenting or improving their productive facilities, is the lever which, in the instrumentation of the *General Theory*, raises or lowers the society's entire unit-time expenditure on the production of goods. It does so by filling a larger or smaller saving-gap between entire expenditure on production and that on production of goods to replace those concurrently bought by consumers.

If so, the central question which needs to be answered is what governs the size of the flow of investment expenditure or alters it from time to time. I shall describe what the *General Theory* offers in answer to this question and then I shall propose an alternative view which avoids some of the difficulties of Keynes's account, while embracing his main theoretical innovation.

KEYNES'S ACCOUNT OF THE DETERMINATION OF INVESTMENT EXPENDITURE PER UNIT OF TIME

If a business man could know for sure by how much in each named year to come the sale proceeds of product of a proposed additional production facility would exceed its operating expense there would be some rate r per cent per annum which, if used to discount for its deferment each of these amounts of net earnings, would bring the total of their discounted values to equality with the money cost of acquisition of the facility, and the rate r could then be validly compared with the market interest rate at which the business man could borrow funds for this investment so as to decide whether the investment would result in a gain or a loss. But so far from being known for sure, the net earnings of any future year are a mere conjecture subject to falsification by endless and unknowable takings-place. What changes of taste or need, what growth of rival firms, invention of new technologies, swings of political opinion; what momentous decisions of which, since they owe nothing to presently discernible, or to *any*, antecedents, no inkling can be gained, are questions whose answers can entirely transform the prospect for the investment he plans, and mean that such investment is hazardous and daunting in its possible results as well as offering immense prizes.

The rate r, based on the grossly irrelevant supposition of assured knowledge of the content of time-to-come, has to be replaced by an expression which allows for the business man's elemental and irremediable lack of that knowledge. Keynes's concept of the marginal efficiency of capital must be supposed to make this allowance by taking a numerical value different from r. His name for this concept suggests that he had in mind a rate that would be uniform at any one time throughout the whole field of investment. But an investment-decision emerges from arcane processes of thought and feeling belonging uniquely to some individual mind in some particular set of suggestive circumstances. There is no market process which could bring these decisions to a common basis. Keynes insists emphatically that the marginal efficiency of capital reflects business men's ideas of the net earnings that proposed additional production facilities will yield in *each* year to come. He also assumes that the marginal efficiency of capital will be a decreasing function of business men's aggregate current expenditure on investment. These two ideas however are incompatible. There is no positive connection between the net earnings of a production facility in a distant year and business men's current aggregate investment expenditure. It is not even evident whether a larger current flow of investment might not through the multiplier-effect increase current net earnings of existing facilities sufficiently to raise rather than depress expectations of what these facilities might earn in distant years, and thus raise rather than lower the marginal efficiency of capital.

UNCERTAINTY AS RECOGNITION OF POLAR CONTRASTING POSSIBLE OUTCOMES

Uncertainty consists in the recognition that plural rival answers to some question must be treated as non-excludable, as *possible*. An action-chooser's choice amongst rival feasible deployments of his resources will depend on the skein of rival imagined sequels that each such deployment seems to make possible. When such sequels can be assigned by the chooser to places on a scale of desiredness – counter-desiredness, perhaps in terms of a proxy variable such as money value, the effect of choosing one deployment rather than another will be to shift the extreme points of the set of points representing the possible sequels of choice. If possibleness is treated as a category rather than as a variable, so that the question whether something is possible can be answered only by yes or no, sequels of choice which are deemed possible must be deemed *all equally* possible, and only the most desired and the most counter-desired sequel of any deployment will be relevant to choice, since interior points of a skein will be *eclipsed* in the chooser's concern by the extreme points. His choice will then fall on that action whose most desired possible sequel most powerfully outweighs for him its most counter-desired possible sequel.

The meaning for choice contained in polar contrasting possible outcomes cannot be conveyed by any single-valued numerical expression. The concept of the marginal efficiency of capital does not tell what *can* occur at best and at worst. The diadic scenario, of neither more nor less than *two* possibilities, is recognized by the Planning Division of Shell Transport and Trading as the efficient guide for the investment decision maker (Wiseman, 1982, chs 2 and 8).

LIQUIDITY-PREFERENCE, THE RECOIL FROM INVESTMENT

Investment is the giving of hostages to fortune. The business man's reluctance to do this, until the inspired moment is glowingly upon him, will lead him to keep his resources organized to give choice its utmost compass of freedom. Such freedom is epitomized in the word *liquidity*, which Keynes brought from the vocabulary and the thought-mould of banking into the wider world of business entire. For the most vital of the *General Theory's* innovations was its profound permeation of economic theory by the idea of liquidity-preference and its far-reaching implications. By imputing the ups and downs of the interest-rate to hopes and apprehensions of the Bulls and Bears in the bond-market, Keynes had made clear in the *Treatise on Money* that the *level* of the interest-rate is governed by uncertainty. We can go further. The very existence of a long-term interest-rate reflects the inherent character of bonds. To buy a bond is to give a known for an unknown sum of money. The buyer when he buys, that is, when he lends, cannot know at what time to come he will need to repossess his money. To repossess it he will have, at that unknowable time, to sell his bond. At what price will it then sell? He cannot now know.

THE THREE PROPERTIES OF AN ASSET AND THE SPECIAL CASE OF MONEY

It is in Chapter 17 of the *General Theory* that Keynes has put forth his most intense, complex and encompassing theoretical effort. Here he has marshalled a system of implicit questions, and their answers, which, granted the capacity for insight, foresight and judgement that the argument imputes to the human brain at its best, shows that it is the peculiar characteristics of money, the high-liquidity, non-price-responsive asset, that account for the possibility of massive general unemployment. The argument takes the form of comparative statics, and we might conjecture that it is for the sake of the theme of Chapter 17 that Keynes invokes the notion of equilibrium in a work whose purpose is to explain the occurrence of massive general unemployment. Surely the explanation can be far more direct.

SUBTLE BLENDS OF MEANING AND A REVOLUTION OF THOUGHT

The General Theory has two personalities. One of them is oblivious of time-to-come and is concerned essentially only with comparisons of economic measurables that can be observed at some one and the same moment. The other personality bursts suddenly into view in Chapter 12 where the meaning of time-to-come with its content of takings-place not yet in being, and not inferable from the present, appears as the *General Theory*'s real and vital theme.

The meaning and force of the *General Theory* lie, at last, in a few words and expressions bearing on the work of the human psyche. The word *sentiment* stands for the subtle blending of the formal account which a business man may give himself of the state and potential movement of affairs, and the feelings which this engenders. Sentiment is both an opinion and a response to it. By means of such a word, whose skein of nuances the reader is left to assimilate for himself, Keynes conveys a rich meaning with formal simplicity.

The word *confidence* is, of all Keynes's terms, the one which travels furthest in its process of development of meaning. It carries us from one personality of the *General Theory* into the other, and to the extremest manifestation of that other, where, with nothing less than a revolution of mental attitude, it silences the voice of rationality and speaks of *animal spirits* (Keynes, 1936, pp. 161–3). Animal spirits crave and insist upon movement: for the business man, movement is enterprise, in especial it is investment. What has animal spirits to do with the bringing of the marginal efficiency of capital down to equality with the rate of interest?

Confidence is that elected self-deception which sanctions the drive of animal spirits. Confidence is the outer garb of animal spirits, the presentable and intellectually decent name for a state of mind which is in some slight degree self-intoxicated. Confidence is not calculable: *business* is not calculable. The *General Theory*, having spent many chapters on the niceties of comparison, and the little less and the little more, suddenly rejects them and explains why *liquidity preference* haunts the investing business world.

Some reality is given to the notion of individual confidence by its claim to measurable effects. To have confidence in some view of things is to accept that view for practical purposes up to some limited scale. Anything in 'the news' which calls that view in question will be a ground for drawing-in such limits. Such drawing-in will become known to other decision-makers, their own hesitations will thus be reinforced, and the process of development of a *conventional* view will have begun.

INVESTMENT, THE STIMULANT AND DEPRESSANT OF BUSINESS

Investment, the expenditure per time-unit on augmenting and improving the society's equipment of buildings and production facilities in general, brings about by a rise or fall of its level a rise or fall also of expenditure on goods meant for immediate consumption. Investment thus, in the Keynesian theme, governs the whole tempo of the economic process. Two questions are thus posed: How are changes in the level of the investment flow themselves engendered? and: Can we regard that engenderment as itself the systematic consequence of still other takings-place, and thus ultimately traceable to an earlier change in the level of investment, so that the course of events as a whole constitutes a *cycle*? If the *General Theory*'s second personality is its true meaning, the motivation of investment must be seen as *original*, as in no way the *consistent* upshot of antecedent circumstances, as indeed *autonomous*, a law unto itself. If so, motivation can fail. Investment can flag, and leave potential resources unexploited. A consistently high level of employment would be the phenomenon requiring explanation. It is perhaps the 1960s rather than the 1930s that should surprise us.

CHANGING THE NATURE OF A DISCIPLINE

How did the *General Theory* come to have two personalities and to which of them are we to attend? Keynes says that the writing of this book was 'a long struggle of escape'. It is in Chapter 12 that the bonds are burst asunder with dramatic, astonishing violence and decisiveness. The *volte face*, the turning away from the marginal efficiency equation and the uncompromising, clear statements in which Keynes seems almost to rejoice, that the business of launching enterprises by investment in their required facilities is not motivated by calculation and a case made out by data, but is the manifestation of a surge of the restless human spirit: this *volte face* occurs with the utmost suddenness. When the *General Theory* is described as 'lacking a clear design' (Professor J.C. Gilbert) or as an 'obscure and discursive work' (Professor Alan Coddington) or as 'an exceedingly bewildering and vexatious book' (Coddington), we may feel that Keynes started to write one book and ended by writing another, and that in turning from reformist to revolutionary he was outpacing his followers and his critics and leaving them to wonder which of many roads to the horizon he had followed and whither he had disappeared.

4. Subjectivism and Post-Keynesianism: Towards a Better Understanding

Stephan Böhm

INTRODUCTION

The title of this chapter may give rise to serious misunderstandings; it requires immediate clarification. In keeping with the general theme of the present conference volume, the tone of this essay is constructive rather than critical. Its aim is not, primarily, to identify and explore the domain of 'subjectivist' elements and their ramification within the 'economics of Keynes', but rather to suggest affinities and, to a lesser extent, to expose disagreements between two bodies of thought which share a healthy scepticism towards neoclassical economics – albeit for different reasons. However, a warning should be issued at the outset. It is by no means a small order to discern the wood from the many trees that have passed through the pulper in the cause of either subjectivism or post-Keynesianism in recent years. A 'fair' representation – in the permissive sense of pleasing everybody – is bound to be illusory.

'Subjectivism' is an elusive concept embraced by a host of writers from a diversity of 'schools', traditions and approaches.[1] It is perhaps only fair to point out, however, that the most outspoken and self-assured champions of subjectivism are to be found among an ever-growing group of authors who profess allegiance to the 'Austrian' tradition, as epitomized in the writings of Ludwig von Mises and Friedrich von

Hayek. Indeed, an all-embracing subjectivism forms the *pièce de résistance* in the Austrian citadel.[2] The prominent display of 'subjectivism' and its likening to 'post-Keynesianism' in the title of this paper provides in itself a pertinent reminder of how prevailing attitudes within the profession have changed, from an outright hostility towards subjectivism[3] to an admittedly still widespread sentiment of benign neglect and blissful ignorance, but also, more importantly, to a greater readiness in some unsuspicious, 'non-Austrian' quarters to appreciate the subtle intricacies of subjectivist reasoning.[4]

But all is not well that ends well. The claim that modern Austrians adhere to a subjectivist position is liable to important qualifications. There is a scramble for the subjectivist's mantle which has been raging for some time now within 'Austrian' circles, and which has only recently become noticeable for 'outsiders'.[5] To paraphrase Sir John Hicks (1979), p. 51), there are two sorts of subjectivists: Open Subjectivists and Particular Subjectivists. The former, under the formidable aegis of veteran Austrian economist Ludwig Lachmann, categorically dismiss the vision of the market economy as an equilibrating system as sheer folly and view themselves as 'radical uncertainty challengers'. This 'irregular and defective' (to use Sir John's words again) strand which elevates subjectivism to an art form[6] clashes head-on with Israel Kirzner's more moderate, 'middle-of-the road' variant of subjectivism,[7] which tries to steer a middle course between *Scylla* – neoclassical determinism – and *Charybdis* – Lachmannian radical subjectivism or, less sympathetically, analytical nihilism – and to have it both ways,[8] as it were.

The argument pursued in this essay is not only that there are at least superficial parallels between Austrian and fundamentalist Keynesian[9] theorizing *vis-à-vis* neoclassical, mainstream economics which warrant closer attention (this is certainly not to deny that those similarities *may* be based on vastly differing visions of the economic process, giving rise in turn to divergent policy stances); but rather that the rift within the Austrian school in some ways mirrors the split within the Cambridge school between the (hyphenless) post-Keynesians and the neo-

Ricardians.[10] From the viewpoint of the history of economic thought it is, moreover, mildly ironic that in this reading Keynes, in his insistence on the rôle of expectations, may turn out to be the 'master subjectivist' who 'promoted the cause of the hermeneutic mode of thought in economic theory' (Lachmann, 1986, p.

161) while the supposedly subjectivist Austrians Hayek and Mises, with respect to expectations, 'failed to grasp with both hands this golden opportunity in the 1930s to enlarge the basis of their approach and . . . treated the subject rather gingerly' (Lachmann, 1976, p. 58).[11]

It would seem to be expedient to invoke Davidson's tripartite characterisation of post-Keynesianism (Davidson, 1981, pp. 158–63; see Kay in this volume) as a basis for comparison between the contending schools of thought. However, these propositions are stated in such general terms in respect of their insistence on the importance of historical ('real') time, expectations and institutions that they are hardly suited to draw any criticism from those favouring the Austrian approach; quite the contrary: they can be assured of their unreserved approval. As O'Driscoll and Rizzo (1985, p. 9) add: 'What is even more surprising is that Davidson's explication of the meaning of these propositions increases, rather than reduces, the area of overlap. It is evident that there is much common ground between post-Keynesian subjectivism and Austrian subjectivism.' O'Driscoll and Rizzo go on to lament that 'Crossfertilization between these two schools is, however, exceedingly rare, although the possibilities for mutually advantageous interchange seem significant'.

O'Driscoll's and Rizzo's plea for 'mutually advantageous interchange' has certainly not passed unnoticed. Recent work by Clark (1987–8), Dow (1983, 1985), Garrison (1984, 1985, 1986, 1987, 1987a), Hodgson (1985), Kregel (1986), and Snippe (1987, 1987a) suggests that there is *some* area of overlap, whose scope, however, varies considerably according to which strand of Austrianism is under review[12] – the 'orthodox' Austrian position represented by Kirzner and Garrison, or the 'kaleidic' view of the world inspired by Shackle and Lachmann. Given the great extent to which O'Driscoll and

Rizzo subscribe to the latter's views (their book is dedicated to Lachmann),[13] their spirited call for a closer link with the post-Keynesians is hardly surprising.

The minimal requirements of 'methodological pluralism' – the view that 'takes as a starting assumption that no universally applicable, logically compelling method of theory appraisal exists' (Caldwell, 1982, p. 245) – dictate that alternative research programmes be made comparable to each other. If the theoretical aims and epistemological constraints of rival research programmes are taken as given, this may not be possible, however. In the best of all worlds vistas of a rational discourse may open up, nevertheless, in that divisive issues come clearer into focus, former lack of appreciation gives way to informed judgement, and former adversaries stop talking *beyond* each other. The doctrine of methodological pluralism should not be misconstrued as a convenient passport to the methodological fairyland of 'Anything Goes'; as Caldwell (1982, pp. 250–2) persuasively argues, critical faculties and the associated methodological standards and criteria need not be suspended under methodological pluralism. Needless to say, within the proverbial confines of one short chapter it is hardly possible to do full justice to the whole gamut of issues that are pertinent to our theme. Instead, potential directions for future research will be delineated. The following account is not so much meant to be a juxtaposition of alternative stands on specific, contested areas (for example, on microfoundations, equilibrium and expectations)[14] as an interweaving of different strands of arguments.[15]

SUBJECTIVISM AND SUBJECTIVISM

The method of subjectivism

The concept of subjectivism permeates modern Austrian economics to such an extent that it owes its historical and methodological identity to a conscious relation with it; Austrian economics *is*, for better or worse, the economics of subjectivism.[16] Before turning to more substantive matters and at the risk of appearing to be excessively pedantic, it may be useful first to pin down what is meant by subjectivism. The tendency for 'subjectivism' to be treated as a received notion is not devoid of pitfalls of its own.

At the most basic level, methodological subjectivism focuses attention on the actor's view of the world; all phenomena – social and natural – are perceived from the perspective of the actor. In the words of Fritz Machlup, an unsung hero of subjectivism,[17]

In the explanation of economic phenomena we have to go back to judgments and choices made by individuals on the basis of whatever knowledge they have or believe to have and whatever expectations they entertain regarding external developments and especially the consequences of their own intended actions. (Machlup, 1982, p. 40)

Stated this way, it becomes apparent that questions concerning the knowledge actors are assumed to possess occupy centre stage in subjectivist economics. The protean quality of knowledge defies the solving of neatly stated 'problems' which are laid out before us in all their essentials, yearning to be exposed to the analytical machinery associated with the rationalist ideal. Economics need no longer be confined to a stale backwater of engineering science; instead, it should be seen – in George Shackle's phraseology – as a branch of *epistemics*, the theory of thought. Subjectivism rests on the premise that the products of the human mind, thought in all its manifestations – to inquire, to reason, to deduce, to wonder, to expect, to imagine, to conjecture, to guess, to envisage, and so on – is the epitome of the human predicament.[18] Reflections on the desired employment of one's own resources and thoughts about others' thoughts – that is, conjectures – about how to apply the resources entrusted to them form the very textural fabric of economics from a subjectivist point of view. The strong anti-materialist or – better, perhaps – anti-realist bias inherent in such a position, namely, that the economist's foremost concern should be with thoughts about tangible objects rather than with those things themselves, flies in the face of stereotyped notions of the discipline and, taken at face value, may seem perverse.[19] It appears to be this sort of 'radical subversion' (Littlechild, 1979) that even those who are, in principle, sympathetic towards subjectivist modes find hard to swallow.[20] More often than not, these harsh strictures can be put down to misunderstandings, however.

Under the doctrine of methodological subjectivism the social scientist is required to decipher the meaning human agents attach to their actions (Langlois, 1985, p. 310). The comprehension of the meaning of actions – as opposed to physical or mathematical relationships – is the method of *Verstehen* (understanding) in the sense of Max Weber.[21] The understanding of social action as the manifestation of the subjective meaning the actor bestows upon his action – that is, the meaning it has for him – raises the following, fundamental problem: Granted that the meaning an action has for an actor is unique and individual because it originates in the unique and individual biographical situation of the actor, how is it then possible to grasp subjective meaning objectively ('scientifically')? (See Schutz, 1953, pp. 27–8.)

The problem can be disposed of by heeding the distinction between 'subjectivity' and the 'subjective point of view'. The term *subjectivity* refers exclusively to the experiences, goals, motives, and so on, of a concrete individual; the subjective meaning inherent in action is always the meaning which the acting person ascribes to his own conduct: it comprises his reasons for acting and his objectives, his perception of the situation in which he finds himself and that of other persons, the definition of his own rôle and that accorded to others in the given situation, and so on. Genuine subjectivity must be sharply distinguished from the *subjective point of view* of the economist-observer for whom subjective meanings are crucial factors in the study of social interactions. Following Schutz (1954, p. 53), these meanings are not private but intersubjective; they are part and parcel of the social reality in which we live and which is sustained by intercommunication and language. In dealing with subjective meanings, the analyst applies interpretative conceptual schemes, 'mind-constructs', specific frames of reference – that is, sets of objective concepts (for example, means–ends frameworks) which refer to the subjectivity of human action. It should be stressed that, methodologically, these concepts differ in no way from those of an objective point of view; the difference bears upon the procedure by which knowledge is obtained. The *subjective interpretation* of social phenomena derives from an objective frame of reference honouring the subjective point of view. 'All interpretation requires a pre-existent structure of thought to serve as a frame of reference' (Lachmann, 1978, p. 67). *Economic understanding* is the result of an economist's subjective interpretation of the phenomena of human action that he studies; as such, it belongs to the objective realm of economic analysis.

The foregoing account, in its desperate brevity, represents a thumbnail sketch of a subjectivist–interpretative type of approach to the methodology of the social sciences, drawing its inspiration from Weber and Schutz. Without having examined the subtleties of and the problems that go hand in hand with it (see Böhm, 1982 for a brief review of some of the main issues), suffice it to suggest that such a position is broadly shared by O'Driscoll and Rizzo[22] and Lachmann and their followers among the Austrians. Whilst all Austrian subjectivists[23] are staunch exponents of methodological dualism – that is, they insist that the appropriate approach to the social sciences be a subjectivist–interpretative methodology with its attendant teleological mode of explanation of human action, as opposed to an objectivist–behaviourist methodology with its causal mode of explanation – there is much less agreement on the crucial issue of empirical testing. On the one hand, Mises's epistemological *a priorism*[24] categorically rules out any rôle whatsoever for empirical testing, whether of assumptions or of hypotheses; on the other hand, O'Driscoll and Rizzo, following Hayek, seem to envisage a moderate rôle for empirical tests in establishing whether or not particular interpretative theories are applicable to specific real-world situations (O'Driscoll and Rizzo, 1985, ch. 2).[25]

Hayek and Keynes

It is interesting to find the Austrians in general agreement with Keynes on important matters of methodology.[26] (See also

Lachmann, 1983, pp. 374–5.) Although methodological pronouncements, with their philosophical foundations having been laid in *A Treatise on Probability*, are scattered all over his works, Keynes's correspondence with Harrod concerning the latter's Presidential Address to Section F of the British Association, 'Scope and Method of Economics' (*Economic Journal*, September 1938), and – in connection with it – concerning the econometric aspects of Jan Tinbergen's work for the League of Nations is suggestively illuminating in this regard.

From that correspondence, Keynes emerges, first of all, as someone who is highly suspicious of what Hayek (1979, p. 24) later was to label as *scientism*, or *scientistic* prejudice – the 'slavish imitation of the method and language of Science'. Keynes (1973a, p. 296) notes that 'economics is a branch of logic, a way of thinking', and that 'attempts . . . to turn it into a pseudo-natural science' should be strongly resisted. And further in this vein (p. 300): 'the art of thinking in terms of models is a difficult . . . practice. The pseudo-analogy with the physical sciences leads directly counter to the habit of mind which is most important for an economist proper to acquire.'

Keynes repeatedly drew attention to the fact that in economics the material under study – human conduct under various institutional contexts – was not sufficiently 'homogeneous' through time to warrant the adoption of the tools of the physical sciences. The 'extreme complexity of the actual course of events' (Keynes, 1936, p. 249) precludes the classification of variables according to some 'objective' yardstick; the division into dependent and independent variables is always subject to the purpose of the analysis at hand, and relative to a given historical context. What may sensibly be considered as a dependent variable in one context, may equally well be treated as an independent variable in another. Since there are no particular factors which are accorded pride of place in his theory, Keynes's account may therefore be interpreted as an interactionist one (Lawson, 1985a, p. 924).

The thesis concerning the 'complexity of the economic material' is also a recurring theme in Hayek's work (see especially Hayek, 1967, ch. 2). Contrary to those critics of 'scientism' who simply throw up their hands in despair proclaiming that 'social science is not "really" possible', Hayek, like Keynes, is concerned with designing a systematic methodology which enables us to do theoretical work in the face of the apparently insurmountable problems posed by the 'complexity' of social phenomena. However vague and ambiguous the term may be, it is fairly safe to maintain that, in a very broad connotation, it encapsulates all those problems which are held to exacerbate the establishment and development of a theoretical social science. More specifically, ever since J.S. Mill's discussion of the moral sciences in *A System of Logic* has it been a familiar complaint that the relevant factors in social–scientific studies are far too numerous ('plurality of causes') to be ascertained and too rapidly in flux to provide the necessary stable conditions for the separation of causes from contingently accompanying factors. It is precisely this problem that Keynes has in mind when he writes:

The object of a model is to segregate the semi-permanent or relatively constant factors from those which are transitory or fluctuating so as to develop a logical way of thinking about the latter, and of understanding the time sequences to which they give rise in particular cases. (Keynes, 1973a, pp. 296–7)

In his 'Degrees of Explanation', Hayek holds that in the construction and application of 'patterns of explanation' for typical complex situations as encountered in economics we are essentially performing a deductive task, which does not provide us with new knowledge:

What will be new about such a 'new' explanation of some phenomena will be the particular combination of theoretical statements with statements about facts regarded as significant for the particular situation (the 'initial' and 'marginal conditions'), not any one of the theoretical statements from which it starts. And the problem will not be whether the model as such is true, but whether it is applicable to (or true *of*) the phenomena it is meant to explain. (Hayek, 1967, p. 7; emphasis in the original)

The assertion that a certain explanatory pattern (or model) is applicable is an empirical, and hence falsifiable statement; in this case, 'applicability' refers to the phenomenon to be explained rather than to a subsumption of concrete initial conditions to the abstract conditions contained in the if–component of a nomological statement. Without intimating that Keynes's is a falsificationist account, it does not seem far-fetched to attribute to him some variant of a moderate 'applicability thesis' when he declares that 'Economics is a science of thinking in terms of models joined to the art of choosing models which are relevant to the contemporary world' (Keynes, 1973a, p. 296). Keynes's theory of induction, as set out in his *Treatise on Probability*, pre-empts a major rôle for testing in the sense of protracted efforts at falsification of hypotheses or models (Keynes uses these terms interchangeably); he is not so much concerned with the validity of the hypotheses themselves as with the degree of belief which it is rational for an agent to entertain, given the available evidence (see Lawson, 1985a, p. 124). In Keynes's logical[27] theory of probability, in stark contrast to the relative frequency concept of probability[28] espoused in the natural sciences, probability does not refer to a property of the physical world but rather to the beliefs people hold about the world. According to Keynes (1973, p. 3), the study of 'conduct' belongs to those branches of knowledge, along with science and metaphysics, which do not lend themselves to demonstrative certainty, and which are, to a greater or lesser degree, inherently inconclusive. Therefore, Keynes goes on to maintain, a theory of probability is required in those fields.

What is particularly interesting to note for present purposes is the intimate link that connects Keynes's view of probability to his approach to economics. The theory of probability judgements underlies his account both of probability and of individual action. 'To believe one thing *in preference* to another . . . must have reference to action and must be a loose way of expressing the propriety of *acting* on one hypothesis rather than on another. We might put it, therefore, that the probable is the hypothesis on which it is rational for us to act' (Keynes, 1973, p. 339; emphasis in the original). Rejecting the causal explanation of action in terms of natural laws, Keynes views economic agents as active, purposive, self-conscious beings whose behaviour is guided by the very hypotheses on which their probability judgements are based. The reasonableness that Keynes ascribes to action must not be construed as deductive logical certainty, however; agents are portrayed as being bounded by limited knowledge of the circumstances bearing upon their actions. On the other hand, they are not perceived as taking a plunge into the void; conventions, social practices and institutions – that is, the social context, or structure, surrounding actions – substitute for partial ignorance (see Keynes, 1973a, p. 124).[29]

Carabelli (1985, pp. 172–4) has commendably drawn attention to the symmetry in Keynes's account that informs the reasoning of both the economic analyst and the object of his analysis, the economic actor. Just as the economist's theories and policy proposals are derived from probability judgements, ranging from 'we have some reason to believe' to 'we simply do not know', individual actions are based on a belief-model conforming to the hypotheses which guide the economist in his work. Thus, both the economist and the actor are assumed to proceed according to essentially the same logic.

Keynes's idea of the relationship between the economist and his subject-matter is mirrored in the way he conceives of the relationship between economic theory and policy. Since the probability judgements guiding individual actions are based on flimsy foundations such as ordinary beliefs, pessimistic or optimistic sentiments, conventional judgements or average opinions, rather than being rooted in infallible certainty, they are liable to change. Given the impossibility of demonstrating its truth, the rôle of theory is to persuade, or to influence public opinion and beliefs. Therefore, Keynes's penchant for interventionism is closely tied up with his 'latent rhetorical bent' (Carabelli, 1985, p. 173). The relationship between the economist and those whose actions he tries to influence – consumers, entrepreneurs, politicians, trade unions, 'the public' – parallels the relationship between an author and his audience. As Carabelli aptly puts it, 'On the one hand, the economist was able to *verstehen* his subject of study. At the same time, he could influence it by his writings. He could change the social understanding of the economic agent and, consequently, change his behaviour and action too. Conversely, the economic agent could react to theory, thus influencing the economist's beliefs' (p. 173). (On this, compare also Hodgson, 1985.)

Turning to the Austrians again, one may safely assume that they find Keynes's well-known references to economics being a moral science most to their liking. In his correspondence with Harrod already mentioned above, Keynes (1973a, p. 297) remarks, 'economics is essentially a moral science and not a natural science. That is to say, it employs introspection and judgments of value.' And again, in what surely is his most outspoken pronouncement in this matter, Keynes rejects the employment of the Newtonian method in economics:

I also want to emphasise strongly the point about economics being a moral science. I mentioned before that it deals with motives, expectations, psychological uncertainties. One has to be constantly on guard against treating the material as constant and homogeneous It is as though the fall of the apple to the ground depended on the apple's motives; on whether it is worth while falling to the ground, and whether the ground wanted the apple to fall, and on mistaken calculations on the part of the apple as to how far it was from the centre of the earth. (Keynes, 1973a, p. 300)

Austrians may draw comfort and inspiration from this remarkable passage, but its subjectivist connotations should not be stressed too strongly. Whilst being true that Hayek and Keynes strikingly share a number of important misgivings about the quantification of economics, the affinity abruptly stops when they consider the implications for public policy of the essentially and irreducibly 'complex' nature of social phenomena.

Hayek's argument concerning the 'complexity' of the social sphere is at heart an epistemological one; it does not primarily turn on insufficient data availability but rather on ways of knowing (as noted by Addison, Burton and Torrance, 1984, p. 6). Hayek's point that the knowledge we can hope to obtain in the social sciences is markedly inferior in scope and precision as compared with the natural sciences is bound to have far-reaching repercussions on interventionist policies. When the endeavours of the investigator are essentially confined to recognizing recurrent patterns in social life, and to construct *abstract* models of social processes, well-meaning public policies aimed at generating *specific* desired effects may turn out to be ultimately self-defeating, owing to the limited knowledge on the part of the practitioners of such policies of the ways in which isolated – that is, directed only at a small section of the system of interdependent actions – commands requiring specific actions make themselves felt on a system-wide level. This is the gist of the Hayekian argument against 'interference' in the market grounded on 'complexity'.[30]

One of the chief results so far achieved by theoretical work in these fields [such as economics] seems to me to be the demonstration that here individual events regularly depend on so many concrete circumstances that we shall never in fact be in a position to ascertain them all; and that in consequence . . . the ideal of prediction and *control* must largely remain beyond our reach. . . . (Hayek, 1967, p. 34; emphasis added)

In stark contrast, Keynes proclaimed the active rôle of the economist in fostering social change (witness his *Essays in Persuasion*). As his eminent biographer (Harrod, 1972, p. 226) pointed out, the 'presuppositions of Harvey Road' encompass the notion that governmental affairs are most smoothly run by a small band of bright people, a kind of 'intellectual aristocracy', chiefly relying on the methods of persuasion in the propagation of their ideas. The agreements reached at Bretton Woods provided a splendid example after which economic government should be fashioned. Keynes's idea of the economist as a trustee, 'not of civilization, but of the *possibility* of civilization' (Harrod, 1972, p. 227; emphasis added) accords well with his view of the constant possibility of change in society.

Hayek on several occasions (see, for example, Hayek, 1967, pp. 89–90; Hayek. 1973, pp. 25–6) refers to Keynes's moral beliefs as a prime example of what he terms 'constructivist rationalism', or 'constructivist fallacy' – a view which emerges most clearly, according to Hayek, from the former's autobiographical essay 'My Early Beliefs', which amounts to a full-scale dismissal of conventional morals. The kind of rationalism espoused by Keynes and shared by many of the most famous spirits of his time repudiated any commitment to abstract moral rules, traditional wisdom and convention; it recognized no inner obligation to conform or to obey, and was thus, strictly speaking, amoral. The rejection of traditional beliefs and moralities entailed the claim that each case should be judged on its own merits, and that all means are justified by the ends pursued.

Two comments may be in order here. First of all, Keynes's denial of the binding nature of *any* abstract rules – moral or otherwise – and its concomitant claim that man is capable to arrange his affairs successfully, without having to take recourse to general rules for guidance and reassurance, in full knowledge of the circumstances pertaining to his actions and of all the alternative courses of action open to him encapsulates Western man's eternal ambition to gain total control over his life. Elsewhere, in strange contrast, we are told that we have to fall back on 'conventions' (see Keynes, 1936, p. 152) in taking decisions, and that 'The social object of skilled investment should be to defeat the dark forces of time and ignorance which envelop our future' (p. 155). This tension, if it is one, between the constant urge to depart from rules, principles or conventions – epitomizing, as it does, a view of man as the assured master of his circumstances – and the dire necessity to cling to those very rules, principles, or conventions for guidance – epitomising, as it does, a view of man as the prisoner of time – points to one of the more enduring enigmatic aspects emanating from the work of the most sparkling of all the great economists.

The second comment concerns a deeply disturbing, even paradoxical feature of Hayek's work. For someone like Hayek who is hailed as the leading classical liberal thinker of our age, and who himself has taken great pains to elaborate on why he is not a conservative, the intensely moralistic stance that he adopts is, to put it mildly, a trifle unsettling at first sight. But here again one encounters a familiar argument. Hayek's defence of traditional beliefs, values and morals against rationalistic criticism is grounded in the thesis that one should not tinker with long-cherished belief structures because that might upset the social bonds upon which society rests. Given that, by definition, only successful societies can survive, and that we are more or less ignorant of the factors contributing towards their success, the escape route seems to be complete. Faced with a choice between the benefits accruing from the protected, community-held system of beliefs and values in a closed society and the Popperian spirit of critical inquiry characteristics of an open society, Hayek plainly opts for the former. Against Keynes and Popper, Hayek seems to hold that incessant rationalistic criticism may be too much of a good thing, and that it may also undermine the moral values on which an open society is based.[31]

Static versus dynamic subjectivism

As adumbrated above, the main task for the theorist seeking to comply with methodological subjectivism is to devise a method which accounts for the subjective meaning of human action in an objective way. This involves, first, the construction of a model of a hypothetical individual mind ('the mind-construct') in terms of its goals, constraints and knowledge, and secondly, relating the activities attributed to such a mind-construct to the observed facts that we wish to explain in an 'understandable' way (see Schutz, 1953, p. 34). There are two related problems that need to be addressed at the outset: first, what typical contents must be imputed to the mind-construct in order to account for the phenomena we wish to explain? and secondly, what is an understandable relation? (See O'Driscoll and Rizzo, 1985, p. 21.)

The activities ascribed to the mind-construct may be said to be understandable if it is at least conceivable that reasonable men, endowed with the knowledge of the hypothetical actor, would act in a way consistent with the abstract model. As Langlois (1985, pp. 310–12) has suggested, the requirement of understandability may, in principle, assume one of two forms. On the first criterion – 'strict' or 'rationalist' in Langlois's phraseology – human action is identified with rational action. Rationality refers to the consistency of actions, and basically it involves a logical operation, the logically correct deduction of conclusions from explicitly stated premises. Thus rationality is not so much a property of the agent as of the (re)constructed problem situation itself. Given a properly specified means-ends framework, all the options available to the agent are pared down to the optimizing – that is, rational – 'choice'. On the second criterion – 'loose' or 'institutionalist', according to Langlois – the concept of rationality embedded in the understandability relation is a much wider one. Just as on the strict criterion, the loose criterion is also centred on a (re)construction of the logic of the situation the agent finds himself in; the difference derives from a notion of rationality that goes far beyond the deduction of logically correct conclusions from premises, and which therefore does not easily translate into optimizing behaviour (see Langlois, 1985, p. 312). Keynes's theory of rationality under uncertainty (see Lawson, 1985), which relies heavily on social practices such as routines, conventions and institutions, may be regarded as fitting an instance as any of the loose, or institutionalist criterion of understandability.

Related to this distinction between 'strict' and 'loose' forms of rationality is the differentiation between 'static' and 'dynamic' subjectivism.[32] Mind-constructs or abstract conceptual schemes such as 'monopolist', 'firm', 'consumer', and so on, are nothing but 'a kind of intellectual shorthand' (Schutz, 1953, p. 27) in which the underlying subjectivist elements of the activities attributed to them (ends, means, motives, perceptions, relevances, and so on) are either held at bay or accorded a catalytic rôle in explanation. The static version of subjectivism emanates from subjective value theory and has squarely been incorporated into neoclassical analysis. The statically subjectivist view of decision-making suppresses the creative and indeterminate elements inherent in choice by treating the mind-construct as a passive transmitting device through which the circumstances bearing upon action are perceived. On this account, choice serves as a mere deterministic link between circumstances and actions. Indeed, if the chosen course of action is already implied in the given configuration of preferences and obstacles, one must no longer talk of genuine choice at all.

By way of contrast, dynamic or 'creative' subjectivism is predicated upon the presupposition that decision-making is not rigidly determined by external events. Dynamically subjectivist choice is inherently indeterminate and, hence, incompatible with perfect predictability. The mind-construct, in that case, is no longer envisaged as a passive filter but rather as an imaginative powerhouse. The outcome of choice can no longer be explained – and predicted – on the basis of the knowledge of the initial conditions and some general law; the point is that even if we had perfect knowledge of the antecedents, choice cannot unambiguously be traced back to them.

Pushed to its limits, this dynamically subjectivist view can be a highly explosive thing. There can be no better way of illustrating this than by reference to the inspired work of G.L.S. Shackle who has relentlessly pursued and endlessly refined this theme with single-minded devotion over the course of half a century. Central to Shackle's vision of the economic process is his notion of social history as being engendered by thought. Choice is a new beginning, a source of events; as Shackle has never grown tired of hammering home to the profession, choice is originative, generative, active, creative, fertile, effective, inceptive, non-empty, non-powerless, history-making . . . (These are only some of the words Shackle uses to invest choice with an aura of fascination and mystery.) Shackle proceeds by inquiring into the consequences of assuming that (at least some part of)[33] a choice of action constitutes a 'cause uncaused' (see Shackle, 1979, ch. 4). If choice does make a difference, the argument runs, if it can be an *ex nihilo* origination, how can there ever be knowledge of the future? 'If future choices will engender history, how can that history be now inferred?' (Shackle, 1972, p. 123). Since knowledge of the contents of 'time-to-come' cannot be derived from present or past conditions, the future is nothing but the 'void'. Indeed, 'To call it the future is to concede the presumption that it is already "existent" and merely waiting to appear' (Shackle, 1972, p. 122).[34]

This decisionist, or voluntaristic, view of history contrasts sharply with an idea of 'history without humanity' – determinism. 'Determinism is the view that history in every particular from eternity to eternity exists *independently* of human knowledge or initiative' (Shackle, 1976, p. 309; emphasis added). Determinism invokes secular social development, whilst non-determinism or decisionism focuses on the present, the 'moment-in-being'. In Shackle's non-determinist account, there is a yawning abyss separating the past from the present; the past is a closed book not making itself felt on the present,[35] whilst the present is the arena of spontaneous creativity. Against a commonly held belief that the present is a kind of imaginary dividing line between the past and the future, Shackle would insist that the present is a 'double cut-off' (1976, p. 310). In an aside on Shackle's conception of the interrelation between the past and the present, Giddens (1979, p. 70) interestingly suggests a close affinity between the former's perspective and that developed by Sartre in his *The Critique of Dialectical Reason*, and he opines that 'it would not be too inaccurate to regard Shackle's work as a kind of Sartrean economic theory'.

Sensing how easily the unwary may become intoxicated by, and addicted to, Shackle's sweet poison, a number of commentators have enunciated grave misgivings about the extremes to which the dynamics of subjectivism is taken here. One of them was worried that the emphasis on subjectivist ideas and their associated implications of uncertainty and indeterminism would 'drive a wedge between behavior and circumstances', and that 'if the wedge were to become comprehensive, they [the post-Keynesians – and the Austrians, one may add] would be left with no theory at all, all behavior would appear equally capricious and unintelligible' (Coddington, 1982, p. 486). Another commentator, echoing Coddington's dire warnings, has aired similar sentiments to the effect that, if expectations and current knowledge were 'nothing more than creative acts of the imagination' (Lawson, 1987, p. 955), this would evoke the spectre of knowledge losing its grip on 'objective reality'.

Conceding that Shackle's position may be extremely vulnerable to this sort of criticism, the case for the subjectivist approach as a whole is not necessarily seen to be thoroughly undermined by it. It would appear that the method of the mind-construct developed by O'Driscoll and Rizzo effectively disposes of the main force of the above strictures. Once it is taken for granted that the chasm separating action and circumstances cannot be bridged by the application of logic alone, and that 'there is more to conduct than passively "recording" circumstances and then, as an essentially computational matter, acting in these recorded circumstances in accordance with one's interests' – as Coddington (1975, p. 152) had observed in a rather different vein – then it follows on from this reasoning that the logic of explanation pertinent to dynamic subjectivism is not adequately captured by the covering-law model of scientific explanation put forth by Hempel and Oppenheim (1948), which was seen to be at the heart of static subjectivism. 'Mind constructs that yield the required behavior as a determinate implication of initial conditions and a theory cannot be genuinely dynamic' (O'Driscoll and Rizzo, 1985, p. 26).

What is clearly required in place of logical deducability is a non-determinist explanatory schema which renders decision-making neither illusory *nor* unbounded. Hence, the argument advanced on behalf of indeterminism should not be construed as a licence for wishful thinking; to the extent that complete unpredictability would eventually paralyze all action, creative decision-making must be restrained.[36] The originative element in choice is superimposed on, and anchored in, the determinate structure underlying static decision-making in the sense that the latter provides a 'necessary empirical foundation' (O'Driscoll and Rizzo, 1985, p. 28) for the former. To put it into sharper focus, the issue is not whether all decision-making is truly 'creative', as Shackle avers, nor even that it is predominantly so, but rather that there must be some room in our theoretical reasoning for its accommodation, at whatever decisive moments and however seldom it may occur. It is not a question of complete determinism versus indeterminism, or total and precise predictability versus unpredictability, but of the *degree* of indeterminism that should be incorporated into a theory of decision-making.

What emerges, then, on the view set out above is emphatically not an attempt to bid farewell to theoretical considerations altogether – as dreaded by the critics – but a controlled effort to devise a theoretical language for the expression of the inherently imprecise quality of many, if not most, concepts encountered in economics (see Coddington, 1975, p. 158). The theoretical aim is no longer predictability based on mathematical probability, but intelligibility or reasonableness based on 'favourable relevance' or 'increased likelihood', in the sense that the observed outcome is 'rendered more likely' – this is not meant to imply a high likelihood – on the given mind-construct model than on any other model (see O'Driscoll and Rizzo, 1985, pp. 26–7).

But there may be a general problem with the type of explanation presented above, which can be highlighted briefly with reference to Popper's method of objective understanding, or situational logic. (To avoid any connotations of determinism, Popper sometimes seems to prefer the term 'situational analysis'.) Drawing on what he takes to be the typical procedure followed by economists, Popper advocates an approach to the social sciences which in its proffered explanations seeks to eschew any 'subjective' – that is, psychological – ideas, and to replace them with 'objective situational elements'; he proposes that social scientists adopt a mode of explanation of individual actions based on the 'logic of the situation' in which the actors find themselves. This involves, first, the 'logical reconstruction' of the problem-situation – an analysis of the situation in terms of the actor's aims, beliefs and constraints – and, secondly, an assessment of the kind of 'logical' response 'appropriate to the situation' as perceived by the actor (see, for example, Popper, 1976, pp. 102–3). To the extent that the observed behaviour corresponds to the logic of the situation, it is deemed to be rational. The rationality principle[37] which is thus invoked in all social science explanations enables us, according to Popper, to render perceived actions 'intelligible' in an objective way.

A serious problem confronting this line of argument lies in its logical inability to explain *actual* behaviour, rather than ascertaining what sort of behaviour would have been appropriate to the situation. The rationality principle invoked by Popper simply does not do as a stratagem for explaining actual behaviour. Another difficulty with explanations of the 'logic of the situation' variety stems from their tautological nature. The circularity of the argument inheres in the procedure to infer meanings or intentions from actions, and then to use them in the explanation of those very actions. Since the overriding concern is with the derivation of actions from assumed subjective variables – goals, motives, intentions, 'theories' concerning the success of an envisaged course of action – there is no independent standard of reference which would ensure that the attribution of those psychological states or dispositions bears a controllable – not necessarily empirically falsifiable – relationship to observed actions.

It may also be worth commenting, at the risk of labouring the obvious, that 'situational logic' easily lends itself, completely contrary to Popper's intentions, to being cast in a behaviourist mould. All psychological elements having been purged from the explanatory schema, there looms the danger of its being subsumed within the covering-law model. A one-to-one correspondence between the circumstances making up the 'situation' and the 'appropriate' action, strung together by the rationality principle, is completely detrimental to subjectivist inclinations. This relates back to the central tenet of dynamic subjectivism already alluded to that indeterminism be viewed not merely as a property of the application of a model but of the model itself (see O'Driscoll and Rizzo, 1985, p. 25, arguing against Machlup).

Analogous comments can be made in relation to Keynes's conception of probable inference. In what he clearly takes to be 'an extension of Keynes's argument'. Shackle (1972, p. 338) questions whether Keynes's notion of probability as a logical relationship between two sets of propositions can conceivably be argued to be devoid of 'judgemental resolve' and imagination. In the demonstrative proof of a syllogism the conclusion is entailed by the premises; in the case of probable inference such 'essential identity' is lacking, Shackle contends. Put in slightly different terms, in Keynes's conception of probable inference the premises do not 'compose' the conclusion; they merely 'suggest' the conclusion. In the 'fabrication' by the reasoner of the required evidential basis lies the essential difference between probable and demonstrative inference. 'Once a complete evidential basis has been assembled, partly by observation and direct knowledge, partly by imaginative hypothesis, then it is the old logic which comes into play, and nothing new is required' (Shackle, 1972, p. 389).[38] Warming up to this theme on another occasion, Shackle (1979, ch. 20) takes the argument one step further by inquiring into the source of the 'conclusions' which are supposed to be supported by various degrees of 'rational belief'. Whereas for Keynes, 'an accession of new evidence increases the *weight* of an argument'[39] (Keynes, 1973, p. 77; emphasis in the original), for Shackle the implication of ' "new evidence" is that of increasing the richness of suggestion on which the chooser can draw in imagining rival sequels to any contemplated course of action' (Shackle, 1979, p. 132). The highest stage in moving along the subjectivist roller coaster is reached once it is realized that the 'conclusions' are founded on a figment of the imagination 'supplied with materials by suggestions from the field, but *not governed in its use of these suggestions by any determining antecedents*' (Shackle, 1979, p. 131; emphasis added). *That* variant of subjectivism is clearly at odds with Keynes's theory of probability, which holds that 'high degrees of rational belief require a close logical proximity between a hypothesis and the evidence – in other words, *that the hypothesis not go very far beyond what is known through past experience*' (Rutherford, 1984, pp. 380-1; emphasis in the original).

It has been the intention of the above account to outline the considerable difficulties of establishing a clear view of the structure of subjectivism. The bulk of this section has been devoted to an exploration of several possible avenues to subjectivism,[40] with pride of place having been accorded to a discussion of the Austrian version of 'dynamic subjectivism'. There is a strong tendency in the profession to dismiss the more ardent exponents of subjectivism as some kind of *raconteurs*, and to view subjectivist theory as somewhat lightweight – little more than economic gossip, some sort of 'economics by the fireside' (to paraphrase the title of one of Shackle's books). Fear of total 'deconstruction' may also be the force behind much of the mistrust subjectivism has to put up with. Needless to say, in that sense the preceding outline is offered as an effort to redress the balance. In particular, it is hoped to have been shown that a commitment to subjectivism does not - *pace* Lawson (1987) - necessarily imply the abandonment of the quest for realist analysis.[41]

We are now in a position to turn to more substantive matters.

THE SYSTEMATIC MARKET PROCESS VERSUS THE KALEIDIC SOCIETY

Occupying the middle ground, or Having it both ways

Economic theory prides itself on conceiving of market phenomena not as some haphazard or random occurrences but as the outcome of *systematic* relationships. 'The observable phenomena of the market are seen not as masses of isolated, irreducible data but as the outcomes of *determinate* processes that can, in principle, be grasped and understood' (Kirzner, 1973, pp. 1-2; emphasis added). Kirzner goes on to maintain that there are, in principle, two ways of focusing on market phenomena, namely, in equilibrium terms and in process terms. The process approach favoured by Kirzner is concerned with elucidating 'how the decisions of individual participants in the market interact to generate the market forces which compel *changes* in prices, in outputs, and in methods of production and the allocation of resources' (Kirzner, 1973, p. 6; emphasis in the original). On this view, the market process is constituted - and impelled - by a systematic discovery of hitherto unperceived opportunities for entrepreneurial profit. From this perspective, the significance of entrepreneurship is seen to be twofold: first, it is held, market entrepreneurship is a disequilibrium phenomenon by definition because only disequilibrium situations present opportunities for pure gain; secondly, and more importantly, what happens in a disequilibrium state can be explained only by referring to what entrepreneurs do.

The 'conventional Austrian position' as expounded by Kirzner (see Kirzner, 1985; 1985a, for an incisive statement) occupies rather modestly, frequently expressed allegations of extremism and radicalism notwithstanding, the middle ground on almost any spectrum of possible theoretical positions. For instance, on the vexing question of 'equilibrating tendencies' it steers a middle course, thus circumventing both the 'neoclassical' view that the economic system, owing to the stability and predictability of its underlying data is at all times at, or in any case close to, a fully co-ordinated state of affairs, with equilibrating tendencies being considered a matter of self-evidence not worthy of any further investigation; and the polar view associated with Shackle and Lachmann,[42] holding that the volatility of the data would render the mere possibility of an overall equilibrating tendency illusory at best. But this 'middle-of-the-road' position should not be construed as signalling roughly equal distance from the two 'extreme' views just mentioned. Kirzner's position is much closer to the neoclassical view; indeed, it is complementary to it. The 'alertness' perspective on entrepreneurial behaviour[43] is claimed to admit of the incorporation of entrepreneurship into standard equilibrium theory (see Kirzner, 1985, p. 11).[44]

According to this view, the spontaneity, creativity and ingenuity inherent in human action do not rule out systematic processes of market co-ordination; quite on the contrary, these processes are seen to depend crucially on the human propensity to better oneself by transcending the perceived framework of means and ends, discovering and creating new opportunities. Far from 'originatively' injecting new elements into market conditions which are in no way related to, let alone determined by, formerly prevailing circumstances (Shackle's concept of 'choice'), the genuine novelty and surprise that we identify with entrepreneurial behaviour may be argued to arise systematically from, and to be related to, earlier market conditions. It is precisely the profit opportunities offered by earlier market conditions that 'switches on the alertness of potential entrepreneurs, generating entrepreneurial discovery' (Kirzner, 1985, p. 11). Thus the initial market ignorance which stands in the way of a fully adjusted state of affairs will not prevail; it is subject to erosion owing to a continuous entrepreneurial discovery process which, in turn, can be imagined to set in motion and to sustain, barring exogenous changes, a tendency towards equilibrium.

Although the concept of the 'entrepreneur' does not seem to figure prominently in the *General Theory*, it is by no means alien to the economics of Keynes. It is well known that Chapter 3 of the *General Theory* ('The Principle of Effective Demand') was provisionally entitled 'The Characteristics of an Entrepreneur Economy' (consult Torr, 1980, for detailed references). As Lachmann observes (1986, p. 120), in the context of a discussion of the different usage of the term 'entrepreneur' in Schumpeter and Keynes, the rich concept of an *entrepreneur economy* 'serves to delineate a class of agents to whom a wider range is open than to other people'. What unites the otherwise vastly different visions of Keynes, Mises and Schumpeter – and what sets them apart from neoclassical general equilibrium analysis – is their insistence on the entrepreneur as the driving force of the economic process. As Hodgson (1985, pp. 15–17) notes, it is not at all clear, however, to whom the expecting agent is meant to refer in Keynes. Although Chapter 12 of the *General Theory* seems to suggest that the entrepreneur is concerned with taking decisions relating to long-term physical investment, there are other passages in which 'entrepreneur' refers to investors on the stock market. Moreover, it is not clear whether Keynes means by 'entrepreneurs' a particular group or class of people, or whether he has in mind 'entrepreneurship', a specific function with which everybody is supposed to be endowed with in varying degrees.

On the other hand, we find Mises arguing, 'In any real and living economy every actor is always an entrepreneur and speculator' (Mises, 1966, p. 252). This is the sort of statement that post-Keynesians will be hard pushed to swallow. The limited range of actions available to different groups of agents is a subject well worth studying. As Lachmann (1986, p. 121) notes, wage earners can only bargain for money wages, not for real wages. The unemployed could live on the moon, as it were, for all the influence they exercize in the labour market.[45]

A further example of the limited set of options confronting agents is provided by modern markets for consumer goods in which the buyer typically no longer participates in the price-making, nor in the production process itself. Until now, modern Austrian analysis has in the main centred on the stabilizing rôle of the entrepreneur. While it is conceded that entrepreneurs may often commit errors and inject further instability and unpredictability into the economic system, this is not held to cancel the co-ordinative function of entrepreneurship. 'Relative to a world of no entrepreneurship, the changes that exogenously impinge on a system are less disruptive. Because of entrepreneurship there is more stability and regularity in the flow of events' (O'Driscoll and Rizzo, 1985, p. 78). What is urgently needed is a systematic account of how the stabilizing and destabilizing effects of entrepreneurship would interact.

The kaleidic view of the world

According to what has been dubbed the 'convential Austrian position', as represented by Kirzner, equilibrium is seen to be a limiting position which, in the absence of changes in the underlying data, would be reached once the entrepreneurial discovery process has run its course. Lachmann categorically rejects this view of the market process as (potentially) terminating in a state of equilibrium and proposes in its stead an ongoing market process, without beginning or end, buffeted by unexpected change, divergence of interpretation and divergence of expectations. 'What emerges is an image of the market as a particular kind of process . . . propelled by the interaction between the forces of equilibrium and the forces of change' (Lachmann, 1976, p. 61). Viewed from this perspective, it is hardly surprising that Austrian economics, at least in one of its important manifestations, took an instant liking to Shackle's vision of the 'kaleidic society'.[46]

The vivid image of the kaleidic society describes the economic system not as a co-ordinated, orderly progressing entity, but as an amalgam of ever-changing expectations and actions.

Each choice is unique in the sense that past experiences can never serve as a certain guide for current behaviour. The metaphor of the kaleidoscope is invoked to underscore that the prevailing pattern of prices and resource allocation is bound to be upset by unexpected change.

Adherents of the 'kaleidic society' place special emphasis on speculative markets in general, and asset markets in particular. Considering that all storable and durable goods constitute potential candidates for speculative behaviour, the inherent restlessness of those markets must pose a major threat for the stability of the economy. Lachmann, in particular, has made it very much his own theme to explore differences in the *modus operandi* of the market process in commodity and asset markets, respectively. As a rule, the more durable the traded goods, the more important are expectations. The *divergence of expectations* is of the essence in speculative markets. Indeed, some of the central institutions of capitalism such as stock exchanges and futures commodities markets could not possibly function the way they do if they depended for their functioning on convergent expectations. It is the central task of those institutions to co-ordinate the divergent expectations of bulls and bears. Without a divergence of expectations, prices would change in such markets without any transactions taking place (see Lachmann, 1986, p. 18). An equilibrium price in an asset market rests on a precarious 'balance of expectations' which cannot last. For the very same reason for which an equilibrium is established so speedily in such markets, it is bound to be upset by the 'daily news'. The volatility in such markets is enhanced by the fact that the whole stock is always potentially for sale, and that it is very easy to 'change sides', that is, to act as a bull in the morning, and as a bear in the afternoon.

Viewed in this light, what can we make of statements to the effect that 'it is one of the functions of a market to make expectations converge', or that 'the market serves as a discovery procedure'? The crucial role of expectations in speculative markets poses a major threat for the vision of the market as a systematic entrepreneurial discovery process because the 'discovery' of future knowledge is even more problematical than the co-ordination of existing knowledge in a highly decentralized system. 'But can the market process diffuse expectations in the same way as it diffuses knowledge where this exists?' (Lachmann, 1976, p. 59). A striking instance of the gulf separating the two strands of Austrianism is provided by their respective stands on the problem of intertemporal co-ordination. Whilst the 'conventional Austrian position' postulates an intertemporal entrepreneurial market process, the Lachmann / Shackle view is squarely post-Keynesian in that it denies the possibility of matching future demand with present investment (on this, see the exchange between Garrison and Snippe; and Kregel, 1986).

The relationship between those two Austrian sub-groups may be summarized by noting that for the convential position the creative subjectivism underlying the kaleidic view and its concomitant denial of systematic equilibrating tendencies is held to put in jeopardy the very possibility of a theoretical science of economics. For Lachmann, put at its starkest, the conventional view smacks of 'late classical formalism' (Lachmann, 1986, pp. 159–62), and its conception of determinate equilibrium is seen to serve as some kind of 'centre of gravity',[47] analogous to its rôle in objectivist neo-Ricardian economics.

CONCLUDING REMARKS

It has been the intention of this chapter to suggest possible links between the Austrian and post-Keynesian research programmes. Instead of focusing primarily on substantive issues in this comparative appraisal, the emphasis was put on subjectivism. Methodological subjectivism was shown to be an enormously varied research strategy encompassing both Austrian and post-Keynesian approaches. In particular, it should be noted that in the Keynesian case the subjectivist commitment is allied – doubtless paradoxically for the purists – to an interventionist stance and a holist conception of society. The implications for economic policy of 'the dark forces of time and ignorance' (Keynes, 1936, p. 155) surrounding individual decision-making stand out starkly; whereas in the Keynesian approach the appeal to uncertainty and imperfect information is invoked whenever chaos and waste are blamed on the decentralization of production and investment decisions under capitalism (see Coddington, 1982, p. 486), the Austrian stance is much less ambitious and is aptly encapsulated in the slogan: 'The less we know, the less we can intervene'.

NOTES

1. Apart from George Shackle's pivotal contributions (for example, Shackle, 1972, 1979), some of the offerings of the 'Stirling school' (Dow, 1985; Earl, 1983; Loasby, 1976), with their skilled fusing of post-Keynesianism of the Shacklean variety with behaviouralist insights derived from the Carnegie school, interspersed with Austrian-type arguments, have been in the vanguard of the subjectivist resurgence. Langlois (ed., 1986) arguably represents the beginning of a most promising line of research bearing upon subjectivist inclinations; it comprises neo-Schumpeterian theory *à la* Nelson and Winter, Austrian theory *à la* Hayek and Kirzner, Oliver Williamson's transaction-cost economics and behavioural theory inspired by Herbert Simon.

   Given the breadth and depth of the recently published *New Palgrave*, one cannot but be disappointed at the omission of a separate entry on 'subjectivism'; indeed, there is no mention of 'subjectivism' in the index either.

2. According to an oft-recurring quotation from Hayek (1979, p. 52), 'it is probably no exaggeration to say that every important advance in economic theory during the last hundred years was a further step in the consistent application of subjectivism'. In a footnote to this remarkable *confessio fidei* Hayek refers to his mentor Ludwig von Mises as the foremost representative of subjectivism.

3. It may be recalled that the term 'subjectivism' was originally meant by Marxists to serve as an invective against the Austrian theory of value (on this, see Böhm, 1982).

4. The recently published, exhaustive study by O'Sullivan (1987) is a case in point.

5. See Yeager (1987) for a warning against exaggerated extensions of subjectivism, and the subsequent exchange between Block (1988) and Yeager (1988). See also Selgin (1988) for a balanced survey of current controversies among Austrians generated by the challenge of the new 'historicism' ('historism' in the sense of voluntarism would be more appropriate). That there is a connotation of modern Austrian economics that implies *total* rejection of received theory has now been officially acknowledged in Israel Kirzner's article on the Austrian

school in the *New Palgrave*, where he notes the historical irony of this situation:

> This line of thought has come to imply serious reservations concerning the possibility of systematic theoretical conclusions commanding significant degrees of generality. This connotation of the term 'Austrian Economics' thus associates it with a stance sympathetic, to a degree, towards historical and institutional approaches. Given the prominent opposition of earlier Austrians to these approaches, this association has, as might be expected, been seen as ironic or even paradoxical by many observers (including, especially, modern exponents of the broader tradition of the Austrian School of Economics). (Kirzner, 1987, p. 150)

6.   For the most representative sources of the genre, see Lachmann (1986, 1986a), O'Driscoll and Rizzo (1985), and some of the contributions, notably those by Richard Ebeling and Don Lavoie, in Kirzner (ed., 1986). Ebelings's and Lavoie's essays are exemplary of the 'interpretative turn' that is currently being staged at George Mason University. The upsurge of interest in the hermeneutical tradition in general and in the works of continental authors such as Wilhelm Dilthey, Hans-Georg Gadamer and Paul Ricoeur in particular links up nicely with the latest methodological fad, the 'rhetoric of economics' approach associated with Don McCloskey and Arjo Klamer. The notion of the economist as being engaged in a permanent conversation, in which he tries to convince his opponents of the soundness of his arguments, is one that many Austrians, along with exponents of other, unorthodox research programmes, find appealing.

  For the uninitiated who are not aware of the hermeneutical overtones in Mengerian economics it may even be more incomprehensible how to square the epistemological *a priorism* of von Mises with the philosophical hermeneutics of Gadamer. Fortunately, this is not the occasion for probing into those weighty issues. Moreover, the jaded continental European observer harbours a sense of *dejà vu*; many of the issues involved in the current modest revival of the interpretative approach in economics have been fiercely debated – if not resolved – in the so-called 'Positivist Dispute in German Sociology' of the 1960s (for key contributions to this wide-ranging controversy, see Adorno *et. al.* (1976), with a substantial introduction by David Frisby). Were it not for the fact that the revival of hermeneutical modes is, of course, intimately related to the gradual shift from a 'positivist' to a 'nonpositivist' conception of science that has occurred over the last decades, a cynic might argue that its timing has everything to do with the belated translation into English of key works in the hermeneutics literature.

7.   For expositions of the orthodox Austrian viewpoint, see, in particular, Kirzner (1973, 1979, 1985).

8. The notion of Austrian economics as the 'middle ground' has first been advanced by Garrison (1982, 1984) and was subsequently taken up by Kirzner (1985, ch. 1).

9. The terminology is, of course, due to the late Alan Coddington (1976); Coddington (1982) was arguably the first author to group Austrians and post-Keynesians together. His trenchant criticism of Austrian nihilism, in particular, has surprisingly not elicited an *immediate* response from those attacked (but compare Shackle's response (1983–4). For a gallant effort to come to the rescue, see Snippe (1985).

10. Compare, for example, Kregel (ed., 1983). For a critique of Keynesian fundamentalism from the neo-Ricardian point of view, see Magnani (1983). The contributions by Hodgson, and Hamouda and Harcourt in this volume are also pertinent to this debate. It is a tribute to Professor Lachmann's wise judgement that as early as 1973 (!) he clearly foresaw the split within the Cambridge school:

> Keynes, for all his interest in macro-economics, owed little to Ricardo and all his life remained a subjectivist who refused to cast the inducement to invest in the mould of a macro-variable such as the acceleration principle. He disclaimed any interest in long-run equilibrium and substantiated this disclaimer by pointing out that in the long run we are all dead. (Lachmann, 1973, p. 18)

With the benefit of hindsight Lachmann observes with respect to the Cambridge school:

> This school . . . has always been a coalition of heterogeneous forces, and it is possible that . . . the defeat of the common (late classical) adversary will lead to a break-up of the alliance. We are dealing here with a coalition between the Sraffa school, whose doctrines may be classified as 'neo-Ricardianism' and which proposes the return to the classical style of thought, that is to say to the objectivism of impersonal social forces, and the post-Keynesians who want to continue Keynes's work. But . . . Keynes was a subjectivist. It cannot surprise us that within this coalition a dispute broke out over the role of expectations the fundamental role of which the post-Keynesians need to cling to, while to the Ricardians they are most distasteful. (Lachmann, 1986, p. 164)

11. Comparing Hayek to Keynes, Lachmann arrives at the conclusion that, 'Rather to the surprise of some of us, Keynes emerges as being more deeply committed to subjectivism than is his Austrian opponent.' (Lachmann, 1983, p. 375)

12. This is by no means to ascertain that awareness of this 'dualism' is equally present with all the authors cited. The exchange between Garrison (1985, 1987) and Snippe (1987), for example, highlights that *tertium non datur* between the Austrian and post-Keynesian

approaches, while Kregel (1986, p. 158), in his incisive essay, refers to Lachmann's work as representing 'an important synthesis of Austrian and Keynesian elements'. Hodgson (1985; see also his chapter in this volume) rejects the 'mainstream(!) Austrian Theory' – along with Shackle's work – for failing to produce determinate results and urges the abandonment of 'subjectivism and the entire project to synthesise the work of Keynes with Austrian theory'.

13. Correspondingly, their book received highly critical (Baird, 1987) and lukewarm (Kirzner, 1985a) review articles from adherents of the mainstream view; on the other hand, it was acclaimed in a review article by Lachmann (1985) and in a review by that noted post-Keynesian, Thomas K. Rymes (1987).

14. That is the approach taken by Dow (1983, 1985) in her studies of schools of thought in macroeconomics.

15. The fact that much more space is devoted to the reconstruction of Austrian analysis is justified on the grounds that post-Keynesianism is dealt with at much greater length in other chapters of this book.

16. On the general theme of 'subjectivism in economics', see the collection of articles in Wiseman (ed., 1983).

17. Anyone who doubts Machlup's credentials as a subjectivist is referred to his magisterial monograph, *The Economics of Sellers' Competition* (1952), which shows him to be imbued with Schutzian methodology. On the influence of Alfred Schutz on Austrian economics in general, see Prendergast (1986).

18. Referring to one of Hayek's seminal contributions (Hayek, 1937), Shackle (1981, p. 254) states, 'In "Economics and Knowledge" Hayek takes what is often called the subjectivist standpoint, the view that for the human being the business of life is *thought*. For the individual in deciding his course, what he thinks is the case, *is* the case' (emphasis in the original).

19. For analogous circumscriptions of the proper province of economics, compare Shackle (1972, p. 246) to Mises (1966, p. 92).

20. In respect of Lachmann's concern with learning Hicks (1978, p. 401) remarks, 'he is so preoccupied with it, with the spread of information, that the production of *things* drops almost out of sight. "Learning by doing" – he welcomes Arrow's slogan; but to react so far against materialism as to make the learning displace the doing must be going too far' (emphasis in the original). In a similar vein, Garrison (1987a, p. 80) notes, 'we may legitimately wonder how far we can push subjectivism without losing sight of the essential objective aspects of economic reality.'

21. To recall, Weber (1962, p. 35) distinguishes between observational (direct empirical) and motivational (explanatory) understanding of the meaning of a given act.

22. O'Driscoll and Rizzo (1985, p. 5) define their position as mid-way between extreme *a priorism* and extreme instrumentalism.

23. With the notable exception of Hayek, who in his sadly neglected (among economists) later methodological work appears to narrow down the radical differentiation between the problems of the natural and social sciences to one of degrees; see, in particular, his 'Degrees of Explanation' and 'The Theory of Complex Phenomena', reprinted in Hayek (1967).

24. See Mises (1966, chs 1–7); for a sympathetic account of Mises's praxeology consult Caldwell (1982, ch. 6).

25. Compare O'Sullivan (1987, p. 160), who attributes 'some version of the applicability thesis' to O'Driscoll and Rizzo. See also Lachmann (1986, p. 34) on the relationship between the analytical social sciences and history.

26. This is in no way to deny that there may be important differences in epistemology. Carabelli (1985, p. 151) labels Keynes's epistemological position as a 'mixture of anti-empiricism and anti-rationalism'. In this connection, see Lawson (1987) for a cogent critique of foundationalism, as attributed to Keynes; and Pheby (1985) for an exploration of Keynes's credentials as a Popperian.

27. Keynes draws a distinction between logical and subjective probability, by which he means 'not . . . subject to human caprice. A proposition is not probable because we think it so. When once the facts are given which determine our knowledge, what is probable or improbable in these circumstances has been fixed objectively, and is *independent* of our opinion' (Keynes, 1973, p. 4; emphasis added). However, see Bateman (1987) for the argument that after the publication of the *Treatise* Keynes, under the influence of Frank Ramsey's critique, was willing to accept a *subjective* epistemic theory of probability.

28. Whilst not adhering to a logical theory of probability in Keynes's sense, Mises also rejects frequency probability ('class probability') and proposes the concept of 'case probability' in dealing with the 'unique events' of human action (see Mises, 1966, ch. 6).

29. On all this, see the illuminating account by Carabelli (1985).

30. Compare Gray (1986, pp. 80–1). There is a related argument here, based on the central planner's ignorance. For a critique, see Dasgupta (1980).

31. For Hayek's most recent forays into the theory of morals, compare, for example, Hayek (1984).

32. On the two levels of subjectivism, see O'Driscoll and Rizzo (1985, ch. 2) and Kirzner (1986, pp. 137–40).

33. Unfortunately, there is hardly any discussion in Shackle of that part of choice which is not a 'beginning'.

34. In an attempt to trace Shackle's philosophical affiliations, the present author has come across the ingenious work by Kern (1983), which explores the ways in which, before the Great War, innovations in technology and culture revolutionized traditional modes of perceiving time and space. See, in particular, the account of the reservations

expressed by Henri Bergson and Emile Meyerson about the naturalistic determinism of Pierre Laplace (ibid., pp. 100–2).

35. Despite striking parallels in outlook in most other respects, the echo of the past seems to be much more powerful in Lachmann's work. For example, the concern with malinvestment and problems of the capital structure in general (1986, ch. 4) is a recurring theme in Lachmann's thought.

36. 'Creativity can exist only within a framework that provides at least some degree of predictability' (O'Driscoll and Rizzo, 1985, p. 11).

37. On some difficulties associated with Popper's rationality principle, see Hands (1985).

38. Whether the introduction of this subjective element would necessarily be 'unacceptable' to Keynes – as Shackle (1972, p. 388) avers – may be open to doubt. Consider the following statement:

What we know and what probability we can attribute to our rational beliefs is . . . subjective in the sense of being relative to the individual. But given the body of premises which *our subjective powers and circumstances* supply to us, and given the kinds of logical relations, upon which arguments can be based and which we have the capacity to perceive, the conclusions, which it is rational for us to draw, stand to these premises in an objective and wholly logical relation. (Keynes, 1973, p. 19; emphasis added)

39. By 'weight of an argument' Keynes denotes the 'balance . . . between the *absolute* amounts of relevant knowledge and of relevant ignorance respectively' (Keynes, 1973, p. 77; emphasis in the original).

40. Four approaches to subjectivism have been identified Keynes's, post-Keynesian (Shacklean), neoclassical ('static subjectivism') and Austrian ('dynamic subjectivism').

41. For example, see the discussion of 'decision weights' in O'Driscoll and Rizzo (1985, p. 31). On the 'realist' conception of scientific theory, see the discussion in O'Sullivan (1987, pp. 38–43).

42. Joan Robinson's more recent writings may also be mentioned here.

43. 'Alertness' refers to the discovery of hitherto unexploited opportunities; these may be offered by current and future conditions.

44. Stated in a somewhat exaggerated way, it is only by incorporating the 'alertness' view of entrepreneurship that neoclassical theory makes sense.

45. The entrepreneurial discovery process in the labour market may be stifled by institutional constraints. There is no way in which the unemployed as individuals could persuade an employer to hire them by offering him terms more favourable than those enjoyed by the presently employed. For Keynes and the post-Keynesians, all this must be anathema; according to them, the level of employment is determined by the state of long-term expectations, and not by anything that goes

on in labour markets. On the relationship between Keynesian unemployment and Kirznerian entrepreneurship, see Torr (1981, pp. 287–8).
46. Shackle (1972, p. 76) describes a kaleidic society as 'interspersing its moments or intervals of order, assurance and beauty with sudden disintegration and cascade into a new pattern'.
47. On the concept of a 'centre of gravity' in neo-Ricardian economics, consult the contribution by Hamouda and Harcourt in this volume.

5. Post-Keynesianism and Institutionalism: the Missing Link

Geoff Hodgson

It is not only neoclassical theory that has internal problems.[1] It is now widely argued, even by sympathizers, that there are fundamental problems with post-Keynesian theory as well (Harcourt, 1982; Tarshis, 1980). Whilst one short essay cannot resolve these matters, it can attempt to investigate the difficulties. The first part consists of a critical survey of the contending or possible theoretical foundations for post-Keynesian economics and the second suggests an alternative line of argument which has not as yet been given sufficient attention. It is to build a theoretical foundation for post-Keynesian theory out of some ideas which are associated with the institutionalist tradition.

THE EXISTING FOUNDATIONS FOR POST-KEYNESIAN THEORY

It is now widely accepted that after the publication of the *General Theory* Keynes's ideas were bowdlerized and synthesized with orthodoxy. Economics itself became an amalgam of neoclassical micro-theory and the Hicks-Hansen version of Keynes. In part this was because Keynes himself failed to develop adequate theoretical foundations for his system, and he leaned too heavily on the marginalist analysis of Alfred

Marshall in his work. The result was what Joan Robinson described as 'bastard Keynesianism'. This, we now know, failed to encompass some of the key ideas in the economics of Keynes: particularly his focus on the potential instability of a monetary economy, affected as it is by decisions in regard to a future about which all agents are profoundly uncertain.

However, this reappraisal of Keynes's ideas (Davidson, 1978; Hines 1971; Leijonhufvud, 1968; Shackle, 1974) came too late to salvage the banner of 'Keynesianism' from the barrage of the Chicago artillery. 'Bastard Keynesianism' was shattered, but the fire was not effective in demolishing the central arguments in the economics of Keynes. Nevertheless, by the early 1970s it appeared that the monetarists had routed the so-called 'Keynesians'; and Keynes was pronounced dead. The subsequent onslaught of the rational expectations battalion consolidated the victory. Since that time the supporters of Keynes have been fighting a kind of guerrilla war from the hills, but unfortunately they are split into different factions with different perspectives and ideas.

The question of the post-Keynesian theoretical foundations

A further difficulty is that neoclassical theory, despite its own internal problems, is still claiming great success in extending its microeconomic analysis, particularly to the macroeconomic sphere. Post-Keynesians have not succeeded in changing the terms of this debate away from the search for 'sound microfoundations'. Furthermore, inspecting post-Keynesian theory, 'microfoundations' of equivalent depth are lacking. Whilst there have been important developments in the post-Keynesian theory of the firm (e.g., Eichner, 1976), and in its macroeconomic theory (e.g., Sawyer, (1982), these are often concerned with the presentation of alternative views on the behaviour and direction of causality of economic variables, particularly by dropping the neoclassical assumption of perfect competition, rather than by examining even more fundamental theoretical assumptions. Indeed, post-Keynesian research programmes in this mould have focused mainly

on the 'empirical' matter of the shape and nature of key
functional relationships, rather than the theoretical bases of
those functions and their associated variables.

Notably, over fifty years after the publication of the *General
Theory* there is still no consensus amongst Keynesians as to what
are the basic theoretical foundations of their economics. Indeed,
Geoff Harcourt (1982) has noted that post-Keynesian economics is often portrayed as being distinguished more by its
dislike of neoclassical theory, than by any coherence or agreement on fundamentals by its contributors.

Fernando Carvalho (1984–5) has usefully surveyed this
diversity by classifying the different treatments and manipula-
tions by various post-Keynesian theorists of the concepts of
the short and the long run. He comes up with a spectrum of
approaches within post-Keynesianism, ranging from the long-
period models based on the work of Piero Sraffa, to the
analysis of George Shackle which concentrates on the
uncaused nature of imagination and expectation and the
indeterminacy of the economic process.[2]

In the present essay we shall not attempt to survey all these
alternatives. Indeed, a slightly different emphasis is posed. At
the core of neoclassical theory lies a formal theory of prices
and resource allocation and a theory of human agency based
on rational maximization. The question is to what extent do
contending approaches offer a coherent and developed alternative to neoclassical orthodoxy at this fundamental theoretical level?

It by no means undervalues the contributions of the many
post-Keynesian theorists to suggest that the greater part of their
effort has not been in response to this particular question. Even
the work of the greatest of the post-Keynesian theorists, including Michal Kalecki, Nicholas Kaldor and Joan Robinson, does
not rest on an alternative and fully developed theory of human
behaviour to rival the neoclassical one.

What is on offer as a theoretical bedrock upon which post-
Keynesianism can build its alternative to neoclassicism? At
present there are three types of analysis which have been said
to provide such a theoretical foundation.[3] They are, first,
work which has attempted to incorporate the notion of effec-

tive demand in the long-period framework developed by Piero Sraffa (Garegnani, 1978, 1979a; Eatwell and Milgate, 1983), secondly, the behaviouralist analyses inspired by the seminal work of Herbert Simon (1957, 1959, 1968, 1983), and thirdly, the contribution of George Shackle (1955, 1969, 1972, 1974) which has synthesized elements of Keynes's theory with the subjectivism of Friedrich Hayek and the Austrian School.[4]

The first and third types of analysis have had the closest explicit links with post-Keynesianism, partly for the reason that they have been created with the development of Keynes's work in mind. In contrast, Simon's work has been connected with post-Keynesianism through the efforts of later commentators (Earl, 1983; Garner, 1982). Notably, Carvalho's typology of post-Keynesian theory does not include behaviouralism. It is to the question of the relative adequacy of these three contending approaches that we now turn.

The Keynes-Sraffa synthesis

A gulf divides the Sraffian theorists from others like Simon and Shackle who emphasize problems of uncertainty and argue that the economy cannot be captured by a static analysis. On one side, Pierangelo Garegnani (1979b, p. 183) echoed by John Eatwell (1979, 1983) denies a 'central role to uncertainty and expectations'. On the other side, Paul Davidson (1978), Alexander Dow and Sheila Dow (1985), Tony Lawson (1985), Brian Loasby (1976), George Shackle (1974) and Hyman Minsky (1976) have all seen uncertainty and expectations as being central both to the work of Keynes and to developments based upon it.

The fact that Sraffa's long-period analysis represents a major amendment to Keynes's theory is stated by Sraffian theorists themselves. For instance, Garegnani (1979b, p. 183) insists that the 'short-period character of Keynes's theory' is a weakness. Following this, Eatwell (1983, pp. 271-2) states that there are 'many parts of *The General Theory* which either do not address or . . . directly contradict the notion of long-period theory . . . it frequently appears that

Keynes is simply presenting a theory of . . . short-period positions'.

An even more important question is to ask to what extent does Sraffian analysis offer a foundation for post-Keynesian theory? By 1973 Joan Robinson was expressing some misgivings about an exclusive focus on the long-period: 'In reality', she wrote, 'all the interesting and important questions lie in the gap between pure short-period and long-period analysis' (Robinson, 1973, p. 60). In 1980 her differences with the long-period theorists had become even more clear: for 'in her debates with Garegnani, and with Eatwell and Milgate, Joan Robinson used her views on the inadmissability of long-period comparisons for describing processes, which she developed in her critique of neoclassical theory, to criticise the central stress by these authors on the notion of centres of gravitation or long-period positions' (Harcourt, 1985, p. 106). Sraffian 'values' or 'prices of production' were rejected because they could not be incorporated in a theory which was set in historical time (Robinson, 1974, 1979b, 1980; Bhaduri and Robinson, 1980).

In one of her later publications Joan Robinson (1979b, p. 180) asked directly what was the meaning of the normal rate of profit in long-period analysis: Does it mean 'what the rate of profit on capital will be in the future or what it has been in the past or does it float above historical time as a Platonic idea?' Garegnani (1979b, p. 185) replied that the normal rate of profit is located in the present: 'It corresponds to the rate which is being realised *on an average* (as between firms and over time) by the entrepreneurs who use the dominant technique . . . it is also the rate of profits which that present experience will lead entrepreneurs in general to expect *in the future* from their current investment.'

This response suggests that long-period analysis is a short-period one as well, for the long-period avarage is seen to bear upon short-period decisions. But how do entrepreneurs *know* what the average rate of profit is, or if the rate of profit in their own enterprise is above or below it? They may know quoted market rates of interest, but they are clearly not the same thing. Consequently, how can entrepreneurs form expectations of a future rate of profit on the basis of this present average rate of profit which is unperceived and unknown? Even if it were known, why should entrepreneurs assume that it would remain the same in the future? These questions are neither raised nor answered in the Garegnani–Eatwell–Milgate extension of Sraffian theory.

Secondly, it is questionable that a Sraffian world of fixed coefficients can represent the long period if this is meant to include capital accumulation and technological change. Sraffian theorists have suggested that these phenomena can be encompassed by the comparative–static analysis of the switching of techniques. But as Joan Robinson (1980, p. 134) puts it: 'It is a mistake in methodology to compare two technical systems . . . and then to switch from one to the other. A switch is an event in historical time which has to be accounted for by introducing historical causation in the story. This is where Sraffa leaves us and hands us over to Keynes.' Technological change is a process, through time, with future consequences which are rarely known with any precision in the present. It involves, for instance, investment in research and development where the payoffs are essentially uncertain, and changes in the social relations of production resulting from industrial struggles or the reorganization of work. A static matrix of Sraffian input–output coefficients cannot represent these processes.

Thirdly, a fundamental issue is elided in the attempt to build the theory of effective demand on Sraffian foundations. Strikingly, the standard Sraffian model does not include money in the proper sense. True, the equations can include a unit of account or numeraire. But this is not money in the full sense, because *any* commodity could serve as such a unit of account. As Keynes (1971a, 1971b) made abundantly clear, money is a *special* commodity. It is, as Marx (1973) put it, 'the God among commodities', and it cannot be associated *arbitrarily* with *any* commodity in the system.

The special status of money results in part from the fact that in a monetary economy barter is not the rule; it is money, and generally only money, which is exchanged for other commodities. If any commodity can be chosen as 'money' in the formal model, then this essentially describes a barter economy in which all commodities are 'money' commodities, rather than a true system of monetary exchange (Clower, 1967). As a result the Sraffian equations apply more to a barter rather than to a monetary economy.[5] As Frank Hahn (1981, p. 130) has admitted, the same is true of neoclassical general equilibrium theory as well. The absence of money on these theoretical systems is indeed a serious problem, for without it there can be no adequate formulation of the principle of effective demand.[6]

Finally, the Sraffian approach does not offer a theory of human agency and interaction. It simply suggests that the long-period positions will somehow reflect and affect the expectations and actions of agents, without explaining how the average rate of profit and long-period prices are attained. Whatever the strengths of Sraffian analysis, particularly its destructive critique of neoclassical and Marxian theories of value and capital,[7] this lack is a serious weakness. In consequence it cannot be claimed that Sraffian analysis provides a completely adequate or entirely appropriate foundation for post-Keynesian theory.[8]

Behaviouralism

From the outset, Herbert Simon's behavioural research programme has emphasized the weight of uncertainty and incompleteness of knowledge that bears upon decision-making, and, by comparison with the task of maximizing on the neoclassical model, the limited computational capacity of the human brain. A key feature of Simon's work is that he rejects the global maximization hypothesis but retains a notion of 'bounded' rationality. Thus, for example, agents may not be able to gather and process all the information for reaching global maximization decisions, but they can make a 'rational' decision within a small set of possibilities. Consequently it is suggested by Simon (1957, 1959) that firms and consumers are not maximizing, but 'satisficing', i.e., simply trying to attain acceptable minima.

Contrary to some neoclassical interpreters, Simon is not simply proposing that agents are faced with additional 'costs', nor even that information is a problem because it is scarce, but there is a central problem of computational limitations for the decision-making agent. Consequently, rationality is not simply 'bounded' in the sense that there is too little information upon which reason can be based, but also that there is too much information to compute or assess.[9]

Like Keynes, Simon emphasizes problems of information and uncertainty. Furthermore, with the rejection of maximization and global rationality there is a similar rejection of any economic analysis which is based exclusively on the concept of a partial or general equilibrium. In Simon's (1976) work rationality is 'procedural' rather than 'substantive' or global.

One limitation of the behavioural research programme is that it focuses almost exclusively on the decision-making of the individual agent. Unlike the work of Keynes and many other economists, the global or system-wide consequences of individual actions do not come into view. In general, behavioural economists fail to deliberate on the unintended consequences that result from the actions of agents interacting with one another. There is supreme emphasis on the explanation of the behaviour of the single agent. However, the prime goal of social science, as exemplified in the work of Marx, Keynes and many others, is to explain the unintended as well as intended results of the actions of many actors. For this reason, despite Simon's emphasis on the problems of dealing with information and uncertainty, behaviouralist theory is inadequate as a theoretical foundation for post-Keynesian economics.

Shackle and post-Keynesian theory

Turning to the work of Shackle, he has based much of his argument on the treatment of uncertainty and expectation in Chapter 12 of the *General Theory* and Keynes's 1937 article from the *Quarterly Journal of Economics*. Shackle's personal contribution has been to elaborate the argument concerning non-probabilistic uncertainty – with his concept of 'potential surprise' – and to attempt to build links with the subjectivist treatment of uncertainty and knowledge in the work of Friedrich Hayek (1948) and others of the Austrian School.

Like both Hayek and Keynes, Shackle emphasizes that the economic future is not predetermined but essentially indeterminate. The future depends on the purposive decision-making of economic agents but the decision-maker is not in possession of anything more than an inkling of the future that has yet to be created. Lack of knowledge of the future means that decision and action must rest on the imagination and expectations of individuals, which are not predetermined but uncaused. They 'do not rest upon anything solid, determinable, demonstrable. "We simply do not know" ' (Shackle, 1973, p. 516). By taking the individualism of much economic theory to its logical limits, Shackle reaches striking and non-mechanistic conclusions: 'In so far as economics is about choice as a *first cause*, that is the coming into being of decisive thoughts not in all respects to be explained by antecedents, it is *essential* to talk in terms of what is foreseen, expected and intended' (Shackle, 1989.)

Thus Shackle's anti-determinism is based on a conception of the essential indeterminacy of human decision-making: of individual decision and action as a first or uncaused cause. There is no equilibrium in the economic process, nor disequilibrium, because these concepts are based on determinate functions of human behaviour which are seen as theoretically misconceived. Given the capricious imagination and expectations of many uncertain individuals, there is no necessary regularity between periods in historical time.

However, Shackle suggests that actions and expectations are, for the purposes of theoretical consideration, *completely* uncaused, and in this respect he differs from Keynes. It is one thing to suggest that human agency presents uncaused causes, another to claim that there are no factors moulding decision and action at all. Keynes mentions such factors, but his account of them is unclear. Most often he states that expectations of the future are based on the 'psychology' of individuals (e.g., Keynes, 1971b, pp. 147, 154; see Hodgson, 1985a) but he does not elaborate this much further. What is evident is that the actual formation of expectations and decisions is exogenous to Keynes's economic model (Champernowne, 1964).

In making the formation of expectation and decision exogenous, both Shackle and Keynes conform to the individualistic tradition in economic theory. Just as neoclassical theorists put the formation and moulding of individual tastes and preferences beyond the scope of their analysis, for Hayek (1948, p. 67) the task of explaining the springs of conscious action is a matter for 'psychology but not for economics . . . or any other social science'. In general, Austrian theorists seem to argue either that individuals bear no significant influence of the environment, or that it is beyond the scope of economic theory to enquire any further as to how purposes and actions may be determined. Whilst the analyses may be different they have a common effect: to exclude such matters entirely from the domain of economic enquiry. Despite his theoretical radicalism, Shackle follows both the neoclassicals and Austrians by taking it for granted that choice is the 'first cause', without asking what are the preconditions of and influences on choice itself.

A consequence of this insular attitude is to disregard the impact of advances in psychology and other social sciences in the understanding of the processes and structures governing human action. Particularly, the link between the cognitive processes and the formation of goals and expectations, on the one hand, and the social and cultural environment, on the other, is downplayed or ignored.[10]

In arguing that the forces moulding expectation and decision cannot be explained at all, Shackle's position is different from Hayek, who suggests that they could possibly be explained by psychology but it would not be legitimate to do so, and from neoclassical theorists, who 'explain' behaviour by reference to all-determining and exogenous preference functions.

By rejecting any determinate explanation of decision-making, both Shacklean and mainstream Austrian theory is incapable of building a model of the economy with a sufficient degree of order and regularity,[11] and as a result cannot generate predictions concerning the future. Contrary to many neoclassical theorists, prediction is not all-important, but that does not mean that we should ignore it entirely. Consequently, Shackle's work shares a limitation of the Austrian approach: 'it over-emphasises the freedom of the agent and under-estimates the influence of conditions other than his own imagination' (Carvalho, 1983–4, p. 270).

A more plausible view is that there are external influences moulding the purposes and actions of individuals, but that action is not entirely determined by them. The environment is influential but it does not completely determine either what the individual aims to do or what he or she may achieve. There are actions which may be uncaused, but at the same time there are patterns of behaviour that may relate to the cultural or institutional environment within which the person acts. Action, in short, is partially determined, and partially indeterminate: partly predictable but partly unforeseeable. The economic future is still uncertain, in the most radical sense; at the same time, however, economic reality displays a degree of pattern and order.

In contrast, in Shackle's subjectivist analysis the role of institutions and culture in shaping human cognitions and actions is ignored. 'Institutional questions tend to be obscured by the Shacklean approach, losing place to a growing emphasis on the process of imagination' (Carvalho, 1983–4, p. 271). Furthermore, by seeing individual action and decision as a completely 'uncaused cause', Shacklean analysis takes a one-sided view of the historical process. True, it looks forward and sees the gulf that separates the unknown future from the present. But it does not look backwards and appreciate the full significance of the past. As Shaun Hargreaves Heap (1986–7, p. 276) elegantly puts it: 'Recognition of historical time matters, not only because it forces an acknowledgement of uncertainty, but also because history's legacy to the present is a set of institutions which structure our perceptions and hence influence our behaviour with respect to that uncertain future.'

Nevertheless, as we shall see below, there are passages in Shackle's work which utilize Keynes's notion of the 'convention' in a sense which moves closer to institutional theory. However, to give these ideas full flight it is necessary to abandon subjectivism and the entire project to synthesize the work of Keynes with Austrian theory.

In a similar vein, Robert Dixon (1986) has noted the failure in Shackle's work to draw out the full implications of the concepts of uncertainty and expectation. The fact that we are uncertain of the future, he argues, results from the fact that it is not under our control. The need for expectation and the existence of uncertainty is not a subjective and asocial datum of the human condition; it results from lack of control over our futures and an inability to shelter from the consequences of the decisions of others. Cast in such a mould, 'Shackle's train of thought leads inexorably to a discussion of control and of power' (p. 589).

THE INSTITUTIONALIST FOUNDATIONS

In finding all three contending approaches wanting, we now turn to a possible institutionalist foundation for post-Keynesian economics. Some connections have already been made by institutional economists, particularly Allan Gruchy (1948, 1949), Wallace Peterson (1977), Dudley Dillard (1980) and Warren Samuels (1986). There is also the extensive work of Gunnar Myrdal and John Kenneth Galbraith, which has in both cases spanned the two traditions.

However, it should be admitted at the outset that there is no single, unified body of institutionalist theory. Indeed, as Myrdal (1958, p. 254) has noted, traditional American institutional economics was marked by a flagrant 'naïve empiricism' and did not give due precedence to matters of theory. A notable exception in this regard is Thorstein Veblen; and there has been increasing attention to the theoretical foundations by institutionalists in recent years. The following account is a summary of the eclectic amalgam of institutionalist theory which I have attempted elsewhere (Hodgson, 1988).

Habits

The high degree of relevance of habits to economics was emphasized by Veblen in several of his works. Indeed, according to him, institutions themselves are comprised of 'settled habits of thought common to the generality of men' (Veblen, 1919, p. 239). The significance of habits has also been recognized by the maverick institutionalist Frank Knight (1947, p. 224). He believed that the forces that help to mould human society 'belong to an intermediate category, between instinct and intelligence. They are a matter of custom, tradition or institutions. Such laws are transmitted in society, and acquired by the individual, through relatively effortless and even unconscious imitation, and conformity with them by any mature individual at any time is a matter of "habit".'

One of the functions of habits is to deal with the complexity of everyday life; they provide us with a means of retaining a pattern of behaviour without engaging in global rational calculations involving vast amounts of complex information. In contrast to the neoclassical picture, fully conscious rational deliberation about all aspects of behaviour is impossible because of the excessive amount of information and the unattainable computational competence that would be involved in processing it. Fortunately, human agents have acquired habits which effectively relegate particular ongoing actions from continuous rational assessment. The processes of action are organized in a hierarchical manner, facilitating monitoring at different levels and rates, and with different degrees and types of response to incoming data. Habits exist in conjunction with a human mind which operates simultaneously at different levels of consciousness and deliberation.

In contrast, and with few exceptions, economic theorists assume that all human action takes place on the same level of reason or deliberation. In a minority view, however, action springs from both deliberative and non-deliberative sources. Below the level of full deliberation there is what Michael Oakeshott (1962) calls 'practical knowledge' and Anthony Giddens (1984) 'practical consciousness'. Such mental activity helps people to 'go on': to act without giving their choices direct discursive expression.

Because the concept of habit suggests that some actions flow from full, conscious deliberation, whereas others do not, we should expect hostility to this idea from both positivists and classic liberals. Positivism fails to find empirical support for the very idea of consciousness; whereas classic liberals eschew the idea that the individual is not fully in control of all his or her acts. In a place where positivism and classic liberalism meet – in neoclassical economic theory – we find a doubled hostility and a categorical rejection of the concept of habit as it is understood in daily life.

The capacity to form habits is indispensable for the acquisition of all sorts of practical and intellectual skills. At first, while learning a technique, we must concentrate on every detail of what we are doing. Eventually, however, intellectual and practical habits emerge, and this is the very point at which we regard ourselves as having acquired the skill. When analytical or practical rules are applied without full reasoning or deliberation then the technique can be said to have been mastered.

In general, neoclassical theory implies that economic behaviour is essentially non-habitual and non-routinized, involving global rational calculation and marginal adjustments towards an optimum. In contrast, the view taken here is that the study of habits is important for economics because it relates to the large amount of routinized behaviour in the economy as a whole.

Whilst inductive reasoning cannot prove that habits exist, a great deal of data can be marshalled to support the idea of the importance of habits in economic life. Regarding consumer behaviour, John Maynard Keynes wrote in the *General Theory* that a 'man's habitual standard of life usually has the first claim on his income' (Keynes, 1971b, p. 97). Since then a number of studies have offered support for this general proposition, particularly James Duesenberry's (1949) now neglected theory of the consumption function. In addition, consumer surveys by George Katona and Eva Mueller (1954), Robert Ferber (1955) and Joseph Newman and Richard Staelin (1972) found that most households did not make purchases after extensive deliberation. Evidence such as this led Richard Olshansky and Donald Granbois (1979) to conclude that a substantial proportion of purchases do not involve decision-making in a meaningful sense.

Business itself is bound by informal customs and rules which are acquired by most participants. In addition, from extensive studies of business behaviour Katona (1975, p. 321) concludes that habitual pricing rules may 'extend to such measures as rebates, markdowns, promotions and clearance sales' and argues that rigid pricing mechanisms may be operative even if prices are changeable. It is widely accepted that labour markets are built upon a series of rigidities of contract and behaviour, underlined by tradition and the prevailing social culture (Dunlop, 1958; Marsden, 1986).

Work itself involves a degree of practical knowledge or know-how which is both acquired and routinized over time. Indeed, the industrial skill of a nation consists of a set of relevant habits, acquired over a long time, widely dispersed through the employable workforce, reflective of its culture and deeply embedded in its practices. Veblen drew our attention to this fact, and devised a theory of economic evolution based on the conflicting habits and expectations of the workforce and the business community (see Veblen, 1964; Dyer, 1984).

Similar ideas have re-emerged in the impressive work on the firm by Richard Nelson and Sidney Winter (1982).[12] Being concerned to show how technological skills are acquired and passed on within the economy, they argue that habits and routines act as repositories of knowledge and skills. In their words, routines are the 'organizational memory' (p. 99) of the firm. Consequently, Nelson and Winter do not simply argue that habits and routines are widespread, in addition they have functional characteristics. It is to some of these we now turn.

Routines, institutions and information

An important enabling function of institutionalized routines is to do with the information they provide for other agents. This aspect of routinized behaviour has received very little attention from economists, yet it is fundamental to the analysis of all social and economic institutions. All organizations gather and process some amount of information on a day-to-day basis, and this may be available within or outside the institution. However, the informational function of institutions is much wider and deeper than this. Through their very existence, and the established, visible character of much of the associated behaviour, institutions actually create additional information as well.

Stabilized and routinized behaviour establishes and reproduces a set of rules and norms 'fixed by habit, convention, tacit or legally supported social acceptance or conformity' (Kornai, 1982, p. 79). These are not necessarily inviolable, but the point is that they help agents to estimate the potential actions of others. One early and neglected statement in this regard is as follows:

One individual can choose or plan intelligently in a group of any size only if all others act 'predictably' and if he predicts correctly. This means, *prima facie*, that the others do not choose rationally but mechanically follow an established and known pattern, or else that the first party has coercive power, through force or deception. . . . Without some procedure for co-ordination, any real activity on the part of an individual, any departure from past routine, must disappoint the expectations and upset the plans of others who count on him to act in a way predicted from his past behaviour. (Knight and Merriam, 1948, p. 60)

The critical point is that both routines and formal institutions, by establishing more or less fixed patterns of human action, actually supply information to other agents. Such inflexibilities or constraints suggest to the individual what other agents might do, and the individual can then act accordingly. Whereas if these rigidities or 'imperfections. did not exist the behaviour of others could change with every perturbation in the economic system, and such frequent adjustments to behaviour might be perceived as random or chaotic.

In other words, institutions and routines, other than acting simply as rigidities and constraints, enable decision and action by providing more or less reliable information regarding the likely actions of others. One consequence of this function of institutions is that in a highly complex world, and despite uncertainty, regular and predictable behaviour is possible. The informational function of institutions and routines leads to patterns of action, guided by the information that the institutions provide,[13] and this has been illustrated in a game-theoretic framework by Andrew Schotter (1981).[14]

If we make the less rigid assumption that individual tastes and preferences are malleable and will change or adapt, then the objectives and behaviour of agents can be moulded or reinforced by institutions. This is partly because institutions have an important cognitive function (Hodgson, 1985b; Hargreaves Heap, 1986). The information they provide is not transmitted raw; it is affected by the structures of those institutions themselves. Such structures do not simply provide information, they influence the processes through which information is selected, arranged and perceived by agents. Furthermore, social culture embodies habits of thought and cognition which mould perception and action in subtle ways (Douglas, 1973).

Markets, prices and norms

Basing himself on Joan Robinson's (1971, 1974) work, Thanos Skouras (1981, pp. 202–4) has developed a line of argument that raises many questions about the neoclassical theory of prices and suggests an institutionalist alternative. Consider the market for a commodity, and assume that it is evident that the quantity supplied exceeds the quantity in demand. A consequent price reduction may result from changes made by individual agents. But, as Skouras argues, there is no necessary reason why people will automatically reduce prices in this way. If, for example, 'historical experience leads buyers and sellers to expect that this is an abnormally low price and that it will most likely be higher in the near future, then the price will not fall' (p. 203). Given such experience and expectations, buyers will be willing to buy more and sellers will be willing to sell less, so that the gap between supply and demand will narrow, and may even be reversed so that demand is in excess. And all this may occur whilst the price remains constant.

What is crucial in Skouras's argument is the idea of an expected normal or equilibrium price which is formed, in part, from historical experience. Furthermore:

The quantity that buyers would be willing to buy and sellers willing to sell at a particular price will be different depending on whether, (1) this price is seen as the equilibrium price, (2) this price is lower than the expected normal price, or (3) the price is higher than the expected normal price. It is evident that in cases (2) and (3) the drawing of demand and supply schedules presupposes a knowledge of the equilibrium price and cannot serve for its determination. Traditional demand and supply analysis, even when enriched by reaction functions giving rise to fluctuations, is built on case (1): buyers and sellers are assumed to react as if any price that is considered might be the equilibrium price. It is in this way that their memory of the past and their expectations about the future are eliminated and it becomes possible to construct curves the intersection of which determines the equilibrium price. (p. 203)

It is, of course, widely accepted that decisions to buy or sell at a given price depend in part on expected prices in the future. But future prices may themselves fluctuate, so the expectation is in the form of a norm, or range of possible prices, that are assumed to prevail at some future period. The question then is how such an expected norm is established.

The obvious orthodox answer would be to suggest some learning experience, based on observations of moving prices. However, if price adjustments were frequent then there are strong arguments to suggest that agents would have difficulty in establishing some expectation of a norm. Ceaseless, incremental price fluctuations may appear to the observer as little more than 'noise', and even if a sophisticated statistical analysis were readily at hand then it would not necessarily produce a reliable result. Most of the evidence of judgement under uncertainty (Kahneman, Slovic and Tversky, 1982) suggests that people do not make such judgements on the basis of Bayesian probability calculations or statistical regressions. Furthermore, given the amount of information involved and the insufficiency of computational speed and capacity (even in the age of the micro-computer), it is difficult to see how people could carry out such computations.

Yet in the absence of such expected norms, decisions to buy and sell would appear hazardous or uncertain. For markets to work, some mechanism to establish norms in the minds and

practices of agents is required. In some cases, crudely interpreted past experience can fit the bill. There are a large number
of day-to-day commodities for which prices are more or less
stable, and without deliberating upon it we learn the price level
and thus come to expect that future prices will be at about a
given level. As Shackle (1972, p. 227) argues in his chapter on
'prices as conventions', prices which 'have stood at particular
levels for some time acquire thereby some sanction and
authority'.[15] And, as Nicholas Kaldor (1985, p. 22) has
pointed out, such norms are functional for the system: 'Belief
in a long-run normal price of a commodity has always been
regarded as an indispensable condition for the reasonable
functioning of commodity markets.'

In many cases, however, prices will not be stable; and may
seem to vary more or less continuously. But even here a broad
or narrow range of prices can serve as a norm or a guide. Prices
are then evaluated in relation to their position within or
outside this range. We can thus generate expectations on the
basis of rough-and-ready experience of price movements
through historical time.

Even if the day-to-day price of a commodity shifts decisi-
vely above or below its preceding norm, as argued above, this
does not mean that the expected price-norm itself will move
automatically in the same direction. Clearly, however, few
prices are permanently stable, and at some time or another
price changes will force norms to adjust. The question then is
through what mechanism is the new norm established?

A partial answer proposed here is that market institutions
themselves have an important function in establishing norms.
This is frequently overlooked because the prevailing conception of a competitive market is one where agents are continuously higgling and haggling, and moving prices incremen-
tally to their mutual advantage. However, even in markets
where price alterations are frequent, trading is often structured and information is published enabling the formation of
norms, so that most agents may accept them as a guideline or
convention.

Take the stock market as an example. This is a case of a
potentially volatile market where minute-to-minute, incre-

mental adjustments in prices are common. Nevertheless, and even after recent changes, stock markets remain highly structured institutions. There are formal arrangements for gathering and publicizing information and for making transactions, and there are extensive informal networks and routines. We may conclude that even in a potentially volatile market where dramatic price changes are possible, trading is structured and information is published selectively so as to help the formation of price expectations and norms. Indeed, the very complexity and volatility of the price of stocks impels the market institution to publish or sponsor a great deal of guideline information so that agents can cope. Furthermore, informal trading networks between agents also help to establish trading conventions and norms.

In other cases, where prices are less volatile, price information can more directly contribute towards the formation of a norm. It is because prices are stable, and are perceived by agents to be in equilibrium, that the task facing market institutions is less daunting in this respect. Nevertheless, market institutions still have a crucial function: by ordering trade under the aegis of some institution, the price and quality of the product may be legitimized at its given level. There is a kind of stamp of institutional approval which may contribute in a powerful manner to the emergence of price norms.

It is important to note that price norms acquire a moral dimension in the eyes of the purchaser, which further helps to reinforce them in the market. In a random survey Daniel Kahneman, Jack Knetsch and Richard Thaler (1986) discovered that an overwhelming majority of respondents would regard a price increase as acceptable if it reflects a real cost increase, but not if it is simply a response to scarcity. (See also Frey, 1986.)

In rehabilitating a type of price norm, in a sense we are returning to the classical tradition of Adam Smith and David Ricardo, with their 'normal' or 'natural' price, and to subsequent developments such as Karl Marx's 'prices of production', and Piero Sraffa's (1960) system of 'values' based on matrices of input–output coefficients.

However, there are important differences between this

tradition and the argument presented here. In the works of Smith, Ricardo, Marx and Sraffa price norms relate to some kind of long-period stationary state where global profit rates and other adjustments are assumed to be fully worked out. In contrast, 'institutional' price norms are the outcome of a process in historical time, depend in part on expectations, and relate to the legitimizing and informational functions of institutions. At best, Sraffian prices are the notional norms which are consistent with a uniform profit rate.

The impossibility of perfect competition

Keynes argues that in a capitalist economy we act very much on the basis of past experience and established convention: 'Knowing that our own individual judgement is worthless, we endeavour to fall back on the judgement of the rest of the world which is perhaps better informed. That is, we endeavour to conform with the behaviour of the majority or the average' (Keynes, 1973, p. 114). This type of argument has clear implications for the question of price and quantity adjustments within market institutions, but these were not developed by Keynes and they remained underdeveloped in economic theory until similar issues were addressed by G.B. Richardson (1959, 1960).

Richardson argues that if neoclassical 'perfect competition' did actually exist it could not function for long. The problem being that no individual agent would be aware of the investment intentions of others. The incentive to invest depends in part on the knowledge of a limited competitive supply from other firms, or the establishment of a belief that others do not possess the information regarding the opportunity that is available to the investor. 'Perfect competition' does not provide this. Precisely because of its 'perfection' it places no limit on the number of firms that can be expected to compete. He writes:

A profit opportunity which is known by and available to everybody is available to nobody in particular. A situation of general profit potential can be tapped by one entrepreneur only if similar action is not intended by too many others; otherwise excess supply and general losses would result. In other words, a general opportunity of this kind will create a reliable profit expectation for a single entrepreneur only if there is some limitation upon the competitive supply to be expected from other producers. (1959, pp. 233–4)

This turns the conventional, neoclassical view inside out. Richardson argues that ' "perfect knowledge" ' . . . would have been no use to the members of the system even if they could ever be assumed to possess it' (p. 236) and the 'conditions necessary for adequate information are incompatible with perfect competition' (p. 233). He suggests that producers obtain information about the prospective activities of those to whom they are interrelated in a number of possible ways. First, there is explicit collusion or agreement; secondly, there is implicit collusion: 'a general understanding that no-one will alter what they are doing'; and thirdly, there are 'frictions', 'imperfections' and 'restraints', which, although they appear to stand in the way of 'free competition', are actually in some measure necessary to make the market system function at all.

Thus the model of perfect competition that is found in mainstream economic theory is unconvincing because it does not work. It is readily admitted by neoclassical theorists that perfect competition does not exist. The point, however, is that it would not be viable if it did.

As a consequence, the mainstream view of rigidities and constraints has to be reversed. Far from always preventing the system from working efficiently, they often play a functional role in a modern economy. This idea has been taken up by some modern post-Keynesians. Jan Kregel (1980, p. 46) argues that because of uncertainty regarding the future: 'the information required for rational decision making does not exist; the market mechanism cannot provide it. . . . The system reacts to the absence of the information the market cannot provide by creating uncertainty-reducing institutions: wage contracts, debt contracts, supply agreements, administered prices, trading agreements.'

Despite not being developed to the full, a glimmer of this argument is found in Chapter 17 of the *General Theory* where it is suggested that the rigidity of the money wage is not necessarily disadvantageous. Keynes argues that if money wages fell easily then this might create disruptive expectations of a further fall. However, these ideas were not fully developed by Keynes, and his microeconomic theory remains largely on marginalist foundations.

The discussion of price norms is again relevant in this context. Without the informational assistance of such norms it would be difficult to establish meaningful expectations of the future. Price norms thus help the market-based economy to operate in a world where agents have limited knowledge.

Consequently, the (partial) rigidity of prices and wages should not be treated as a restrictive assumption to be imposed upon a 'more general' model. Rigidities are not a 'special case'. These so-called 'imperfections' help to impose coherence and order on the market system. Markets function coherently *because of* institutional rigidities and 'imperfections', and not *despite* them as neoclassical theorists presume.

The potential for cumulative instability

Whilst we carry the burden of the past in the form of the institutions that mould and dominate our lives, institutional economists such as Veblen never overlooked the processes through which institutions and habits may change: 'The situation of today shapes the institutions of tomorrow through a selective, coercive process, by acting upon men's habitual view of things, and so altering or fortifying a point of view or a mental attitude handed down from the past' (Veblen, 1899, p. 190).

Furthermore, in stressing the importance and functional character of habits and routine, it should not be overlooked that conscious choices and purposive action are involved as well. Thus the 'selective, coercive process' is not confined to a fixed groove. Institutions change, and even gradual change can eventually put such a strain on a system that there can be outbreaks of conflict or crises, leading to a change in actions and attitudes. Thus there is always the possibility of the breakdown of regularity: 'there will be moments of crisis situations or structural breaks when existing conventions or social practices are disrupted' (Lawson, 1985, p. 920). In any social system there is an interplay between routinized behaviour and the variable or volatile decisions of other agents. This non-deterministic view stresses both the weight of routine and habit in the formation of behaviour and the importance of some elements of strategic deliberation and their possibly disruptive effects on stability. Such a tension between regularity and crisis is shown in the following quotation from Veblen:

> Not only is the individual's conduct hedged about and directed by his habitual relations to his fellows in the group, but these relations, being of an institutional character, vary as the institutional scene varies. The wants and desires, the end and the aim, the ways and the means, the amplitude and drift of the individual's conduct are functions of an institutional variable that is of a highly complex and wholly unstable character. (Veblen, 1909, p. 245)

With these ingredients it is possible to envisage processes whereby for long periods the reigning habits of thought and action are cumulatively reinforced. But this very process can lead to sudden and rapid change. The very ossification of society could lead to the decimation of the economic system from more vigorous competition from outside, or there could be an internal reaction leading to a newly modernized order. Conversely, a recklessly dynamic system may suffer from lack of continuity of skill or outlook, and reach an impasse because in its own breakneck pace its members were left without enduring values or goals.

In Veblen's view the economic system is not a 'self-balancing mechanism' but a 'cumulatively unfolding process'. Economic institutions are complexes of habits, roles and conventional behaviour. However, because of the momentum of technological and social change in modern industrial society, and the clashing new conceptions and traditions thrown up with each innovation in management and technique, the cumulative character of economic development can mean crisis on occasions rather than continuous change or advance.

Despite the geographical and intellectual remoteness of Keynes's work from that of the American Institutionalists, there are similarities here with the analysis in Chapter 12 of the *General Theory*. Here Keynes emphasizes the 'precariousness' of the 'convention' upon which decision and action are based, and the possibility of cumulatively violent changes in mood and expectation. At the same time, however, he cautions that 'the state of long-term expectation is often steady, and, even when it is not, the other factors exert their compensating effects' (Keynes, 1971b, p. 162).

The evolutionary character of institutional economics

Ever since the classic articles of Armen Alchian (1950) and Milton Friedman (1953) neoclassical theory has relied on a Darwinian analogy in its analysis of competition or even individual rationality. However, as Sidney Winter (1964) demonstrates, the appeal to Darwinian notions of evolution is unsuccessful because the mechanisms involved in the sustenance and procreation of such maximizing behaviour are not specified. For instance, in the case of the firm the neoclassical 'natural selection' theory lacks a viable mechanism to transmit the characteristics of surviving firms from one generation to the next. In the natural world, according to many biologists, such a mechanism is the gene. This is believed to contain the hereditary information which is passed on from each organism to its successors.

Within an institutionalist perspective, organizational structures, habits and routines play a similar evolutionary role to that of the gene in the natural world. To some degree these have a stable and inert quality and tend to sustain and thus 'pass on' their characteristics through time, and from one institution to another.

For example, the skills learned by a worker in a given firm become partially embedded in his or her habits. Thus these act as carriers of information, 'unteachable knowledge' and skills. The idea that routines within the firm act as 'genes' to pass on skills and information is adopted by Nelson and

Winter (1982, pp. 134–6) and forms a crucial part of their theoretical model of the modern corporation. However, routines do not act as genes in the strict biological sense. In contrast to Darwinian biology, the inheritance of *acquired* characteristics is possible. Thus the evolutionary process in society can find a more adequate analogy in the earlier biology of Jean-Baptiste Lamarck. Unlike orthodox Darwinian biology, economic evolution is not always gradualistic, and rapid 'mutations' are possible as rapid transformations in the social, economic and technological culture lead to the rapid acquisitions of new skills and routines.

CONCLUSION

Three major theoretical perspectives have been offered as a foundation for post-Keynesian theory: the behaviouralist, the Shacklean and the Sraffian. It has been argued here that all three, despite their positive points, have their limitations and flaws. Furthermore, a relatively unexplored alternative foundation can be found within institutionalist theory, and this may have the benefit of incorporating some of the acceptable features of the other three perspectives.[16]

Interestingly, the research agenda that is promoted by this linkage of institutionalist and post-Keynesian theory includes a focus on the relationship between, on the one hand, the long-period and the durable aspects of habits and routines, and the short-period and the aspects of cumulative instability and indeterminacy in the system. The differing treatments of the short and long period can be related in part to different emphases within the hierarchy of decision and action. Further theoretical work should aim to resolve this issue within a comprehensive theoretical framework.

NOTES

1. I am grateful to participants of the 'New Directions' conference, especially Geoff Harcourt, Neil Kay and Ingrid Rima, for comments on an earlier draft of this paper.
2. Carvalho (1984–5) surveys these approaches within post-Keynesia-

nism: (1) the long-run, Sraffian models of Eatwell and Garegnani; (2) the Kaldor–Pasinetti model where long-run growth rates are moveable; (3) the Kaleckian alternative, which combines both long and short run models, with an emphasis on cyclical movements; (4) the 'historical' approach of Davidson, Kregel and Minsky where uncertainty undermines the usefulness of long-run or gravity centre models; and (5) the indeterminate economics of Shackle.

3. Harvey Leibenstein is on the editorial board of the *Journal of Post-Keynesian Economics* and some may argue that his X-inefficiency theory (Leibenstein, 1976) should be included in this list. However, as Leibenstein (1983, p. 841) himself admits, there is no finished theoretical basis for the X-inefficiency idea in his writings.

    Furthermore, the idea has little to do with the economics of Keynes. Apart from the rejection of the maximization hypothesis, there is very little that is radical in a theoretical sense. Notably, X-inefficiency itself is defined in relation to neoclassical norms, and the policy imperative is that those norms should be attained as far as possible. Leibenstein argues that neoclassical theorists are wrong because they fail to acknowledge the existence of X-inefficiency, but he then seems to draw the conclusion that policies must be so designed that it is minimized and that reality then conforms to the neoclassical model.

    Whilst the X-inefficiency idea points to the existence of slack and spare capacity, there does not seem to be a recognition that in a world of uncertainty and ignorance some slack capacity is *necessary* to deal with contingencies; a firm that rid itself of slack would be inflexible and less likely to survive. Leibenstein's argument, however, is that slackness and inefficiency should be abolished or minimized through the competitive pressure of the market. It is implied that any remaining slack or excess capacity is a regrettable residual rather than to some degree a functional necessity for the firm. For these reasons there are serious limitations in making the X-inefficiency idea a main theoretical foundation for post-Keynesian economics.

4. Note also the synthesis by Peter Earl (1983) which attempts to combine behaviouralism with a Shackle-inspired view of the economic process. Joan Robinson's work has spanned different perspectives by moving away from Sraffian long-period analysis towards a rejection of equilibrium theorizing and an emphasis on historical time. (See Robinson, 1974, 1979a, 1980; Harcourt, 1985.)

5. Elsewhere (Hodgson, 1981; 1982, ch. 15) I have attempted to graft some notion of money on to the Sraffa system using a joint-product framework. The attempt was tentative, and the aims of the article were mainly to suggest that there was a problem in the orthodox Sraffaian system and to set an agenda for future research. In the single-product model devised by Carlo Panico (1980, p. 376) money appears simply as an interest payment, not as a store of value nor as a portion of capital which could be advanced by the industrial capitalists.

6. In fact, without the concept of money, the concepts of supply and demand are inseparable and devoid of independent meaning. This is because *in a barter economy* a 'commodity which is supplied, is always, at the same time, a commodity which is the instrument of demand. A commodity which is the instrument of demand, is always, at the same time, a commodity added to the stock of supply. Every commodity is always at one at the same time matter of demand and matter of supply' (James Mill, 1821, p. 190). In a monetary economy, however, demand and supply are distinguished from one another and, contrary to Mill, Say's Law does not apply (Hodgson, 1982, pp. 67–8, 122–3).

7. For an account of the Sraffa-based critique of neoclassical theory see Harcourt (1972). For the impact of Sraffa on Marx see Steedman (1977) and the discussion in Hodgson (1982).

8. Recently, G. Dumenil and D. Levy (1987) have attempted to construct a more dynamic model based on Sraffian foundations. However, the objections raised here still remain; crucial problems of information and knowledge are assumed away, and money proper does not exist in the model.

   For a further discussion of the limitations of the Sraffa-Keynes synthesis see Harcourt and O'Shaughnessy (1985).

9. Note in this context Ronald Heiner's (1983) work on the origin of rules, norms and 'predictable behavior'. Like the work of Simon, one of its valuable features is its stress on the difference between computational capacity or ability and the complexity of everyday choices and problems in economic life.

10. On this and related topics see also Hodgson (1985b, 1986, 1988).

11. In later works Hayek has moved away from mainstream Austrian theory, and its classic liberal presumptions, by accepting – with his concept of 'spontaneous order' – a function for institutions and routine in maintaining order in social and economic life. Note, however, that this idea is one-directional in its scope. An order is defined as a state of affairs in which people can '*form correct expectations*' because of the existence of some pattern or regularity in social life (Hayek, 1982, vol. 1, p. 36). Thus when Hayek writes that 'a spontaneous order results from the individual elements adapting themselves to circumstances' (p. 41) he means that behaviour may adapt given the information and constraints that are presented. The adaptation in behaviour results primarily from a change in information or perception, not from a change in the individual himself or herself.

    Thus, characteristically, Hayek still regards individual purposes and preferences as being exogenous to the system. He does not acknowledge that norms and conventions may actually result in the adaptation of the character and purposes of the individual. But order does not simply affect expectations, it affects individuals themselves. As Anthony Giddens (1982, p. 8) puts it, *both* human subjects and social institutions are '*constituted in and through recurrent practices*'. Thus, despite his laudable appeal to an evolutionary conception of the emergence of social institutions, Hayek does not consider the evolution of purposes and preferences themselves.

12. Surprisingly, despite some considerable similarity between Nelson and Winter's approach and the theories of Veblen and the early American institutionalists, Nelson and Winter make no reference to any of Veblen's works. In fact, the Nelson–Winter approach is much more institutionalist than the so-called 'new institutionalism' of Oliver Williamson (1975, 1985) and others.

13. Several writers have made this point. See, for instance, Geoffrey Newman (1976, p. 474), Lawrence Boland (1979, p. 963), Herbert Simon (1983, p. 78) and Richard Langlois (1986a, p. 237).

14. However, in a game-theoretic framework the model of the agent is still that of maximizing 'economic man'. Furthermore, Schotter (1981, p. 160) underlines a standard assumption of game theory that agents make use of '*all* relevant information', and nothing is ignored in the determination of their optimal strategy. However, as Simon argues, such global calculations are impossible because of the limited computational capacity of any computer or human brain.

     True uncertainty does not play a central role in game theory because the actors are assumed to be aware of both the menu of strategic options and the payoffs in each case. As Shackle (1972, ch. 36) points out in his critique, game theory excludes the phenomenon of tactical surprise: 'Surprise is the exploitation of the opponent's lack of knowledge, or of his reliance on what he wrongly believes to be knowledge' (p. 423). In reality, Shackle argues, the 'most powerful resource available to a real-life contestant may be to exploit the ignorance of . . . contestants concerning the ultimate conditions of the contest' (p. 426). For this reason the structure of competition and markets is not adequately represented by the game-theoretic tableau.

15. Shackle (1972, pp. 226–7) notes the work of Hugh Townshend, a pupil of Keynes, in this context. Townshend (1937, p. 168) writes that

     in regard to actual money-prices, there is nothing save the force of habit, operating through conventional prejudices about the normality, or propriety, of certain price-levels for certain particular variables, . . . and through habits and conventions which limit the velocity of circulation of money on the one hand and its volume on the other, to prevent them from varying arbitrarily, even in the shortest period. In long periods they do in fact vary arbitrarily – that is to say, in a way not governed by regular law, and therefore unpredictable. Thus a convention of stability is necessary for any dynamic economic theorising.

     Keynes was aware of this article and did not distance himself from it. For Keynes's correspondence with Townshend see Keynes (1979).

16. There are other links between post-Keynesianism and Institutionalism which have not been discussed here, particularly in regard to a system-

wide or organic view of the world. See Gruchy (1948); Brown-Collier, (1985). For more general discussions of closely related interest see Eichner (1985) and Foster (1987).

6. The Macroeconomics of Keynes: An Evolutionary Perspective

John Foster

INTRODUCTION

The argument presented in this paper is, perhaps, surprising. It is that the macroeconomics of Keynes, as set out in the *General Theory of Employment, Interest and Money* (hereinafter GT), is compatible with an evolutionary perspective on the macro-system. This is a surprising proposition because the GT is usually regarded as being about the short run, leaving aside any concern for the long run over which structural change is viewed as important. One of the main reasons why it is now possible to view the GT as evolutionary in nature is because, in biology itself, views of how the evolutionary process itself proceeds have changed. The Darwinian view of this process, which has little in common with the GT, is now under attack from a new vision of evolution where it is argued that the process is one of long phases of harmonious interaction punctuated by short phases of catastrophe. This new view is felt to be particularly appealing in analyzing the evolution of human-created structures.

The organization of the paper is as follows. In the first section, the reasons why the GT has lost its central place in macroeconomics are discussed. In the second section, it is argued that Keynes's analysis of the 'supply-side' is widely misunderstood because it is not recognized that the principle of effective demand, as a proposition pertaining to historical time, cannot be placed in an abstract aggregate demand/

supply framework. The third section goes on to argue that the principle belongs in an evolutionary framework. What such a framework actually is in the macroeconomic domain is discussed in general terms and the merits and shortcomings of the GT in such a framework are evaluated. The final section looks to the future, discussing how we can build on the GT to produce a macroeconomics which is more explicitly evolutionary in character, and capable of addressing the economic problems of the 1980s rather than those of the 1930s.

KEYNES'S MACROECONOMICS IN DECLINE

Today the GT is widely perceived as a book which is not very relevant to the problems of the 1980s' macroeconomy. An examination of recent North American texts in macroeconomics reveals that there is little or no discussion of the GT, only some presentation of new Keynesian ideas which have grown out of the monetarist–Keynesian debate of the 1970s. More often than not, inclusion of these ideas is only for the purpose of highlighting the validity of simple, sharp new Classical logic. The GT is no more than a historical curiosity, long ago judged to be analytically and methodologically unsound, not by new Classical economists, but by 'Keynesians' such as Tobin, Modigliani, Patinkin and Friedman in his 'we are all Keynesians now' days.

Those of us who see the GT as a durable contribution often find ourselves dismayed by this trend, but such a reaction is unwarranted for it is remarkable that a book, centrally concerned with the problems of inter-war years and the drive to make stabilization policy intellectually respectable, should still be discussed at all. Since the 1970s, there has been a distinct change in emphasis in writings on the GT. A decade ago there existed a belief that if, somehow, the GT could be viewed from a different direction or interpreted in a new way we could come to understand the causes of stagflation. The 1980s have been different, now discussion of the GT resides more firmly in the history of economic thought. When in 1983 Victoria Chick published her excellent book, *Macroecono-*

mics After Keynes its time had passed, not as a valuable book for students to read, but as a contribution to a great debate at the heart of macroeconomics.

Serious interest in the GT is now largely confined to the post Keynesian school but, even in a group with such a direct lineage back to Keynes, we have witnessed a growing preference for expressing some of Keynes's ideas in the context of Michael Kalecki's medium-run model.[1] It is true that such a shift has its attractions for post-Keynesian's, given the existence of distributional models of the long-run developed, for example, by Kaldor and others.[2] Keynes's refusal to depart in any formal way from the short-run perspective had always presented a medium-run void which could be filled by adopting the Kaleckian approach, encapsulating short-run problems of effective demand while meshing nicely with long-run distributional models of growth.[3]

In Cambridge, resistance to this trend came from Joan Robinson who always insisted that Keynes had something to say which was more general than Kalecki. Thus she was able to tolerate, more than other post-Keynesians, the ambivalence in Keynes's writings, understanding well the Marshallian tradition within which Keynes had formed his habits of thought.[4] She understood that the Classical components of his thoughts were Marshallian rather than Walrasian and, as such, rendered Walrasian generalizations in IS–LM Keynesianism inadmissible. It is quite astonishing how accurate were her predictions, many made in the 1950s, as to the future course of macroeconomic theory and policy, once Keynesianism had gone down the wrong track.

Despite her strident defence of Keynes, both against Keynesianism in one direction and neo-Marxism on the other, it is true to say that Joan Robinson never succeeded in providing the necessary developments of the GT to establish an alternative framework of analysis. She knew that it was the shift from abstract to historical time which provided the starting point in this quest and that, in the principle of effective demand, Keynes had provided a logical proposition, set in historical time, which could be built upon.[5]

The centrality of the principle of effective demand in the GT is evidenced by the fact that it was the one proposition that Keynesians, post-Keynesians and monetarists retained in their analysis, enabling them all to advocate stabilization policy in one form or another. The abstractness of Say's Law had been replaced by the historicalness of the principle of effective demand. Only the new Classical school, which has risen to prominence over the past decade, rejects the principle of effective demand. They have done so by forcing monetarists and new Keynesians to admit that, in fact, what they call effective demand is no more than disequilibrium of notional aggregate demand in abstract time. The application of rational expectations to a stochastic aggregate demand / supply model is all that was necessary to argue that such disequilibrium is random in character in the short run. Therefore the Classical long run which new Keynesians and monetarists felt their models were equilibrating towards is left as the only persistent force.[6]

It is the abandonment of the principle of effective demand that has led to the demise of the GT. It is now retained in its correct form only by the post-Keynesian school whose analysis has become more disengaged than ever before from that of the three other aforementioned schools of macroeconomic thought.[7] As monetarists and new Keynesians lose logical battles on ostensibly Keynesian issues such as the existence of involuntary unemployment and the efficacy of monetary and fiscal policy, it is becoming clear that there now exists only two distinctive schools of thought in macroeconomics: post-Keynesianism and new Classicism. They are distinctive because of their polar opposite premises concerning, first, the degree to which economic co-ordination occurs through the auction-market process and, secondly, the degree to which we can rely on the *homo economicus* assumption concerning the individual as a basic analytical building block.[8]

As custodians of the principle of effective demand, the post-Keynesians bear a heavy responsibility. It is all too easy to construct dynamic models where defined 'common consciousness' groups such as capitalists and workers struggle for distributional shares. However, such analysis, placing power at the centre of the stage, threatens to replace analysis entirely by history since the outcome of struggle is highly history specific.[9] The course of the macroeconomy becomes the province of political scientists and theory the playground of game theorists. In reading the GT one always gains a strong impression that it was this kind of shift in 1930s' economic thought that Keynes was attempting to prevent.[10] He implied that the problem was not one about conflict between groups but rather one concerning system malfunction in a macroeconomy which had undergone structural change, not clearly perceived in the economic orthodoxy of the time.

One clear distinction between new Keynesians and post Keynesians is that the former try to argue for wage rigidity as the cornerstone of their arguments concerning the existence of involuntary unemployment whereas the latter argue more broadly from a non-market clearing perspective.[11] To post-Keynesians, wage rigidities of the relativistic kind proposed by Keynes are entirely normal manifestations of a world where bargaining and power-relations dominate. Therefore there is no need to perform gymnastics in order to make wage rigidity compatible with a market-clearing *homo economicus* world. However, post-Keynesians seem to underestimate the centrality of wage rigidity to Keynes's own vision of the macroeconomy.

If we suppose that the GT is attempting to persuade us that there was a malfunction in the 1930s' economic system, which could be given historical dimension in the principle of effective demand, and that the source of this malfunction was in the erratic behaviour of investors, then wage rigidity can be viewed as no more than an expression of the fact that systems tend to behave in asymmetric ways in expansion and contraction. This is an *evolutionary* position which is not considered explicitly as such in either new Keynesian or post-Keynesian thought. Keynes focused on wage rigidity in particular because the variable of key concern was unemployment in the labour sector.

That Keynes had an evolutionary perspective on the macroeconomy is a proposition that requires some justification. However, we ought to recall, from the outset, that his teacher, Alfred Marshall, was a profoundly evolutionary thinker who made repeated pleas to economists to analyze the economy as an organic system, in the manner of biologists.[12] Keynes's insistence, in his debates with Dennis Robertson, that little could be said beyond the short run reflects a position that the long run is not the province of useful economic theorizing.[13] Of course, such a position can be classified as no more than pragmatism but the GT is surely testimony that Keynes was attempting to offer more than that.

KEYNES'S VISION OF THE 'SUPPLY-SIDE'

Before we can see clearly how the GT fits into an evolutionary perspective it is necessary to spend some time on the question of aggregate supply. One of the main thrusts of the new Classical critique of Keynesianism is that it lacks a supply-side. Indeed, given that new Keynesians are quite happy to argue in terms of aggregate demand and supply, such a criticism seems well-founded. It is very difficult in the abstract aggregate supply / demand framework to specify both given the degree of interdependence of demand and supply at such a high level of aggregation. Either aggregate demand is taken as passive (through the operation of rational expectations) in the supply-side analysis of new Classicals or aggregate supply is passive (through continuous availability of extra capacity) in the demand-side analysis of Keynesians. Compromises result in garbled new Keynesian and monetarist stories where price and quantity combinations cannot be identified.

Is it true that the root of new Keynesian difficulties was in Keynes's neglect of the supply-side in the GT, setting Keynesianism off on the wrong foot? Post-Keynesians would probably answer with a majority 'no' simply because they do not subscribe to the aggregate supply / demand dichotomy and see it as distinct from the principle of effective demand. However, trivialization of the principle can still occur in post-Keynesianism, not from supply-side arguments, but from arguments that long-run theories of economic development are pre-eminent.

Once we are in historical time and faced with a short-run

where outcomes of struggle are history-specific, it is inevitable that some kind of longer-run historical determinism will be applied in order to say anything at all about economic development. In the Kaldorian long-run and the Kaleckian medium-run theories, inadequacy of effective demand in the short run is a minor issue compared with savings rate changes induced by redistribution and variations in the degree of monopoly. Kaldor–Kalecki structuralism tends to stifle Keynes's insight almost as much as new Classical economics because it makes no allowance for the *spontaneous* development of the macroeconomy. Investment is determined by profit in the long run and induces oscillations through the accelerator in the medium run.

The role of 'animal spirits' in providing the creative stimulus to private sector development is removed.[14] Keynes's rich insight as to the socio-psychological nature of anticipations and the developments of such insight by George Shackle, for example, become relatively unimportant.[15] Some structuralists explicitly accuse Keynes of being overly 'psychologistic' and neglectful in paying attention to the imperfectly competitive nature of the economy so central to Kaleckian analysis.[16] Yet if the rational expectations hypothesis has told us nothing else, it has emphasized that the myths we hold in the short run about the long run can alter the structure of the economic system as time passes.

If this is true, then Keynes was correct not to subscribe to structuralist determinism beyond the short run, he was correct in choosing, as his depiction of the economy, the prevailing myths as to its structure, he was correct in ascribing such importance to animal spirits and he was correct in arguing that the principle of effective demand was of pre-eminent policy importance. As such Keynes's position is not compatible with that of the Kaldor–Kaleckians who seem to misunderstand the nature and purpose of Keynes's writing on the 'supply-side' in the GT.

Effective demand is a magnitude which is observable in historical time, unlike its abstract aggregate supply and demand parents. Thus, when Keynes discusses aggregate supply he does so in a theoretical manner which is necessarily static in nature. It is not the objective here to offer an intensive account of how Keynes envisaged aggregate supply, for that has already been done with great thoroughness, particularly by Victoria Chick. We need not do so for Keynes did not give it too much attention.[17] Essentially, Keynes followed the Marshallian 'short run' by fixing a factor (capital) and assuming diminishing returns to labour along a production function.

Now, although Keynes went to great lengths on the demand side to get his analysis into historical time, his Marshallian supply-side analysis remains in abstract time – a contrived short run created by taking capital out of the picture and having producers wholly concerned with their derived labour demand, remaining in equilibrium through their profit maximizing urges. Meanwhile, on the demand side, these same producers participate in the dynamics of historical time, altering their flows of expenditure on capital in ways so powerful that the stability of the whole economy is affected. This schizophrenia among producers, on the one hand obsessively concerned with changing their capital stock and, on the other, calmly maintaining static equilibrium in factor markets as if capital was fixed, is entirely the product of pushing together a historical time short run with an abstract time short run. It was a very necessary division for Keynes's model because it enabled him to track demand-side instability reliably to employment.

Historical time dynamics were avoided in the Marshallian theory of the firm and its demand for labour but not on the other side of the labour market. Actual earnings in any period were associated with aggregate income and, in turn, expenditure. Thus, there was no guarantee that wage cuts would stimulate employment, but, perhaps more significantly, Keynes introduced historical time behaviour in labour supply whereby money wages are fixed because of a very real world concern for relativities.

In abstract time this looked irrational in comparison with the neat marginalist principles being continuously practised on the other side of the labour market. The historical time vision of labour supply was further developed by Keynes in his view that real wages could be cut by raising prices, again suggesting abstract time irrationality. Of course, there was nothing irrational about ignoring prices in the Great Depression compared with, say, the 1970s. However, irrespective of the historical time antics of labour supply, whatever labour was supplied, at whatever wage, would be fed into the timeless productive structure to compute an output. Thus, an aggregate supply curve could be envisaged which intersects with an aggregate demand curve at effective demand which could be below full employment.[18] This 'supply curve' constitutes more of a 'capacity-utilization' curve prevailing in conditions where the assumptions underlying neoclassical production theory are breached.[19]

The resultant model was extremely successful in achieving Keynes's primary objectives. The fact that an abstract time production sector meshed uneasily with the historical time analysis of effective demand was not an immediate problem for Keynes. In fact it may have been something of an advantage in the eclectic mixture that it produced. Although the revolutionary aspects of his model all lay in the macroeconomic, or holistic characterizations of behaviour set in historical time, the very essence of historical time is that the world changes and characterizations become dated. Although the central theory of effective demand did not date because its logic applies to any monetary economy, Keynes's holistic characterizations of investor optimism / pessimism, labour supply responses and speculator behaviour in financial markets all gradually become obsolete or heavily qualified. This was not the case with the supply side analysis of the productive sector in abstract time. The abstract principles involved were immune to historical obsolescence.

Keynes had not gone far enough in his historical time analysis and the points of interface between history and abstraction remained blurred. For example, the interaction between producers' behaviour with regard to capital formation and the direct implications for patterns of demand in the labour market were not tied together even though both involved profit. The role of flows of credit in capital formation, emphasized in the *Treatise on Money*, were underplayed in favour of liquidity considerations necessary to maintain current production. In the labour market the implicit contractual arrangements which lay behind sluggish wage change were not developed by Keynes. It is clear why; admission that contractual commitments existed into the future would vastly complicate and even destroy the marginal productivity theory of labour demand and Roy Harrod had warned Keynes of the consequences of that.[20]

Keynes was able to clothe his macroeconomic analysis with historical time expectations and anticipations but could not provide anything more than comparative statics to analyze macro-dynamics. The temporal fabric of contract, custom and commitment, within which expectations and anticipations naturally reside, was missing. The debate as to whether Keynes was a special case of the Classics or vice versa is in this sense irrelevant. Keynes could never be a special case of the Classics, for the Classical system cannot admit historical time and, equally, it is trivial to argue that Classical analysis can be a special case in historical time. Keynes's analysis was a special case in a more general, and yet to be discovered, historical time analysis.

So what we have in the GT is not a supply-side story at all but rather a capacity-utilization story, depicted in familiar Marshallian language. It is often forgotten that Keynes was primarily a monetary economist who had devoted little time to developing his own analysis of the functioning of the real economy. This explains his adoption of short-run Marshallian theory as an adjunct to his main message concerning effective demand. Furthermore, it is likely that Keynes looked on this body of theory quite differently to authors of modern texts on microeconomics.

One of the great truths of economics which has endured as a logical 'law' is the idea that 'bygones are bygones'. This 'law' was popularized by Alfred Marshall to model the firm's production behaviour in a real world of fluctuating prices and revenue. In textbooks it is frequently used to demonstrate the marginalist proposition, yet it is a proposition which is much more about fixity, or commitment in historical time. Indeed, it is this fixity that makes the problem tractable and easy for the student to comprehend. The student also knows that once we move into the orthodox long-run, marginalist propositions become much more difficult to sustain and relate to everyday historical experience. Marshall was clearly attempting to offer a formal approach to analyze an evolutionary problem: the constraining influence of past decisions and present commitments.

To develop Keynes's Marshallian depiction of capacity utilization we should not follow the Kaleckian route, of replacing Keynes's competitive model of supply with imperfect competition. The problem is not choice of structure but rather how to improve on the evolutionary dynamics pioneered by Marshall, which underlaid Keynes's analysis.[21] In order to do this we need to look towards the new evolutionary approaches in microeconomics; for example, Nelson and Winter's rules-of-thumb, Simon's bounded rationality and Williamson's transaction cost theory of institutional adaptation.[22] It is in this evolutionary tradition that we can find general principles which can augment the principle of effective demand to provide a macroeconomics which is cast in historical time but also has a forward-looking perspective which is not institutionally and behaviourally static.

KEYNES'S GENERAL THEORY IN AN EVOLUTIONARY FRAMEWORK

Up until now an attempt has been made to argue that the GT exhibits features which are compatible with an evolutionary perspective on the economic system. In this section an attempt will be made to provide a depiction of what an evolutionary approach to macroeconomics actually is.[23] With such a perspective we can enquire into the *adequacy* of the GT and its policy prescriptions in evolutionary terms.

In general terms, an evolutionary approach places at the centre of the stage structural change. Such change is not a random process but traces out a sequence of historical events which have coherence. Evolutionary processes are often associated with Darwinian 'natural selection'. However, the depiction of evolution as the outcome of continuous struggle is, nowadays, something of a special case. To quote Kenneth Boulding, evolution is more about 'survival of the fitting' than survival of the fittest. Evolution as a process concerning creativity and co-operation can be traced, as a concept, back to Peter Kropotkin. However, today biologists such as Eldredge recognize that such harmonious phases of evolution are likely to be punctuated by brief periods of catastrophic change.

The advantage of the Kropotkin / Eldredge approach for economics is that it permits us to argue that we can have protracted periods of harmonious expansion in the level of economic co-ordination as innovators make creative advances following a fundamental breakthrough. There is ample scope for Keynes's 'animal spirits' to translate themselves into economic progress while, at the same time, the onset of inertia and associated crises in confidence create the necessary conditions favourable for another fundamental shift in the knowledge set. Given that this new approach to evolution acknowledges that developmental paths involve planning of co-ordinated effort, structural change no longer proceeds 'automatically' in the Darwinian manner and it is necessary to include, explicitly, the role of consciousness. In other words, anticipations, in an environment of structural change, require to be analyzed. Thus, the insights of Keynes concerning anticipations and their development by, for example, George Shackle, become relevant to an evolutionary perspective, for such anticipations are, without doubt, more firmly cast in an environment of structural change than the rational expectations of new Classical economists.

It is this division between those who view anticipations as being formed about a future which is either structurally fixed or structurally changing that it is of central interest here. It is not the purpose here to stray too far into the rapidly growing area of evolutionary economics or the related area of technological innovation.[24] All we require is some kind of taxonomic framework within which an evolutionary approach can be placed in contrast to the non-evolutionary static equilibrium approach.

Essentially, any evolving system has a productive structure

which emits characteristics which are both qualitative and quantitative. This is a stock. Apart from absorption of energy, there are two distinct types of activity that the system can engage in. First, there is defensive maintenace activity to keep productive structure intact and, secondly, there is creative developmental activity which enables the system to mutate in the face of inevitable entropy of productive structure.

We can identify a system at various levels of aggregation in the economy. Systems operate in a 'hierarchy of consciousness' in the sense that each system tends to subscribe to a higher level of consciousness which provides an umbrella under which the system can operate. Simultaneously, the umbrella consciousness has certain power over the subscriber. Thus, micro-systems, such as individuals, do not have independent consciousness, as postulated in neoclassical micro-theory, but are rather a unique configuration of higher consciousnesses plus an idiosyncratic component which may be quite small.[25] Equally, it can be argued that the appropriate units of consciousness, for analytical purposes, are collective ones and, as evolution proceeds, subscription to such collective consciousness will change. On the periphery of the economic system, consciousness units are likely to mutate rapidly but, at the core, adaption will be slow and conservative, simply because the periphery requires the continuity and security that such core conservatism provides.

We can define macro-consciousness as that which operates at the highest level in the economic system. The shared consciousness of a whole population in culture, custom and law which has, as its custodian, government. Government oversees the economic system and ensures that appropriate myths are perpetrated to enhance co-ordination using agencies such as universities or the Church for this purpose. Government must also ensure that, as the underlying structure of the economy evolves, its functions, both as a provider of infrastructure and as a custodian of mythology, should change. Typically, given its core responsibility to provide certainty and continuity, government finds such adjustment difficult, particularly when constitutional change is required. Even in a democratic system the conflict of vested interests can result in inertia and ultimate catastrophe in the form of structural fragmentation.

It was precisely this short-run evolutionary situation of structural fragmentation that Keynes was preoccupied with in his macroeconomic analysis. He was concerned with macroeconomic structure and the problem that existed in macroconsciousness which resulted in stagnation. Keynes did not disaggregate in order to isolate one 'problem' group that, in some causal sense, was the source of the prevailing malaise, but rather engaged in a particular disaggregation to demonstrate the *interdependency* contained in macro-structure. Or, at a more basic level, through the principle of effective demand, he established that macro-structure had a holistic identity that was not reducible into microeconomic parts. Keynes did identify the cause of stagnation of macro-structure in the interplay of investor pessimism and speculator liquidity preference. The effect was unemployment of resources. Although Keynes tended to have sympathy with the plight of nervous investors and antagonism towards speculators who earned predative gains from structural decline, he clearly saw the situation as a crisis of macro-consciousness that government was capable of rectifying.

For Keynes, the key to this structural problem lay in the interaction of stocks and flows in macro-structure. Investors, already committed to discrete capital stocks, feared shortages of liquidity when flows of income were disturbed, while at the same time, part of the stock of liquidity was demanded by speculators wishing to capitalize on the chain reactions between nervous investment cuts and income–expenditure flows. The authorities' attempts to engage in monetary control created inconsistencies between sub-macro-consciousness, with creative 'animal spirits', on the one hand, and the predative speculative urge on the other. This schizophrenia had, in the nineteenth century, led to business cycles but, after the experiences of the 1920s, it had given way to a dull and protracted pessimism on all sides, in the banking system, in investment, among speculators and in government itself.

Keynes suggested that conditions were so bleak that even if the authorities tried to release extra liquidity they might find themselves in an expectational trap. Orthodox macroeconomics deals with flows, measured in monetary units, over time. The macro-system, thus depicted, is analysed in terms of flow equilibrium. Flow shocks disturb this equilibrium, setting off disequilibrium adjustment processes which culminate in the restoration of new flow equilibria. This is the method of 'comparative statics' as practised in orthodox macroeconomics. Even though macro-structure is 'looser' than the structure dealt with in Newtonian physics, there is still a role for this kind of method over short historical periods. In order to engage in 'comparative statics' the structure through which motion flows must be held constant, otherwise the equilibrium method cannot be used. This is the true static nature of the model in evolutionary terms. This fixed structure consists of a set of institutional arrangements, socially determined, plus a set of behavioural assumptions concerning individuals or groups. In this respect orthodox Keynesian macroeconomics adopts the same method as neoclassical market analysis.

The difficulties involved in assuming fixed economic structure have been alluded to frequently in the history of economic thought. Keynes himself saw difficulties in using the equilibrium method beyond the short run because of the inherent structure-altering effects of capital investment which, in turn, was not viewed as determinable in terms of quantifiable behavioural rules. Although Keynes had essentially saved the equilibrium method by taking it from its redundant Walrasian market context and applying it to short-run income–expenditure flows, he remained cautious as to its usefulness. The long run was the province of evolution and economic structure was not exempt from evolutionary tendencies.

Keynes's use of the equilibrium method for studying the short-run characteristics of macro-system was wholly appropriate for his task at hand. The economic structure upon which he employed such a method was portrayed as having evolved from the Classical conception in two ways. First, 'credit money' had come to be vitally important in facilitating the circular flow of income and expenditure. Secondly, the degree of contractual commitment and interdependence which had come to exist in an economy, which could no longer be characterized by a system of markets, meant that the system responded asymmetrically to expansionary and contractionary shocks. A monetary shock of a deflationary nature could result not simply in a disequilibrium process to re-establish a new flow equilibrium at a new set of prices but a temporary collapse of structure itself. Equilibrium of flows in this revised structure – 'underemployment equilibrium' – was perfectly possible in the absence of an income-expenditure 'stabilizer'. The structural breakdown described by Keynes was not analyzable using 'comparative statics', since the two equilibria in question related to different structures. Keynes solved this problem by suggesting a stabilizing structural change, i.e., the introduction of a government with a stabilization policy, which would then make the underemployment equilibrium a point of disequilibrium in the new scheme of things, and permit equilibrium analysis to be used. With this social innovation, the equilibrium method could then be used to discuss the equilibrating policy responses to macroeconomic shocks.

That Keynes was referring to disequilibrium only after structural fragmentation had been avoided by a structural development is not a point which is made particularly explicit in the Keynesian exegesis literature.[26] In particular, the new 'disequilibrium approach' seems to be founded on an association of market disequilibrium with a very special case of structural fragmentation; i.e., temporary market failure. Not surprisingly, neoclassical economists have made short work of such a contention with the introduction of an expectational dimension to markets. While, at the same time, those wedded to structural change, more even than Keynes, reject the disequilibrium approach on the opposite grounds. Whether or not Keynes was correct in his continued use of the equilibrium method in one structure in preference to another is not something that can easily be evaluated. In an evolutionary context, adherence to any fixed economic structure will ultimately become an obsolete position yet may yield great benefits for a long time. It is these very benefits which permit the evolution which leads to obsolescence.

The motional flows which interested the Classical economists were flows of quantities, regulated by price fluctuations and accompanied by a faith that the latter would ensure flow equilibrium in economic (Walrasian) structure. The behaviour of economic agents in such a model consists of sets of optimization rules which render microeconomics and macroeconomics indistinguishable. The spatial dimension of motional behaviour is removed by assumptions concerning the qualitative homogeneity of different individuals, firms, etc., and the temporal dimension by assumptions of perfect knowledge, full adjustment, and so on. Keynes, on the other hand, introduced the motional behaviour of economic agents directly into his model. The consumption and production aspects of economic agents' behaviour were given explicit dimension over time in expenditure and income. Determination of output flows is not the outcome of some esoteric price interaction but is ground out of the historical dynamics of income and expenditure interactions. The multiplier is a thoroughly dynamic equilibrator. In a spatial sense, Keynes also extended the motional picture of behaviour. Consumers, investors and money holders, even though an economic agent could be all three at once, were separated by Keynes as key interactors in analyzing behaviour from a macroeconomic perspective. Individuals were not so much independent entities whose behaviour could be aggregated to the macro level. Rather, individuals were divided into distinctive macro-consciousnesses. Keynes had prised apart the old division between individualism and class collectivism by presenting individuals who were members of several relevant groups at once.

The picture that Keynes presents in his model is extremely well tailored to investigating the short-run behaviour of an interdependent system in historical time. 'Equilibrium' is not something which is left to the 'magic' of the market, but involves certain motional decisions by government over time. *Ex ante* forward-planning decisions by firms and consumers are reconciled by government from its vantage point over the whole system. With nervousness concerning structural failure removed, aspirations and activity could be brought together in contractual union. Equilibrium is thus translated into the historical context of observable behaviour over time. Disequilibrium relates, not to whether everything which has been produced is sold, but rather whether or not income is sufficient to ensure that the aspirations of consumers and producers coincide. The latter is not the same as the former because the latter also relates to making plans in the security that they will be realized.

This forward-looking dimension of Keynes's conception of macro-equilibrium has not been done justice to in orthodox Keynesianism, as Shackle has emphasized, essentially because it is qualitative. The 'animal spirits' which dictate fluctuations in investment expenditure in turn affect income. This precipitates appropriate stabilization action which can be viewed as the enactment of a particular forward-looking commitment by the authorities at the core of macro-consciousness. The disappearance of Keynes's forward-looking perspective in the Keynesian orthodoxy can be attributed to a lack of identification of Keynes's stock-flow dichotomy with the core-peripheral or evolutionary perspective discussed here. Relativistic tension between core and periphery does not appear explicitly in Keynesian stock-flow analysis.

What Keynes emphasized was structural stabilization rather than structural development on the evolutionary path of the macro-system. Keynes had an idealistic notion of how government, at the core of macro-consciousness, would carry out its stabilization responsibilities. He did not address the problem that, in the course of development, stabilization policy would become a vehicle for social restructuring developments and provide a permissive regime for inflation. Keynes was much more concerned with the prospect that, in the long run, falling rates of profitability would stultify investment, forcing the state to intervene increasingly. In all this Keynes remained speculative, for such long-run projections were beyond the compass of his model and of any reasonable logic in an unknown evolutionary future. What was important was that Keynes had managed to influence that future by providing macro-consciousness with a suitable logic which would ensure the active pursuit of stabilizing intervention for the first time in history outside of national emergency conditions.

BEYOND THE GENERAL THEORY

We have seen how Keynes offered theoretical backing to a policy innovation which became part of a new interventionist mythology. With an implicit contract to stabilize the economy in place, the Anglo-American economies entered a period of unparalleled economic progress. Businessmen could expand with the confidence that recessions would be weak and short-lived while a rich flow of government contracts in education, housing, health, defence and infrastructure ensured that many large firms did not have to look far for their profit. It would be fair to say that the benefits of the stabilization policy innovation far exceeded Keynes's own expectations.

However, it became apparent very early in the postwar period that the absence of a developmental dimension to Keynesianism would prove to be an increasing problem as the years passed. The UK abandoned industrial policy as a central priority at an early stage in the postwar era and the US never really had one in the first place. This difference between the Anglo-American economies and other countries was to become apparent in the 1960s, not just in comparison to the reconstructed economies such as West Germany, but in comparison to, for example, France, which achieved a higher growth rate than the latter in that decade.

In evolutionary terms, stabilization policy ensured that government became increasingly preoccupied with maintenance at the expense of stimulating creativity in the productive sector. Indicative planning, the provision of incentives to productivity, legislation to deter rent-seeking, particularly in the property sector, were of a low priority. The onset of stagflation and regression to pre-Keynesian ideas concerning theory and policy in the face of inertia is what would be expected in evolutionary terms. A crude but crucial social innovation ran out of steam while those who had benefited from it adopted protective strategies.

The first step in rectifying this situation would be to change the way that we define the structure of the macro-economy. The Keynesian division of aggregate expenditure cannot identify how expenditure flows are divided into creative, production and maintenance categories. All investment is not creative, much of what is recorded as production is the product of rent-seeking activity. If we are, indeed, heading for an evolutionary catastrophe, we do not have the data breakdowns to see it coming. An economy which indulges in overmaintenance at the expense of creativity can convey an illusion of tolerable prosperity as it rolls towards the cliff edge.

Time does not permit much more in the way of speculation as to how progress could be made except to emphasize that the way ahead lies in the direction of policy innovation rather than through theoretical breakthroughs. As was the case with the GT, appropriate economic logic and mythology will be forthcoming once the correct policy is identified. In the area of macroeconomic policy, it seems clear that discretionary intervention has had its day and that the principle of automatic stabilization requires consolidation and development by macroeconomists. Exactly what needs to be done will have to be the subject of another paper.

In conclusion, an attempt has been made to argue that Keynes's macroeconomics is compatible with modern evolutionary approaches which do not rely on deterministic Darwinian theories of continuous struggle. Once we view the process of evolution in the economic domain as one fuelled by creativity, which is translated by co-operation into economic development, then Keynes's macroeconomics and interventionist strategy becomes very evolutionary in nature. The problem with Keynes's analysis is that it remains short-run in evolutionary terms, even though there were good reasons for such a perspective at the time the GT was written.

This short-run emphasis in the GT was the factor that led Schumpeter (1974) to dismiss the GT as unimportant. Similarly, Samuelson could see little contribution to the advance of economic theory in the GT although he sympathized with Keynes's policy prescription.[27] Attempts to develop Keynes's model into the long run by Harrod further undermined the GT for it was empirically implausible that 'knife edge' instability should exist. Harrod's mistake was not to see that it was *entirely inappropriate* to extend Keynes's model into the long-run without extending the depiction of consciousness contained in the *GT*.

Keynes offered fragments of insight into how consciousness as to the future of structure influenced the short-run development of structure and how the communality of macro-consciousness induced inertial qualities in the evolutionary process. The rational expectations point was well understood by Keynes and, indeed, it is now well recognized by Robert Lucas that rational expectations implies an evolutionary perspective, although the one favoured would be in the spirit of Alchian (1950).[28]

The most prominent developer of Keynes's vision of consciousness has been George Shackle. The interplay of visions of the future and action in the present, conditioned by commitments from the past in a world of historical rather than abstract time has been recognized explicitly. It is upon post-Keynesian contributions such as his that we must build in order to extend the GT into an evolutionary approach to macroeconomics. Perhaps then the 'generalization of the GT' which Joan Robinson wished to see will, at last, occur.

NOTES

1. See Sawyer (1982) who lists four reasons why the Kaleckian approach is better suited to analyzing the dynamics of the macro-economy than the Keynesian approach.
2. See Kaldor (1955) for the seminal contribution.
3. Taylor (1983) provides a good example in the context of economic development.
4. See the Introduction in Robinson (1978) and also Robinson (1980), essays nos 6 and 18.
5. See Robinson (1980) pp. 78–80.
6. It was Barro (1979) who, in his conversion from Keynesianism to new Classical macroeconomics, spelt this out most clearly.
7. See, for example, Stein's (1982) attempt to place competing schools of thought within a monetarist framework. The post-Keynesian school doesn't even get a mention, never mind special case status!
8. See Hollis and Nell (1975).

9. Taylor (1983) admits that the Kaleckian dynamics which he utilizes tend to have very history-specific and location-specific characteristics.
10. 'Is the fulfillment of these ideas a visionary hope? Have they insufficient roots in the motions which govern the evolution of political society? Are the interests which they will thwart stronger and more obvious than those which they will serve?' (Keynes, 1936, p. 383).
11. For example, compare Azariadis and Stiglitz (1983) with Eichner (1979).
12. 'The mecca of economics lies in economic biology rather than economic dynamics.' (Marshall, 1959, p. xii).
13. 'Keynes hardly ever peered over the edge of the short period to see the effect of investment'. . . . He used to say: The long period is a subject for undergraduates. He dealt only with forward-looking expectations of profits which would never be exactly fulfilled. All the same, he hankered after the concepts of a normal rate of profit and value of capital though he could not get them clear.' (Robinson, 1980, p. 80).
14. See Dow and Dow (1985) for emphasis of the central importance of animal spirits in the GT.
15. See Shackle (1974) for the fullest exposition of his view of the 'Kaleidic' method in the GT and how it could be developed.
16. See Hodgson (1985).
17. 'Keynes seems to have assumed that the supply-side was easily understood (How wrong he was!)' (Chick, 1983, p. 82).
18. It was not until Davidson and Smolensky (1964) that there was any clear way of looking at the GT from an aggregate demand / supply perspective. See Tarshis (1989a) for the view that the aggregate demand / supply framework can only be meaningfully applied to the macroeconomics of Keynes if explicit account is taken of his view as to the degree of employer–worker co-operation in the economic system.
19. Joan Robinson (1980) also preferred to call it a 'utilisation function' rather than a 'supply-curve' (p. 79).
20. See Chick's (1983) quote (p. 132) of Harrod's warning to Keynes on this matter.
21. Joan Robinson (1980) also felt that the precise structure of the productive sector which Keynes appended to his model was of no great importance. 'Keynes inherited from Marshall the notion of rising short-period marginal costs but this is inessential: the modern treatment of the subject would have suited him better' (p. 79).
22. A particularly useful review of evolutionary approaches is offered by Clark and Juma (1987). See also Hodgson (1989) and Kay (1989) for penetrating appraisals of how these 'institutionalist' approaches link with the post-Keynesian tradition.
23. For a fuller exposition of the ideas set out briefly below see Foster (1987) chs 6–9.
24. See Coombs *et al.* (1987) and Metcalfe (1987) for reviews of the analysis of technological innovation from evolutionary and non-

evolutionary perspectives.

25. This view of the 'collectiveness' of consciousness was pioneered in the GT: in the method of categorizing aggregate expenditure, in the depiction of interdependent behaviour amongst speculators and in explanations of wage rigidity. Although developed by, for example, Duesenberry (1949) in the area of consumption expenditure, the common consciousness hypothesis had all but disappeared from Keynesianism by the end of the 1950s. Tarshis (1989a) also argues that Keynes's view of common consciousness has faded away since the 1930s. He is particularly interested in Keynes's view of the co-operative economy and its implications for how we analyze the interaction of aggregate demand and supply.

26. Neither Chick (1983) nor Samuels (1986), in his appraisal of what aspects of Keynes's theories continue to merit our attention, draw out this evolutionary dimension of the GT.

27. 'It is remarkable that so active a brain would have failed to make any contribution to economic theory . . .' Samuelson (1946), quoted in Moggridge (1976, p. 156).

28. See Alchian (1950).

7. Endogenous Money Creation and Idle Balances[1]

Alexander C. Dow and Sheila C. Dow

INTRODUCTION

A key feature of post-Keynesian monetary theory is the endogeneity of money supply determination, and the analysis of this process in terms of credit creation.[2] The capacity of the financial system to expand credit in line with demand, and the inability, for various reasons, of the monetary authorities to limit that expansion in any direct way, have profound implications for our understanding of the process of income generation and distribution and for monetary policy prescription. These implications have been well-rehearsed and are not our concern here.[3]

The focus of this paper will be on the implications of credit endogeneity for liquidity preference theory and vice versa. Implicitly or explicitly, adoption of an endogenous credit analysis is often taken to preclude the significance of liquidity preference.[4] Rousseas (1985, 1986), while allowing liquidity preference some significance, nevertheless tries to steer attention away from liquidity preference to velocity. For Kaldor (1982a, 1983), Keynes's use of the liquidity preference function was a tactical mistake, in that it paved the way for its incorporation in the neoclassical synthesis as a stable demand for money function, with the interest rate as one of the arguments. Indeed it is sometimes implied that liquidity preference theory is unacceptable to post-Keynesians on that account (see Minsky, 1982, p. 93). The demand for credit is offered as an alternative to liquidity preference theory which avoids identification with neoclassical economics (see, for example, Rousseas, 1986, p. 100). In the meantime, orthodox monetary theory has moved progressively away from the preoccupation with some sort of liquidity preference theory which arose from the publication of Keynes's *General Theory*.

This apparent rejection by post-Keynesians of liquidity preference theory is understandable if 'liquidity preference' refers to the demand for non-interest bearing money only. Then liquidity preference determines the rate of interest on interest-bearing money and other close substitutes for non-interest bearing money. This narrow notion of liquidity preference is not of much interest, since money as a store of value falls outside its scope. In addition, if it is observed that the monetary authorities can, and normally do, set short-term rates in any case, the liquidity preference theory of interest becomes irrelevant.

Keynes in the *General Theory* (Keynes, 1936, p. 167) did equate money and liquidity with non-payment of interest. Nevertheless, liquidity preference explicitly encompassed demand for inactive as well as active balances (Keynes, 1973, p. 223). Therefore, translating Keynes's liquidity preference concept into an institutional context where money (in M_3 and broader definitions of the money stock) includes interest-bearing deposits, we arrive at a theory of choice between those assets and other less liquid assets. Indeed this is simply a translation of the Keynes of the simplified world of the *General Theory* back to the Keynes of the *Treatise on Money*, where he explicitly discusses the speculative demand for money as a demand for (interest-bearing) savings deposits (Keynes, 1971a, pp. 32, 223–30).

Liquidity preference, then, in practice determines the difference between the interest rate on liquid deposits and on less liquid substitutes. The monetary authorities set the rate at the short-term end of the spectrum; liquidity preference (along with other considerations) determines the mark-up to long-term rates (see Rousseas, 1986, ch. 3, for a mark-up theory of interest). Indeed the liquidity preference concept can be expressed in its broadest form as a preference for a liquid asset over any illiquid assets, be they bonds, shares, commercial or industrial loans, or capital goods. Liquidity preference in this broad sense is regarded by many as being of fundamental importance to Keynes's writing, or as its 'soul', as Shackle (1973, p. 27) puts it. Further,

If we sought to condense Keynes's whole thesis concerning employment into a single sentence, we might say that he ascribes the possibility of involuntary general unemployment to the existence of a liquid asset in a world of uncertainty. (Shackle, 1973, p. 28)

Indeed Keynes himself was quite explicit on this point:

The investment market can become congested through a shortage of cash. It can never become congested through a shortage of saving. This is the most fundamental of my conclusions within the field. (Keynes, 1937, p. 669)

Further, while the Keynes of the *General Theory* assumed also that the money supply was given, it is clear from the *Treatise on Money* (Keynes, 1971b, e.g., p. 189) that Keynes was well aware of the scope for endogenous credit growth. It can be argued that Keynes's stance in 1936 was a tactical one (see Harcourt, 1986, p. 19) or was a reasonable simplification of contemporary reality (see Chick, 1987). In any case, as we shall see, Keynes's exogenous money assumption simplifies, without altering the result of, a more holistic analysis of finance. But, since it is scarcely likely that Keynes would make his most fundamental conclusion dependent on either a strategic or an empirical simplification (see Kriesler, 1987), he must have had in mind the possibility of a shortage of cash as a result of increased liquidity preference, a greater desire to hold idle balances.

The paper will proceed by considering the issue in terms of whether, and in what ways, a change in liquidity preference may influence the level of output and employment when the supply of credit is endogenous. The term endogenous is used in the sense of being determined, at least partly, by the private sector. It will be argued that the supply of credit and liquidity preference are interdependent, in such a way that the supply of credit is by no means fully accommodating.[5] After enumerating the avenues of influence of liquidity preference, therefore, an analysis of a monetary production economy will be outlined briefly to demonstrate how the theories of endogenous credit creation and liquidity preference can be incorporated holistically, rather than in the manner of alternatives. To organize thought in terms of mutually exclusive categories, or duals, is the unfortunate but common result of the influence of dualistic orthodox methodology. The distinctiveness of liquidity preference theory can be understood in terms of different organizing principles, which allow for grey areas and different categorizations for different problems (see Dow, 1987).

Interdependence of demand and supply is central to so much else of post-Keynesian theory that it is a natural development for post-Keynesian monetary theory also. While it has been understandable, in the face of monetarist beliefs, to focus on the process underlying credit, and thus deposit, creation as being endogenous, it is important also to reassert the significance of liquidity preference as part of the same process.[6]

Discussing the significance of liquidity preference in terms of the older concept of idle balances helps to focus the issue.[7] As Keynes used it, the concept referred to an *ex ante* desire to hold a stock of wealth in more liquid form, as a result either of lack of confidence in predictions, or of an expectation firmly held of a fall in the price of less liquid assets. The wish to hold assets 'idle' was a wish to avoid the commitment of wealth to finance the purchase of illiquid assets, i.e., productive, employment-generating expenditure. If there were a wish to hold assets idle, an interest rate rise would be required to discourage that wish; at the same time, however, investment plans would be discouraged.[8]

But if all demand for credit can be met at a going interest rate, how can idle balances possibly matter? Demand for idle balances can be satisfied, and potential investors can turn to the banks for as much finance as is required at the going rate of interest. If this is the case, it would appear that the only significance of the financial sector is that the monetary authorities have the power to set the interest rate, which in turn is the benchmark for assessing the profitability of planned investment projects.

We turn now to consider in a partial analysis six of the ways in which an exogenous increased demand for idle balances, or increase in liquidity preference, can nevertheless affect expenditure plans and outcomes, even when the monetary authorities stand ready to provide banks with all their reserve needs at a particular interest rate. The purpose of such a partial analysis is to highlight the several forms which liquidity preference may take. These six strands will be brought together in the following section.

AVENUES OF INFLUENCE FOR IDLE BALANCES

Consumers' liquidity preference

One avenue of influence involving liquidity preference operates through firms' profitability and thereby retained earnings: the lower are retained earnings relative to investment plans and need for working capital, the greater the demand for credit to provide an alternative source of finance. Actual and expected retained earnings can be influenced by the liquidity preference of wealth-holders through the effect on consumption plans of changing expectations as to the value of wealth (including human capital). A rise in liquidity preference generally reflects an expected fall in the value of wealth or an increasing lack of confidence in expectations. Either eventuality would, according to Keynes's theory of the consumption function (Keynes, 1936, pp. 92–4), lead to a fall in consumption and thus a fall in retained earnings; this result is likely to be particularly strong in the case of consumer durables. The direct consequence for firms of a rise in liquidity preference which discouraged consumption, then, would be an unplanned increase in stocks and thus a rise in the demand for credit to finance working capital.

This outcome would be offset to some extent by reduced demand for consumer credit. Furthermore, a sufficiently sustained weakening in consumer demand would also reduce the marginal efficiency of investment, ultimately reducing the demand for credit to finance new investment projects. As output fell in line with consumer demand requirements for working capital would be reduced and bank loans for this purpose repaid (other things, like firms' liquidity preference, remaining unchanged).

Firms' liquidity preference

In considering firms' expectations, at one remove from wealth-holders' expectations, it becomes relevant to think in terms of firms' own liquidity preference, referring to expectations as to the value of firms' assets. Even if consumption plans were not to change, an increase in the liquidity preference of firms could result from mistakenly pessimistic expectations of consumption plans or a loss of confidence in expectations. At one end of the spectrum, an increase in firms' liquidity preference takes the form of a desire to hold their financial portfolios in more liquid form. At the other end, it takes the much more significant form, for production and employment, of an unwillingness to buy new, illiquid capital goods. Again, the effect would be a reduced demand for credit, no matter how elastic its supply.

Firms' asset choice is not limited to that between liquid assets and new capital goods, but extends also to existing (financial and physical) capital. Thus, the possibility of capital gain from the takeover of undervalued equity in other firms can be a particular focus of firms' liquidity preference. Firms with sufficient market power to avoid their own liquidity problems will thus have a demand for idle balances to finance takeovers, the more other firms face liquidity and confidence problems which drive down their share prices. A shortage of liquidity among some firms, therefore, can generate an increased demand for liquidity among others, to finance takeovers.

Financial structure

A change in liquidity preference among wealth-holders has a direct effect also on firms' financial structure. Firms face a lesser willingness on the part of wealth-holders to hold or acquire equity, in particular, but also debt (other than bank credit). If bank credit is perfectly elastic at an interest rate determined by the monetary authorities, then firms can obtain finance in the form of bank credit as the terms of other forms of debt and of equity borrowing deteriorate. The argument put forward by Modigliani and Miller (1958) that firms' capital structure has no influence on investment plans requires among other things a static, certain (if not risk-free) equilibrium environment.[9] The post-Keynesian argument that such an environment precludes features which are fundamental to the operation of monetary production economies is too well-rehearsed to require restatement here.[10] But it is worthwhile to spell out the corollary, that a change in financial structure is likely to affect investment plans.[11] Further, given the final point made in the previous section about takeovers, a change in financial structure which encourages a change in industrial structure will itself have profound effects on the organization and level of production.

Focusing here solely on the increased reliance on bank finance which results from an increase in liquidity preference, it can be seen that the liquidity of firms' financial structure diminishes; bank credit is shorter term than equity or debt and is subject to interest rate changes beyond the borrower's control. The shorter term of bank credit might be of no significance if banks always accommodate demand (although see the following two sections). But Minsky (1982, pp. 90–116) has demonstrated the significance of exogenously determined interest payments relative to a given cash-flow. If interest payments rise significantly relative to cash-flow as a result of a change in monetary policy, firms are forced to increase their borrowing to cover the interest payments or, if they have the market power, to increase their product price mark-up to increase retained earnings. Neither avenue can leave investment plans completely untouched. It will be important, therefore, in the more general analysis below to consider how far an increase in liquidity preference can be expected to be associated with efforts by the monetary authorities to raise interest rates.

Banks, risk assessment of firms

Implicit in the notion of the interest rate maintained by the monetary authorities is the existence of a structure of rates, with different rates reflecting different risk premia. But if risk assessment is not objective, then actual interest charges are determined by the necessarily subjective assessment of risk by bank managers; such assessment is influenced by the same forces of uncertainty as liquidity preference. Further, while a high assessment of risk theoretically generates a credit offer with a correspondingly high risk premium, in practice credit may simply be refused.[12]

The corporate finance literature primarily presumes an objective basis for risk assessment, thereby allowing the significance of differential and, more important, uncertain and changing risk to be diminished. It becomes straightforward to subsume different classes into one, with correctly estimated risk premia bearing the full burden of default risk. It is then legitimate to refer to 'the' interest rate on bank credit. But an objective basis for risk assessment is rarely available for this to be the case in practice. In particular, changing macroeconomic conditions will alter bankers' perceptions of risk, and their confidence in these perceptions. To the extent, then, that risk assessment is subject to systematic variation, there is likely to be systematic adjustment of risk premia (regardless of monetary policy), and thus to the mark-up on the rate set by the monetary authorities. There would also be systematic rationing of credit as potential borrowers become marginal, as assessed risk systematically increased.

Financial institutions' liquidity preference

Just like non-bank wealth-holders, banks too are subject to liquidity preference in structuring their portfolios (see Radcliffe, 1959, pp. 133–4 on the liquidity of financial institutions). Thus, quite apart from the question of how the riskiness of particular projects is assessed, banks will vary their propensity to make advances of a given expected riskiness depending on expectations as to the value of alternative assets and the degree of confidence held in those expectations. Thus banks may be unwilling to undertake new, fixed interest medium-term commitments with corporations if they anticipate a rise in market interest rates and/or the emergence of high capital gains on investments. This will be the case particularly when banks have found their earlier risk assessment of advances to have been overoptimistic: repeated experience of defaults is bound to encourage a move towards more liquid portfolios,[13] in addition to an increased mark-up to loan rates. Indeed, Strange (1986) chronicles the progressively shortening term of international bank lending, reflecting a preference for greater liquidity among financial institutions (regardless of borrowers' preferences) in the face of increasing uncertainty arising from the institutional arrangements which have evolved in international finance over the last two decades.

International sources of credit and liquidity

When considering banks seeking more liquid assets, it becomes particularly limiting to consider only domestic assets. Similarly, firms and wealth-holders can choose to switch into foreign assets, or seek credit from foreign financial institutions. Foreign currency deposits with domestic or foreign financial institutions can offer liquidity which is more or less than domestic currency deposits, depending on the state of the local currency. For major currencies, which trade in active markets, and in which a high proportion of trade in goods and assets takes place, other currencies may be less liquid than the local currency; a preference for other currencies would arise more from an expectation of exchange loss than an increase in liquidity preference as such. The US dollar is the clearest example. Even here, however, if a rise in liquidity preference takes the form of a preference for foreign over domestic assets, it will itself cause expectations of exchange depreciation which will then generate further capital outflows. But for other currencies, and particularly for financial institutions for whom foreign exchange transactions are a relatively simple matter, capital outflows are even more likely as a direct consequence of increased liquidity preference; i.e., in an international context, foreign currencies can become more 'money-like' than domestic currencies. The case is most extreme where the local currency is tied to one of the major currencies, so that that foreign currency is always the first refuge of liquidity preference; such a situation is typical of many developing countries.

The consequences for domestic activity of increased liquidity preference, taking the form of an increased demand for foreign exchange deposits, depends partly on the exchange rate regime. If the monetary authorities are supporting a fixed exchange rate, then capital outflows will be matched (if they are sufficiently large to bring the exchange rate close to one of the intervention margins) by injections of new money by the monetary authorities. But these must be of minor importance for the supply of credit if banks in any case can always acquire additional reserves from the monetary authority. If the exchange rate is allowed to float, however, much depends on whether the exchange depreciation following a rise in liquidity preference is expected to continue or be reversed quickly. If the former, capital outflows will continue in order to avoid exchange loss, and the exchange rate depreciation will indeed continue. This could eventually have a beneficial effect on firms' estimation of MEI, leading to an increased demand for credit to finance new projects. This benefit only accrues, however, if export and import demands are sufficiently price elastic and if trade is denominated in domestic currency. For natural-resource-dependent developing countries, whose exports and imports are denominated predominently in foreign currency, the exchange depreciation will, if anything, discourage investment plans.

As we turn now to consider foreign exchange as an alternative source of credit, it is worthwhile to continue to focus on the situation of natural-resource-dependent developing countries, since their situation illustrates most clearly the limits to credit availability.[14] Potentially, the more open an economy, the greater the scope for credit availability (if indeed there are domestic limitations, as we have suggested here). Let us consider the Eurodollar market as a potential source of accommodation of credit demand.[15] Broadly speaking, in the mid-1970s there was an excess of liquidity in the Eurodollar market which was made available to developing countries in the absence of pressing demand from developed countries. Indeed, the banks to some extent created the demand for credit among developing countries (see Darity, 1986). Only towards the end of the 1970s, when it became apparent that the country risk assessment conducted by individual banks failed to take account of the macro implications of lending on such a scale, did bank willingness to lend to developing countries diminish; the resulting debt crisis ensured that subsequent new lending to developing countries was almost exclusively devoted to protecting earlier loans. It cannot reasonably be argued that, before the mid-1970s, developing countries had only limited credit demand, that the increase in bank credit thereafter was solely demand induced, and that now demand has again contracted or the objective risk situation has changed fundamentally for the worse.[16]

The criteria now used by banks in deciding whether or not to extend credit to developing countries include measures of liquidity held by the potential borrower (see Sargan, 1977). However, the essence of Keynes's concept of idle balances is that it reflects an aspiration rarely fulfilled (see Dow and Dow, 1987). If an increase in liquidity preference within a developing country leads to private sector capital outflows, then foreign exchange reserves are reduced, one of the standard measures of country liquidity, so that an increase in liquidity preference is seen to lead to a reduction in credit availability.

While each of the factors discussed above is sufficient to show that liquidity preference has a bearing on the volume of credit, it is time now to bring them together in order to pick out the systematic relationship between the supply of credit and the demand for liquidity. We turn to this task in the next section.

THE INTERDEPENDENCE OF THE SUPPLY OF CREDIT AND THE DEMAND FOR IDLE BALANCES

Each of the items discussed above is sufficient to demonstrate the interdependence of the volume of credit and the demand for liquidity. Particularly if the liquidity preference of firms and banks is taken into account, together with that of wealth-holders in general, it has been shown here that the supply of credit is not always fully accommodating and, indeed, that it is influenced by liquidity preference.[17] Further, it has been shown that an interest rate set by the monetary authorities is consistent with varying rates on bank loans, depending on the state of liquidity preference. In this section, we draw together the various items to establish a pattern in this interdependence. In particular, it will be shown that, when the supply of credit is generally not fully accommodating, it is the result of the same forces underlying increases in liquidity preference.

Emphasis was placed in the previous section on the significance of the asset price expectations, and thus liquidity preference, of different groups in the economy; wealth-holders in general, firms and financial institutions, residents and non-residents. Considering the expectations of these groups in the context of the business cycle, we can abstract from the problems of differential liquidity preference and consider the broad sweep of the cycle as being characterized by falling liquidity preference in upswings and rising liquidity preference in downswings.

Starting in the middle of a strong upswing, then, it is reasonable to regard all expectations as being optimistic, with respect to the prices of domestic assets. If wealth-holders are optimistic about the future value of this wealth (because of increasing employment and thus income, and asset prices), they will plan to consume more, raising firms' retained earnings and thus liquidity. A strong increase in consumption, as is normal in an upswing, will also encourage animal spirits, raising firms' MEI, and encouraging investment plans (see Dow and Dow, 1985). In addition, in order to raise further the value of their wealth, there will be a greater willingness among wealth-holders to acquire equity and long-term debt thus allowing firms to improve their gearing ratios. If banks too share this optimism they will be more sanguine about default risk and be more willing to lend, at a reduced risk premium, to particular firms. Rousseas (1985, p. 57) notes that for the US over the period 1954–84, the mark-up from borrowing to lending rates was counter-cyclical. This tendency for perceptions of borrowers' and lenders' risk to increase together in a boom period was noted by Keynes (1936, pp. 144–5). Further, the banks' own reduced liquidity preference will encourage a reduced propensity to hold investments against direct lending to firms. Finally, if domestic asset prices are confidently expected to rise relative to foreign assets, there will be an increased net foreign demand for domestic securities which will be stronger the more confidently any resultant exchange rate rise is expected to persist. The upswing is thus characterized by a rising demand for credit to finance new projects, a demand which is accommodated with enthusiasm by the banks and by wealth-holders, domestic and foreign. This process reflects, and is facilitated by, the fall in liquidity preference which results from increasing confidence in high returns on non-money assets. Put another way, credit is expanding in response to demand at the same time as the income velocity of circulation is also rising. (This conclusion counters the conventional one that velocity rises as a consequence of shortage of finance.)

The motivation for the rising demand for credit is monetary accumulation, which is achieved by rising monetary value, whether or not real production has increased. In particular, as the upswing proceeds, the highest returns will be expected from non-reproducible assets – old financial assets, as well as physical assets like real estate. Even if the monetary authorities maintain a fixed interest rate, entrepreneurs will perceive that judicious financial investment offers better returns than productive investment. Banks, and non-bank wealth-holders too, are concerned ultimately with monetary returns, and will create credit for or invest in, respectively, non-productive assets if they yield the highest returns. As Rousseas points out, echoing critics of the Banking School philosophy (see also Dow and Earl, 1982, ch. 17, and Dow, 1986):

As endogenous as the money supply may be, however, it does not mean that accommodation to the 'needs of trade' takes place smoothly or equitably or that it is without cost in terms of distortions in the flow of credit. The problem of controlling the paths it takes by controlling the flow of credit through the economy remains – a problem most post-Keynesian monetary theorists have ignored. (Rousseas, 1985, pp. 59–60)

The consequence of a concentration of credit creation to finance trade in non-reproducible assets is a speculative bubble, with ever-increasing prices of these assets. Even if they have not sought to increase interest rates before this stage, the monetary authorities normally attempt to burst the bubble by raising interest rates. Not only does such an action further discourage productive investment but it also makes highly-geared financial structures very vulnerable to cash-flow problems as Minsky has made clear (see Minsky, 1982, pp. 90–116).

If the exchange rate is floating, the interest rate rise will drive up the exchange rate; if it is fixed, the rise will be counteracted by additional capital inflows. Either way the boom will be encouraged by foreign demand for domestic assets as long as domestic asset prices, in terms of foreign currency, are expected to continue their rise. Any weakening of the boom will dominate other considerations, however, encouraging capital outflows.

As asset prices slow down their rate of increase and the financial structure becomes more fragile; disappointed expectations of continued accumulation will encourage an increase in liquidity preference. Consumers facing a reduction in employment and/or incomes will weaken demand, increasing firms' requirements for bank credit to finance working capital, and reducing firms' MEI estimations. The exception will be firms with market power, for whom retained earnings are a significant alternative source of finance. For them, the response is more likely to be a rise in product prices by raising mark-up, combined with attempts to increase market power by taking over firms more financially vulnerable. Liquidity preference will be rising significantly for this latter category of firm, although their financial structure is becoming less liquid. Banks, facing the prospect of default by borrowers in financial difficulties and capital losses on their own investments, may begin rationing credit, implicitly if not explicitly, by exaggerated risk aversion. This effect will be stronger the more attractive alternatives exist for placement of funds in international markets. Indeed, financial institutions are more likely to turn their attention to foreign currency markets as a source of liquidity as well as higher returns.

The overall picture, then, is of credit creation accommodating demand when liquidity preference is low, but not when liquidity preference is high. This phenomenon adds additional force to the production cycle, and indeed determines to a considerable extent the level of output and employment at which the peak occurs. The strength of the speculative bubble further influences the strength of the downturn. This influences the capacity of individual firms to sustain production levels. However, it also influences the degree to which the downturn induces the desire and capacity for take-overs, and thus industrial concentration. The more concentrated is production, the greater the tendency for firms to finance out of increased mark-up rather than new credit, promoting stagflation. There is of course a parallel phenomenon in the financial sector, where liquidity problems faced by those with a high incidence of default will encourage takeovers, and the growing capacity of the financial sector to pass on higher interest costs (see Rousseas, 1986, pp. 50–60).

CONCLUSION

Keynes chose to write the *General Theory* in terms of a given money supply and non-interest-bearing money and concentrated on the capacity of changing liquidity preference to alter the rate of interest, which then affected the level of productive investment. As should now be well known from the *Treatise on Money* and following the publication of Keynes's papers (see Rotheim, 1981), Keynes's understanding of financial markets and the process of a monetary production economy was profound; he intended much more by his theory of liquidity preference than the simple, separable demand for money function which it became in the neoclassical synthesis.

The part of the monetary process picked up by Kaldor and others in their criticisms of the monetarist version of the synthesis was financial innovation and credit creation. Such a counter was required to the translation of Keynes' treatment of the money supply as a given into Friedman's monetary rules. Rather, what Kaldor, in the spirit of Radcliffe, advocated was that interest rates should be maintained at such a level as to induce the full-employment level of expenditure. Then the full burden of causation is placed on expenditure unconstrained by finance.

But, as the brief account above is designed to show, the cycle in MEI and thus investment is not only exacerbated by a cycle in liquidity preference, but can also itself be partly understood in those terms (i.e., a choice between new capital goods and other assets). In other words, an understanding of animal spirits, demand for credit, and supply of credit can all be enhanced by considering the changing propensity to hold idle balances. An account can be given without liquidity preference, but it is the weaker for it; moreover, an assumption of an infinite elasticity of supply of credit at a given interest rate is a simplification which itself requires justification. But it is more important than that; without explicit consideration of liquidity preference (together with an analysis of market power among and between financial institutions and corporations), it is hard to understand the financial developments which so powerfully dominate cyclical activity.

Certainly the capacity to create credit independently of any particular national state has increased since Keynes wrote (see Chick, 1986.) But to accept a perfectly accommodating credit supply assumption in such circumstances is to ignore the monetary aspects of a monetary production economy and thereby, incidentally, to make a complete break with Keynes. Far better, surely, to analyze the forces behind credit creation, and activity in the markets for financial assets, and the relationship between financial markets and production. The choice between endogenous credit creation and liquidity preference is a spurious one. To advocate emphasis on either supply or demand is to fall into the alien, orthodox habit of thinking in terms of mutually-exclusive duals. A complete analysis of a monetary production economy requires attention to both, and an emphasis on their interdependence and its consequences for production and employment.

NOTES

1. We are grateful to Geoff Harcourt and to two anonymous referees for comments.
2. The key figures associated with the development of this feature are Kaldor (1970, 1981, 1982b) and Moore (1981, 1983, 1984). Excellent reviews of the overall literature may be found in Lavoie (1984, 1985a).
3. See Kaldor (1982b) and Jarsulic (ed., 1984), for example.
4. Arestis (1987), for example, does not include liquidity preference in his survey of post-Keynesian monetary theory. There are notable exceptions who make the significance of liquidity preference explicit: Chick (1983), Davidson (1972, 1986), Kregel (1984–5, 1986) and Wells (1983); see also Cottrell (1986), Dow (1986, 1986–7), Dow and Earl (1982), Gedeon (1985) and Lavoie (1985b).
5. Rousseas (1986, ch. 5) points out the likelihood of a less-than-fully-accommodating supply of credit, and its importance for the design and effectiveness of monetary policy, without exploring the reasons for credit limitations.
6. Interdependence of demand and supply is already present in post-Keynesian discussion, notably of the finance motive. See Davidson and Weintraub (1973) and Weintraub (1980). Here we incorporate liquidity preference explicitly into that interdependence. See Dow and Dow (1987) on liquidity preference and the finance motive. This broader interdependence features in Davidson (1972).
7. See Dow and Dow (1987) for a full discussion of the use and interpretation of the idle balances concept in Keynes's time, and its relevance to the analysis of the modern financial system.
8. See Wells (1983) for a statement of liquidity preference in these general terms of asset choice.
9. See Archer and D'Ambrosio (1983, Part *IV*) for a selection from the Modigliani and Miller debate.
10. See Davidson (1978) for the fullest account of post-Keynesian monetary theory; see also Chick (1983), Dow and Earl (1982) and Rousseas (1986).

11. Minsky (1975, 1982) has developed the fullest theory of financial structure within a post-Keynesian framework. The discussion below draws inspiration from his work.

12. It surely cannot be suggested that credit is fully accommodating to the extent that no potential borrower is ever refused credit.

13. An increasing liquidity preference among banks in the current economic climate can explain the increasing reliance on securitization, i.e., making negotiable loans.

14. The issues being raised here are really too complex for a subsection of a paper; see Dow (1986–7) for another partial treatment.

15. The Eurodollar market is a particularly interesting case, given the absence of reserve requirements. If any market can fully accommodate credit demand it would be this one. See Dow (1986).

16. To explain the debt crisis away as a result of managerial error, with the implication that all credit-worthy borrowers will be accommodated in the future, is also unsatisfactory. It is the essence of the monetary process that lenders' (and borrowers') expectations may be confounded.

17. This conclusion is supported by recent empirical work conducted by Eichner (1979, 1986, ch. 7) and Foreman *et al.* (1984). But the evidence of only partial accommodation is put down to the limited influence of the monetary authorities, rather than any endogenous response to changing liquidity preference.

8. Bounded Rationality, Psychology and Financial Evolution: Some Behavioural Perspectives on Post-Keynesian Analysis[1]

Peter E. Earl

INTRODUCTION

For most post-Keynesians, a decision to explore possibilities for making use of ideas from psychological and behavioural economics would represent a new direction in their research. In this chapter I attempt to make a case for taking this kind of direction in the context of post-Keynesian monetary theory. I shall be considering the distinctive implications of behavioural literature on decision-making for the analysis of portfolio choices – where to store one's wealth, whether or not to borrow or lend, whether or not to speculate actively in the pursuit of capital gains – in an increasingly deregulated monetary environment where technological advances are also serving to change opportunity sets.

One reason for economists not typically seeing behavioural theory and post-Keynesian monetary economics as natural bedfellows may be that they do not normally regard these branches of economics as sharing a common core. Central to the behavioural research programme is the notion that decision-makers suffer from bounded rationality: their mental capacities prevent them from seeing problems in all their complexity and working out optimal solutions to them. Central to post-Keynesian monetary theory is the notion of liquidity preference. However, recent work by Boland (1986, pp. 148–54) makes it difficult to maintain that these two core notions are anything other than ripe for integration. He argues that in taking up positions of liquidity – or more generally, of flexibility – decision-makers are choosing to operate inside the boundaries of their capabilities. Saving is not undertaken just to earn interest as part of a long-run consumption optimization plan. Much of it represents an attempt to 'leave a little room for error or for the unexpected' (Boland, 1986, p. 149). Recognizing their own fallibility as decision-makers, wealth-owners hold back from commitment, hoping to avoid pushing their luck too far. In doing so, they reduce the supply of funds to others or curtail demands for goods and services. In the language of behavioural economics, then, we might state the basic message of Keynes as follows: the more (less) that decision-makers worry about the possible consequences of their own bounded rationality and the more (less) they feel the future is full of imponderables, the more (less) they will retreat into positions of liquidity, of flexibility.

It is doubtful that Keynes himself would have had any objections to a marriage of these two research programmes. Recent work by Dow and Dow (1985) has highlighted Keynes's own rejection of the 'pretty, polite' techniques of orthodox decision theory in favour of a psychological approach to portfolio choice, hinted at through his stress on the roles of 'animal spirits' and of rules of thumb as devices by which choosers delude themselves into thinking they know more about the future than they justifiably claim to know. However, post-Keynesian economists hitherto have not generally displayed an inclination to expand upon this theme in Keynes's work to add to the power of their analysis of financial markets. Many may feel that existing post-Keynesian critiques of the conventional wisdom on monetary base control, financial deregulation and so on should be effective in their own right, and that their chances of acceptance could be hindered if mainstream economists are being told they need to embrace psychology and abandon their core optimization assumption as well as to bring their institutional understandings up to date and shake off what Bootle (1984) has aptly characterized as the 'legacy of gold'.

A PSYCHOLOGY-FREE PERSPECTIVE ON RECENT MONETARY DEVELOPMENTS

It is perfectly possible to present without reference to behavioural and psychological economics a powerful case for seeing the money stock as endogenous and for seeing as 'absolute baloney' (Goodhart, 1984, p. 200) the conventional money-multiplier analysis that still dominates textbooks and monetarist thinking. In attempting to make a thoroughly up-to-date case against doctrine that is founded on the commodity money notion, one could argue broadly along the following lines (see also Kaldor, 1982; Moore, 1979, 1983; Rousseas, 1986).

Over the past three decades, financial markets have undergone dramatic changes. Here, deregulation and information technology have played major roles. We live now in a world in which even the lay-person's image of financial markets involves thoughts of rooms of computer screens, telephones and telex machines, with transactions costs reduced so far by the new technology that expectations of tiny percentage changes in relative prices of assets are worth trading against. Computers facilitate these trades not merely by providing instant access to information about relative prices, but also by serving as means for recording deals. (Even at the more mundane level of housing finance computers have opened up scope for more frequent changes in interest rates, owing to their capacity to spew out personalized letters to borrowers). Whole new classes of financial instruments have come into being as transactions costs have fallen, producing remarkable pyramids of assets: for example, traded options on equities, or 'funds of funds' that enable small savers to spread risks associated with using units trusts as substitutes for personal attempts to play the markets.

As transactions costs fall, and institutions are given greater freedom in respect of the markets in which they operate, it becomes ever more questionable to argue in the monetarist vein that aggregate demand for goods and services is constrained by the size of any particular monetary aggregate. A squeeze on the ability of banks to lend, for example, may be followed rapidly by increases in earnings being offered by non-bank financial intermediaries (NBFIs), as they attempt to gather funds to satisfy those whom the banks have turned away. Deposits move from wealth-holders' accounts in banks to the bank accounts of NBFIs and thence to the accounts of sellers of goods and services financed by loans from the NBFIs. Broad money grows, and with it expenditure. Thus, as far as the authorities are concerned, 'success' in imposing a particular 'narrow money' target may be achieved simultaneously with a total failure to engineer a desired slow-down in expenditure growth. Alternatively, rather than the demand for finance being met via NBFIs, direct lending may take place: for example, children may borrow from their parents, or companies may issue debentures and short-term promissory notes instead of increasing their borrowing from banks.

Increases in access to information about financial possibilities and in the ability of wealth-holders or their agents to switch between markets are problematic for economists and for financial institutions alike. Both groups have to contend with a world where the potential for financial fluidity (and often its actuality) is enormous. Such structural breakdowns as have already occurred have played havoc with the orthodox, econometrically orientated monetary economist's need for stable parameters, and they may raise doubts about the worth of building policy recommendations even upon those relationships that have not yet softened. As far as the financial institutions are concerned, the developments may be seen as pointing to the need for innovative policies aimed at producing longer-term ties between themselves and their customers – or they may seek to reorientate their roles to become providers of information services and arrangers of transactions rather than engaging in deposit-taking and loan-making activities.

Clearly, the recent developments that have reduced transactions costs in financial markets and led to the proliferation of niche-filling financial instruments have served to add weight to arguments that post-Keynesians have been making at least since the time of the Radcliffe Report (1959) as more and more liquid substitutes for bank deposits appear, the task of defining 'the money supply' in an operational manner becomes all the more impossible. The important things to worry about are how liquid decision-makers feel, and how willing they are to part with some of their liquidity in exchange for possible interest earnings or physical goods and services.

BOUNDED RATIONALITY, CONFIDENCE AND CREATIVITY

The moment that post-Keynesians start arguing that portfolio compositions are determined by a willingness to part with liquidity, they are using the notion of confidence to drive further wedges between the size of the monetary base, broader monetary aggregates and the pace of expenditure. At that point, a failure to introduce elements from behavioural economics and psychology makes their critique of orthodoxy vulnerable to the kind of objection voiced by Coddington (1983), namely that the whole thing becomes nihilistic if fluctuations in aggregate expenditure are said to be rooted, not in changes in objective economic circumstances, but in 'the spontaneous and erratic workings of individual minds' (Coddington, p. 53).

Consider how a decision-maker may try to form conjectures about her uncertain future environment. It is impossible to know in advance what will happen; at best, one can try to construct a list of states of the world that might eventuate. Oversight could mean that this list includes neither the event that actually happens, nor the possibility that the decision-maker finds herself surprised because an unanticipated event occurs. Those possibilities that *are* imagined may vary in their implications for the chooser but there may be costs associated with seeking to hedge against all of them. Mindful of such costs, the decision-maker may prefer to adapt her portfolio quite closely to those possibilities which seem difficult to dismiss, and leave herself uninsured against those events that seem harder to take seriously as prospects (cf. Heiner, 1983, pp. 576–7). (Some events that are difficult to imagine may, of course, be taken very seriously and insured/hedged against, because they would be ruinous to the chooser if they did actually happen.) The next task, then, is to decide how hard it is to dismiss each imagined possibility.

If the decision-maker thinks things through carefully, she may well follow the logic used by Shackle (1979) and take the view that she has no ground for dismissing a possibility unless she can see something which could block its occurrence. If she can see all manner of things that could get in the way of a particular happening, then she may feel justified in labelling it as 'practically impossible', or 'unbelievable' in prospect. On the other hand, if she can think of nothing which could happen to stop a particular outcome, then she may label it, possibly along with many other rivals against which it is proving equally problematic to argue, as 'perfectly possible'. But here the thoughtful decision-maker may well realize that she has not really solved her problem of deciding what to believe. The event-blocking possibilities themselves can only be taken seriously if nothing seems likely to get in *their* way: in other words, a problem of infinite regress stands in the way of attempts to form the judgements upon which confidence may be based.

The infinite regress problem seems potentially paralyzing for the decision-maker who tries to think carefully about how the future could look. Indeed, the more creative the person's style of thinking, the wider the range of states of the world she may find herself worrying about and the harder she may find it to make even slightly conclusive arguments against anything. Now, of course, there are some occasions in which uncertainty does seem to exert a paralyzing power and people retreat into positions of particularly great liquidity. But most of the time people seem to be able to place boundaries of some kind on what they believe could happen if they attempt to allocate resources or engage in particular forms of social interaction. Though the world could behave in an endlessly kaleidic manner and lurch around wildly if decision-makers formed their beliefs and choices at random rather than avoiding commitment to anything at all, this is not what one usually observes. In practice, something gets in the way of the infinite regress and random choices, and this 'something' needs to be introduced into post-Keynesian analysis in order that unduly nihilistic conclusions are not drawn from attempts to analyze the nature of choice.

The behavioural theorist's answer to the question of how decision-makers sidestep the infinite regress problem centres on the notion of bounded rationality. The decision-maker is constrained in her deliberations by her own cognitive hardware and by the time pressure under which she takes her decisions. Although it might seem that modern computer systems overcome some human information-processing bottlenecks, it it far from obvious that they contribute to a net lessening of the decision-maker's difficulties, particularly in the world of high finance where computers have facilitated all-day trading in financial assets on globally integrated markets. The age of information technology has increased the need for instantaneous decisions and may have replaced one kind of information overload (raw data) with another (larger volumes of processed data). Here it is perhaps worth noting Lester Thurow's claim, in his address to the 1986 meeting of the American Association for the Advancement of Science, that a major reason for the fall in productivity in the United States is the introduction of computerized information systems and *more* layers of top management to cope with their output. One could also note the questions raised about the contribution of 'programmed selling' – where, in effect, portfolio decisions are delegated to computers – to the global stock market crash in October 1987.

The limitations in the decision-maker's ability to dream up and keep vast numbers of conflicting possibilities in mind will ensure that she is blind to many possible events. To avoid getting bogged down in philosophical worries, a decision-maker, like an economic scientist, will use some kind of system – or *methodology*, in the sense of a body of methods rather than the science of methods – for dealing with inconsistent ideas and reacting to recognized anomalies. In other words, she will use a collection of rules that reject some ideas as unbelievable and allow others, out of the limited set she bothers to consider, to seem in some degree credible (see Earl, 1986, ch. 6). A core of basic assumptions about the world will be used to provide some kind of dogmatic starting point for the formation of other images.

A significant implication of decision-makers using *systems* of rules to guide them in the gathering and interpretation of economic information is that it would *not* be appropriate to see them as forming their expectations, and hence their choices, in a spontaneous and erratic manner. This is so even though their images of the world are subjective, personal constructs that may bear little resemblance to 'rational expectations' which neoclassical economists, with access to identical information sets, would choose to construct. Furthermore, it should be recognized that the possibility of decision-makers using 'objective' information in different ways does *not* necessarily mean that market behaviour is going to be impossible to anticipate with tolerable accuracy. What it does mean is that, to form such expectations themselves, post-Keynesian economists will need to start studying the actual belief-forming methodologies used by decision-makers. In doing so, post-Keynesians must get used to thinking of markets as institutions populated by traders whose opinions differ, just as opinions of economists differ, because they are using different rules for making sense of the complex world with which they have to contend.

The idea that economic analysis should be based on a single type of hypothetical 'representative' decision-maker is, of course, an aspect of neoclassical methodology that Keynes himself abandoned. This is clear from his analysis of the determination of asset prices in speculative markets, which emphasized that differences in opinion about possible price movements play a vital role in reducing market instability. But so far his lead has not been followed – even in post-Keynesian economics – to produce anything comparable with the marketing literature's world of multiple lifestyle categories. It is most encouraging to see Boland (1986) recently urging neoclassical economists themselves to study the incidence of different expectation-forming methods.

Obviously, the bounded rationality of post-Keynesian economists will make it impossible for them to take account of all the idiosyncracies in ways of thought that traders bring to bear in financial markets: like market researchers, they will be forced to do sample survey studies and use simplifying stereotypes, segmenting their populations of market participants into groups with approximately similar ways of thinking (for example, 'chartists' and 'fundamentalists') and of gathering information about the 'state of the news'. Inevitably, these segmentations will in some respects be rough and ready; it will be necessary to force-fit some sampled individuals in order to keep the number of segments manageable. But this need to make abstractions should not be a worry so long as it leads to acceptable predictions. Economists should remember that during internal debates in their own profession they habitually perform such pigeonholing operations, confident that they can predict the behaviour of particular kinds of economists who seem at least to share major analytic building blocks and who tend to employ similar routines for dealing with criticism and anomalies. (For example, a neoclassical economist may label me as a post-Keynesian, may use Joan Robinson as a post Keynesian stereotype, and then may quite often – though not always – accurately anticipate how I construe economic phenomena.) All I am suggesting here is that post-Keynesians should start paying attention to the methodologies used by their diversely minded subjects for coping with economic problems, and not just to those used by their peers.

Information gathered on the systems of rules by which participants in financial markets tend to organize their ideas could probably be turned into sets of computer programmes, one programme for each stereotypical financial decision-maker. It might then be possible to run interactive simulations involving these representations of groups with different decision methodologies, with market outcomes being dependent not merely upon the decision rules ascribed to particular participants but also on the size and initial composition of their portfolios. The significance of a succession of particular exogenous shocks could thereby be investigated in addition to whether or not the system behaved explosively or achieved convergence following a single initial shock. It should not be impossible to model which kinds of changes in the 'state of the news' may be likely to turn particular kinds of speculators from 'bulls' into 'bears', or vice versa – that this would be a valuable exercise is clear from the way that the rapidly unfolding events of 'Black Monday' (19 October 1987) and its aftermath were associated with great differences of opinion about how far expectations should be revised downwards in particular markets, with some people switching between markets sooner than others, if at all, and in different directions. (There is an obvious and somewhat ironical sense in which the sort of simulation work I am proposing is something of a laboratory version of the alleged programmed selling phenomenon of 'computers talking to each other around the world' in the Crash of 1987, except that one would be dealing with rather more complex programmes.)

Such a foray into the 'artificial intelligence' arm of the behavioural research programme seems a potentially instructive but demanding kind of investigation that could be necessary if we wished to try to *model* the ups and downs of financial markets in order to overcome tendencies among orthodox economists to see nihilism as the necessary implication of allowing expectations to be subjective constructs. However, if we wish merely to make pronouncements on how seriously one should take, for example, post-Keynesian hypotheses about the general possibility of financial instability, then it may be enough to look for ammunition in the broader literature on the psychology of decision-making or in existing applications of this literature by behavioural economists.

A pair of recent contributions are enough (in terms of my own system of rules for forming judgements) to prevent me from being optimistic about the ability of wealth-holders to avoid making the kinds of decisions that lie at the heart of Minsky's (1975, 1986) analysis of how the volume of lending can explode in waves of euphoria and collapse in a tide of pessimism. Nisbett and Ross (1980) have highlighted the shortcomings of methods that people use for drawing inferences. For example, instead of treating observations that are statistical outliers as precisely that, people tend to give them undue weight because of the vividness of the images to which they give rise: vivid images drive out less vivid ones from the boundedly rational mind. In an excellent paper Kaish (1986) uses cognitive dissonance theory to explain why the behaviour of speculators can seem horribly akin to that of skaters on an ice-covered pond: the more skaters on the ice, the more may would-be skaters be inclined to infer that it is safe to join in, even though one could also infer that the greater number of skaters, the more likely the ice is to crack. Dissonance theory argues that people do not tolerate inconsistent cognitions, and seek to remove inconsistencies with as little bother as possible. In the case of the skating allegory, Kaish (1986, p. 36) notes that, as the ice gets more crowded, someone who is already skating could (1) dismiss warnings about the possible dangers of staying on the ice; (2) keep telling herself how cold it has been recently, and therefore how thick the ice could be; or (3) get off the ice and warn others to do likewise. Unless over-crowding is already causing a problem, option (3) involves the most bother and is therefore the one least likely to be adopted.

Bringing the Nisbett and Ross/Kaish perspectives together, we might note that a warning of a possible disaster may need to be especially vivid if it is to displace feelings of euphoria or complacency in the minds of decision-makers. If the treasurer of a country with a serious balance of payments problem out-lines how a descent to 'banana republic' status could follow from a failure to make major structural changes, the impact upon financial markets may be much more vivid than a speech which just portrayed matters in terms of figures. However, it might still be dismissed by those non-financial firms that would find it very difficult to implement the strategic changes.

PORTFOLIO CHARACTERISTICS AND PORTFOLIO PREFERENCES

Having used the behavioural/psychological literature to ana-lyze the formation of expectations, some post-Keynesians might well want to go no further in the direction of integrating the two research programmes. They might suggest that, given her expectations, a wealth-holder's choice of portfolio could be explained in terms of her initial endowment of assets, the set of options open to her, and her preferences. Post-Keynesians could borrow tools from modern neoclassical economics to show how, on the basis of these four elements, wealth-holders could come to make choices of the kind that have been observed during recent structural changes. The obvious thing to do would be to present portfolio choice in terms of Lancaster's (1966, 1971) characteristics space analysis of demand. It could be shown how, with different kinds of preferences and different perceptions of the position of the efficiency frontier, wealth-holders would construct different portfolios. One could also show how financial innovations could affect choices because of their impact upon the chooser's efficiency frontier.

That such an approach to portfolio choice has not become a standard part even of orthodox treatments of monetary theory is surprising; the packages offered by financial institutions differ not merely in terms of rates of return and riskiness but also in terms of ease of access (number of branches, locations, opening hours, number of autotellers, chequing facilities, electronic funds transfer at point of sale facilities), friendliness of service, charges for cheques, penalty clauses for premature withdrawals, availability of complementary services such as travel or insurance, and so on. So far, though, one is left able mainly to note the recognition of this in the marketing literature, and consequent empirical work (for example, Anderson, Cox and Berenson, 1976). Scope for using the neoclassical 'characteristics space' treatment of demand to describe the allocation of funds between different financial assets (and choices by borrowers amongst rival sources of funds) could be taken as indicating we have no need to delve further into the behavioural literature to explain observed portfolio choices that prove so inconvenient for orthodox modes of thought on monetary policy. I will now attempt to demonstrate that this would be an inappropriate inference to draw.

INFORMATION OVERLOAD AND PORTFOLIO CHOICE

The length of the list of characteristics associated with financial packages and institutions is something that would immediately put the behavioural economist on guard. The task of choosing an N-dimensional portfolio may become overwhelming if N is a large number and one tries to consider all possible trade-offs, weighing up the pros and cons of particular asset mixes along the lines of the Lancaster theory, until one finds the best package. The behaviourally inclined post-Keynesian would expect portfolio choosers to try to reduce their task to a manageable one by a variety of simplifying tactics. These turn out to be not without relevance to policy issues.

First, while trying to think in terms of some kind of overall score for each option examined, the decision-maker may abandon the attempt to find the optimal mix of assets and simply look at a sequence of possible portfolios until she encounters one which she judges to score sufficiently highly. At that point she may stop search and appraisal and make a commitment, unless she employs some kind of subsidiary rule such as 'examine two more packages, just in case . . ., and then choose the best so far discovered'.

Such 'satisficing' appraisals would probably involve the investigation of discrete combinations of assets, rather than marginally different sets in contractual savings deals, for example, one would expect nicely rounded figures – $100 per month in A and $100 a month in B versus $150 a month in C plus $50 per month in D. Widespread use of such rounded numbers in contractual savings arrangements could produce discontinuous movements in aggregate consumption expenditure whenever changes in incomes were seen by savers as enabling themselves to move up to a larger rounded figure for the amount they could afford to squirrel away. For people thinking about getting into debt, rounded numbers could also play a trigger role, which, given the divisibility of loans, one would not expect from the standpoint of conventional theory: for example a person may actively start trying to fix up a loan only when she feels she can afford $X00 per month, with the result that a pay increase triggers a change away fom consuming many low value goods and towards an indivisible loan-financed item she has been looking forward to buying for a long time.

The use of a satisficing scoring system seems widespread in the case of the market for personal loans. Officials of financial institutions do not interview all would-be borrowers in a particular period and then, on the basis of the latter's different risk characteristics, choose the optimal group to whom funds will be provided. Competitive pressures force them to simplify and offer very speedy replies (cf. Winter, 1964). A useful discussion of such procedures is provided, complete with a sample scoring questionnaire, in work on Australian credit unions by Crapp and Skully (1985, pp. 83–5, 193). They note how credit decisions are based on the following factors (p. 83):

- Stability of residence (buying, renting, boarding)
- Stability and position of employment
- Dependents
- Credit rating obtained from a commercial credit reference bureau
- Stability of character
- Security offered
- Ability to repay whilst still maintaining an accustomed life style (often expressed as a debt ratio where all monthly outgoings as a proportion of net weekly pay after tax should not exceed a designated percentage)
- Purpose of loan
- Current assets and current outstanding liabilities.

Several possible answer categories are allowed in each case and points are assigned to them; For example: Where do you live? With relatives? (2 points) In a rented house or flat? (4 points) In your own house or flat? (8 points). Ruthlessly applied, such a scoring system deprives the loan applicant of finance if her total falls below a particular target. It can also produce some decisions that in these times of rising personal bankruptcies, are very worrying. If I have already been granted access to four credit cards, but have so far not used them much, I am, other things being equal, more likely to get a personal loan than someone who only has two credit cards, despite the fact that the latter person is less able to run amok with a credit-card-financed consumption binge and then find the monthly repayments overwhelming. Indeed, an Australian current affairs television programme (*Sixty Minutes*, 17 May 1987) showed how in an actual finance company scoring system emphasis on an unchanged source of income and residence produced the bizarre result that a long-term unemployed person would pass a loan test that a graduate army officer would fail!

Somewhat implicit in the discussion immediately above (as well as in the earlier section on confidence) is a second method of simplification. Decision-makers can reduce the volume of information they need to handle by using particular attributes of a case as proxies for many more. Crapp and Skully (1985, p. 85) stress that established credit ratings may often displace the use of a scoring system in loan appraisals; this can fail to take account of recent or highly conceivable changes in a person's financial position. Worse still, we should note that a bankrupt Australian couple interviewed on the television programme said that they judged that if the banks and finance companies were prepared to let them add successively to their debts, then it was obviously thought likely that they (the couple) would be able to cope with the burden. If decision rules such as these are being employed, then it is a small wonder that households nowadays make up 70 per cent of Australian bankruptcy cases. Whether or not such shortcomings in the judgemental processes of individuals have Minskian system-wide implications may depend on the extent to which finance companies set not merely their interest rates but the size of their reserve positions in the light of cautious estimates of the probability of default and of the probable resale value of repossessed goods. In relation to this, I cannot resist a conjecture that, instead of being a proxy for ability to pay, the finance companies' emphasis on stability of residence may well be a proxy for the ease with which their 'repo man' will be able to catch up with those who fall behind with their payments.

A third method for dealing with information overload in multi-dimensional portfolio choice problems is to use decision heuristics that avoid the need for weighing up the pros and cons of possible bundles of assets and liabilities, and which instead treat the problem of choice one dimension at a time, in a filtering manner. For example, there is what I have elsewhere (Earl, 1986, chs. 7–9) labelled the 'behavioural lexicographic' routine. Here the choice process is akin to a series of hurdles. Wants are ranked in an order of priority with aspirations being set, experimentally, for each want. Plans which fail to meet the minimum expectational standard on the first characteristic test are excluded from further consideration, and the remainder are subjected to the second test, and so on until only one plan remains (or until the end of the list is reached, in which case a contingent tie-break routine is employed to define a choice). Such routines may be responsible for behaviour at odds with the principle of gross substitution, and studies of their frequency of use may therefore shed a good deal of light on debates between post-Keynesians and orthodox monetary theorists about the existence of gaps in the chains of substitution between assets of various kinds (cf. Karacaoglu, 1984). For example, depending on where wealth-holders draw their lines labelling commitments as 'too risky', we may find reinforcement or challenges to our views about scope for engineering reflations by open market operations. If a person is not borrowing because she fears she may lose her job, and if reduced interest rates do nothing to allay these fears, then she may continue to judge it insufficiently safe to commit herself to increased borrowing. On the other hand, post-Keynesians should stand ready to concede that their views on the elasticity of broad monetary aggregates could look less credible were it discovered that borrowers and lenders were reluctant to deal with some NBFIs; for example, some of my part-time money and banking students have been employees of finance companies and have often said how difficult it is to persuade people that finance company debentures are suitably safe channels for their savings. Like the fear of hanging, perceptions of unacceptable scope for monetary loss may concentrate wonderfully the minds of wealth-holders (cf. Blatt, 1979).

ATTITUDES, PRINCIPLES AND SELF-CONTROL

Lexicographic kinds of choices need not arise simply as results of attempts by portfolio choosers to make multi-dimensional problems more manageable. It may be the case that decision-makers are simply building their lives around particular broad principles which they rank hierarchically. Economists seem to be coming to recognize this even more slowly than Barclays Bank recognized that it might pay to distance themselves from the apartheid regime in South Africa. Prior to their disinvestment, Barclays had, according to the *Guardian Weekly* (30 November 1986), lost a number of bank accounts from Labour councils and some charitable business. But the most serious damage that the South African connection has done to the bank has been the relatively small number of young graduates and undergraduates who have opened accounts at Barclays. Rather more alert to the implications of wealth-holders with consciences have been the growing body of entrepreneurs who have set up ethical investment funds, achieving competitive returns despite their policies which avoid putting money into companies involved in the production of weapons, tobacco, alcohol, toxic wastes, environmental destruction and so on.

The role of principles in portfolio choice is just one aspect of a much bigger topic: how people's attitudes, hang-ups and views of their own strengths and weaknesses affect the kinds of consumption and savings behaviour in which they engage. Changes in the use of consumer credit may reflect shifts in long term attitudes, as well as innovations in the supply of credit instruments. For many people in the past, the idea that they might borrow probably carried implications which raised excessive feelings of guilt – confusion over self-identity (for example, 'I thought I wasn't the sort of person who ... ') – that could be quelled by acting out a role consistent with their self-expectations (that 'I'm a patient, prudent sort of person'). Such a psychological perspective suggests that attitudes, rather than interest rates, could have been a decisive barrier to increases in the rate of expenditure. Now attitudes are different. As *The Economist* (6 April 1985) put it, 'The big spenders of today were born in the baby boom that followed the second world war. They are not constrained by the cautious attitude to credit that their parents carried with them from the 1930s, epitomised by the Lancashire housewife who did not use the washing machine until the last instalment had been paid'. On the side of market innovations we can note Maital's (1982, pp. 138–9; 143–5) psychological analysis of how credit cards have enabled people to buy things on credit without having to display themselves to onlookers (or themselves) as the sort of people who have to borrow, and without having to go through the anxieties of facing up to mysterious and, until recently, stern-faced bank managers. At the time of purchase, it is unclear whether the credit card is going to be used as such or merely as a debit card, with payment to be made in full when the next statement arrives. Cognitive dissonance may allow the shopper to convince herself at the time of purchase that she is doing the latter, while the sales campaigns of the credit card organizations encourage their customers to think of their credit cards as smoothing devices, not as somewhat pricey substitutes for personal loans. 'Access, your flexible friend' is a slogan that presents the card as a substitute for a precautionary demand for money, but the fact that Access statements do not distinguish between contingently necessary purchases and longer-term borrowings enables users to shunt to the back of their minds unease they feel about the latter types of items.

The integration of psychological perspectives and institutional material allows further question marks to be raised about whether financial deregulation is to be encouraged or whether there is a growing need for watchdog agencies. Once we recognize the limited capacities of consumers to formulate and solve long-run household management problems, and once we note the possible malleability of consumer perceptions in the face of images from advertisements, credit cards can seem potentially dangerous pieces of plastic, that distract weak-willed and myopic individuals from the task of providing for future expenditure needs. The extent to which consumers need to be protected from themselves is something which post-Keynesians cannot pronounce upon in this context until there has been some assessment of how far consumers recognize their own fallibility as financial managers and accordingly set themselves constraints in the form of contractual savings schemes (cf. Thaler and Shefrin, 1981). Certainly, the existence of such devices as Christmas Club accounts – that pay lower rates of interest than some easy-access accounts but lock funds away from temptation – implies that banks and some of their customers both recognize the problem of a lack of self-control.

SATISFICING AND SPECULATION

The increase in speculative activity observed in recent years has certainly been aided by financial deregulation and technological changes which opened up options previously non-existent or which could only be taken advantage of if one were a very large trader and thereby able to economize on transactions costs. However, behavioural and psychological economics suggests a possible cognitive reason for changing propensities to speculate. Once again, our starting point is the fact that although uncertainty makes an optimal allocation impossible to identify, portfolio managers may at least be able to say that they judge particular portfolios to be sufficiently likely to produce outcomes that they regard as satisfactory. (Note the double-edged nature of satisficing as it is here portrayed: tolerance extends both to likelihood and to desired performance; see further, Earl, 1986, ch. 8.) Changes in their behaviour may arise not necessarily as a result of changes in their menus of possibilities but, rather, as a result of their encountering problems in using their hitherto-favoured strategies for meeting their aspirations. These problems may arise either because attainments are falling or because things have happened which they see as implying a need to raise their aspirations.

Consider the following recent observation by Carew (1985, p. 135) concerning changes that have taken place in the nature of portfolio management over the past thirty years:

Gone are the days when portfolio management meant buying parcels of securities from time to time and sitting on them till they mature. No-one can afford such a passive approach; the objective now is to buy to trade, taking a view on the direction of interest rates, maximising opportunities to arbitrage between different markets (locally and overseas), between different securities and different maturities, buying in and selling out when rates and timing look right.

Carew's comments were made with respect to the financial markets of Australia, but I have no doubt that they would be applicable to other nations with well-developed financial markets. Post-Keynesians may find them rather puzzling, given that fifty years ago Keynes was arguing that the professional speculator is *forced* to concern himself with the anticipation of impending changes, in the news or in the atmosphere, of the kind by which experience shows the mass psychology of the market is most influenced (1936, p. 155, italics added). Carew's comments give the impression that it is only recently that something has happened to warrant the stereotyping of financial market participants in Keynes's terms. By implication, she is suggesting that thirty years ago one did not have to adopt the role of an active speculator. (It might also be tempting to argue that speculation on price movements was not even possible until recently in the Australian case, as before 1983–5 the money markets were heavily regulated. This seems a doubtful rationalization given that there was ample scope for speculation with equities.) The following satisficing perspective, coupled with the recognition that there existed a ready supply of assets (for example, five year local government bonds) with maturity dates that came within the planning horizons of portfolio managers, makes the passive 1950s situation readily explicable.

Keynes's portrayal of the workings of financial markets was obviously coloured by his own philosophy for making money in them – very much that of the active speculator – but to a behaviouralist it seems to neglect the costs of behaving as he did or of delegating the task to a professional, for example, by buying into a unit trust. Satisficing theory notes that it may well be the case that many individuals feel able to achieve entirely adequate (according to their own criteria) returns on their wealth without placing it in the hands of someone else and even without taking an active interest in possible movements in financial markets. If they never sell assets before they mature they may incur opportunity losses, but they avoid some of the costs of speculation: not only do they avoid brokers' fees and the risks of judging price movements incorrectly, they also avoid building their lives around worrying about the state of the market.

Even if some people do decide to place their wealth with life assurance companies and unit trusts rather than personally managing their portfolios, there is no guarantee that the professional managers will be always particularly active and speculate as Keynes himself did. The reason for this is that, to stay in business in a particular risk area of the financial markets, fund managers merely need to offer relatively competitive rates of return; they do not have to maximize returns. (The rate of return which they feel they must offer is likely to be determined by their conjectures of what they must at least offer to keep would-be entrants out of their part of the financial market, rather than the rate of return that other incumbents seem able to achieve; cf. Andrews, 1949, ch. 5; Davies and Davies, 1984, and note the extent to which financial deregulation may have increased the pressure on incumbent fund managers to seek higher returns as a means of preserving their market positions.) If fund managers generally are able to meet customers' aspirations without taking greater capital risks through speculation, an individual fund manager may be under no pressure to behave differently. In the absence of pressure from suppliers of funds to generate a better yield, pressure for professional portfolio managers to engage in more active policies is unlikely to be felt unless a particular institution is able consistently to generate above-average return without being seen by the public as engaging in much more risky activities. To seek to improve the yield of one's fund by engaging in more risk-taking when there is no pressure from customers or a market leader to do so could seriously misfire if one ends up getting labelled as a higher-risk operation.

A passive portfolio strategy might work very well in times of low inflation: interest rates may be barely positive in real terms but could suffice to enable passive wealth-holders to meet their targets for the real value of their future consumption potential, given the rate at which they find it acceptable to add to their wealth via current saving. However, if inflation suddenly accelerates, as it did in the late 1960s, the passive approach may begin to seem unsatisfactory. In this situation, satisficing theory predicts that the negative real rates of return will prompt search for alternative ways of keeping the value of their wealth intact. The solution to the problem may be seen as lying in a more active approach, whereby capital gains are used as a substitute for inadequate interest earnings. Interestingly enough, such a change of strategy may help perpetuate the negative real interest return that prompts its initial use. For example, consider a middle-aged couple who have been cautiously (and, some would say, foolishly) building up retirement funds in a deposit account at a bank. If they switch their wealth to a unit trust, then they do not reduce the supply of bank deposits in general and do not add to pressures forcing banks to raise their deposit rates.

Behavioural theory points to two main possibilities that could be worth investigating in respect of tendencies to continue engaging in active portfolio management even after the initial motivating force may have evaporated. Consider again the scenario in which accelerating inflation prompted active speculation. If the inflation rate comes down, continuation of an active policy may lead to the attainment of returns that are in excess of the wealth-holders' targets. In this situation one possibility is that aspirations could rise into line with attainments. If so, a resurgence of inflation could lead to search for even higher yields from speculation. If ways of achieving them were discovered, there would be no need for wealth-owners grudgingly to lower their sights. In this case, some kind of ratchet effect would be in operation, somewhat akin to that in Duesenberry's (1949) analysis of savings behaviour. Alternatively, the deceleration of inflation might lead to a reduction in the extent of active speculation, and a retreat to somewhat less risky modes of portfolio management. This would seem likely in situations where the wealth-owner's aspirations were hierarchically ordered (as is assumed in the 'behavioural lexicographic' model of choice) and where she had been able to continue to meet her financial yield goal only at the cost of compromising a lower order goal (for example, her tolerable number of sleepless nights spent worrying about her exposure to financial risks!).

Knowledge of the reference points people use in forming their portfolio aspirations would seem worth acquiring. To the extent that people act as in Duesenberry's view of consumption and set their aspirations in the light of what people they see as similar to themselves seem to be able to achieve, we should be less surprised to see an interest in speculation tending to come in the sorts of waves hypothesized by Minsky. Prior to the disappearance of the fortunes of many yuppies in the Crash of October 1987, the following kind of logic may have been quite commonly employed by those jumping on the speculation bandwagon: 'People around me are playing the markets, and I shall be left behind in the status race if I do not follow suit. The fact that members of my reference group are bragging about how their conspicuous consumption has been financed by successful speculation suggests that I ought to be able to speculate successfully too: they are no smarter than I am and no more able to obtain inside information, so if they can do it, despite little prior experience, why shouldn't I be able to do at least as well?'

CONCLUDING COMMENTS

The plasticity displayed by financial systems, and the evolutionary paths these systems trace in relation to the emerging profile of aggregate demand, do not result simply from technological or regulatory changes but are constrained by what wealth-holders are able to believe, including their beliefs about what they should be able to achieve. The standard post-Keynesian analysis of financial behaviour in terms of confidence, animal spirits, uncertainty and so on has highlighted the subjectivity of beliefs but in doing so it has left itself open to charges of nihilism owing to its failure to explain what delimits the apparently infinite number of responses a creative decision maker can make to any given situation. In this chapter I have attempted to show how bounded rationality and the consequent use of decision rules and satisficing routines may provide such closure, as well as showing how these factors may impinge on the evolution of financial systems. The analysis complements the broader thesis put forward by Heiner (1983), who argues that the possibility of prediction in economics *only* arises because people use routine methods for coping with problem events that are, strictly speaking, unique occurrences.

To rebut fully the assertions of those, such as Coddington, who have accused post-Keynesians of nihilism, it is unlikely to be enough just to show that, in principle, economic modelling is compatible with a subjectivist view of expectations once a behavioural perspective is introduced. The sceptics will demand to see such modelling undertaken in practice. To narrow down the directions in which monetary systems may evolve as financial entrepreneurs and central bankers attempt to change the set of options open to wealth-holders, post-Keynesian economists will have to begin to engage in studies of *how* decision-makers *actually* make up their minds about what could happen and what might be adequate courses of action for them to select. If they only add a behavioural perspective to their work by incorporating theoretical insights from behavioural economics and from psychology, they will still be left able only to discuss what Coddington (1983, p. 99) called the 'texture' of events. But, even then, they should be in a stronger position than hitherto in some policy debates – for example, over the need for prudential control of financial institutions and the regulation of consumer credit.

While advocating that behavioural research methods become part of the toolkit for applied work by post-Keynesian economists, I remain enough of a follower of Shackle's wise words to want to make it clear that I hope such behavioural investigations will not be used as a basis for claims that one can precisely foretell the future. Whenever post-Keynesians seek to draw from such investigations aggregative implications about possible responses to changes in the 'state of the news', they should be explicit about scope for error due to the use of simplified stereotypes. Following Shackle, they also should always warn that creativity in the minds of decision-makers has the potential to prompt choices vastly different from those so far observed. Hence policy recommendations based on behavioural studies should themselves contain room for manoeuvre, in case portfolio choices take surprising turns (cf. Hart, 1945, 1947). I believe post-Keynesians could do much to restore the tarnished public image of economists if, instead of trying to divert attention away from debatable assumptions underlying their conjectures, they presented their policy advice in a way which highlighted the uncertainties that have proved difficult to dismiss and explained why, therefore, inflexible or finely tuned policies could be dangerous.

NOTE

1. The author is grateful for the comments of two anonymous referees, but naturally takes responsibility for any errors, omissions and excesses that remain in the final version.

9. Post-Keynesian Economics and New Approaches to Industrial Economics

Neil Kay[1]

In this chapter we suggest that some recent developments in industrial economics following on the work of Herbert Simon exhibit interesting parallels with post-Keynesian economics in terms of the issues and concepts identified as having central importance for economic analysis. First of all, it is argued that there is a high degree of sympathy between Simon-influenced approaches in industrial economics analyzed in those terms, and secondly, it is suggested that the principles driving post-Keynesian economics are reflected in much of the new industrial economies, even though the substance of analysis may be superficially very different in the respective arenas.

In the first section we shall suggest how reaction to neoclassical theory has resulted in a broadly based alternative perspective in industrial economics, in the second we shall explore possible connections between these alternative representations and post-Keynesian economics, and in the third we give a more detailed account of how one such industrial economics approach looks at corporate behaviour in a world of uncertainty.

THE NEOCLASSICAL APPROACH AND ALTERNATIVES

The traditional neoclassical microeconomic approach is characterized by one basic question; what is the optimal product-

190

Table 9.1 Neoclassical and Alternative Perspectives

Neoclassical perspective	Alternative perspective	Selected analysis
Short/long run	Innovation	Schumpeter, Nelson & Winter
Optimizing	Satisficing	Simon, Cyert & March
Product	Resources	Penrose
Market	Hierarchies	Coase, Williamson
Price	Technology	Schumpeter, Nelson & Winter

market price? (Kay 1984). This question can be further subdivided into identification of short or long run optimal product-market price. The criterion used is P = MC (price = marginal cost); questions in such areas as competition, monopoly, externalities and public goods are analyzed in terms of whether or not this criterion is satisfied, and, if not, what can or should be done with it.

The neoclassical question can be decomposed into its five components. The *short/long-run* time dimension assumes we do not encounter problems of the *very* long run in which technological change takes place; *optimizing* presumes decisions can be expressed in constrained maximization terms[2]; the *product* orientation serves as the basic building block; *market* exchange is the basic form of economic organization; and *price* is necessary and sufficient information for decision-making purposes (Kay, 1984).

Significantly, each of these components of the neoclassical question has been criticized as implying an inadequate description of the economic process. Table 9.1 provides a selective description of major sources of criticism in this arena.

Schumpeter (1954) focused on the process of technological change in industry and analyzed the role of innovation, a phenomenon excluded from the short/long run static technology perspective of neoclassical theory. Nelson and Winter

(1982) follow in the Schumpeterian tradition in their development of an evolutionary theory of economic change. The optimizing component was criticized by Simon (1957 and 1976) who suggested that many decision-making situations were characterized by genuine (by implication, Knightian or Keynesian) uncertainty, and individuals frequently satisficed rather than maximized in such circumstances. Cyert and March (1963) developed this approach into a behavioural theory of the firm. Penrose (1959) described the firm as a bundle of resources rather than an arbitrary aggregation of product markets as in neoclassical theory; her focus was on the firm as an enduring and continuing institution, rather than a neoclassical device definable in terms of its end result. Williamson (1975, 1985) argues that market exchange is not in practice the sole form of economic organization, but that maternal organization or hierarchy may provide a genuine alternative over a wide range of economic activity. Finally, returning full circle to Schumpeter, Nelson and Winter, technological competition rather than price competition may be the driving force behind the growth of firms and industrial development.

The picture painted of the firm in these alternative frameworks is substantially different from that in neoclassical theory. A composite picture of the 'alternative' firm would depict hierarchically organized resources precoccupied with problems of innovative activity in the context of genuine, non-measurable uncertainty. By way of contrast, the neoclassical firm is an optimizing 'black box' whose role is to set and/or react to market price. The firm is not of interest as a resource allocating device in its own right, but as a means of serving the markets role as the method of resource allocation.

In fact, while the composite picture of the 'alternative' firm provides a useful contrast to the neoclassical firm for illustrative purposes, analysts have tended to be selective in terms of which components of the neoclassical perspective they have departed from; for example, Schumpeter still used product-markets as basic units of analysis, while Cyert and March's satisficing approach examined product-market pricing behaviour. Alternative perspectives have often concentrated on the implications of specific limited deviations from the neoclassical perspective, rather than complete abandonment of all components of the traditional perspective.

However, it would be a mistake to believe that the five components of the neoclassical question can be treated more or less independently of each other; it may not be possible to drop one or other of the components without affecting the status or viability of the others. For example, it is difficult to consider problems of innovation without questioning the relevance of maximizing behaviour (though some neoclassical theorists somehow manage this); abandonment of the strict knowledge conditions usually associated with optimizing behaviour also tends to encourage reconsideration of the neoclassical presumption that price is the only relevant informational variable; also, focusing on hierarchies leads naturally to emphasis on the nature of resources in internal organization; and so on.

If there is one central or core issue to which all the others tend to be connected, it is represented by the optimizing/satisficing dyad in Table 9.1. This issue relates to whether or not problems of bounded rationality are likely to be significant in particular situations. Simon's concept of bounded rationality refers to language or cognitive limits on decision-making ability; individuals are intendedly rational but limitedly so. Once bounded rationality enters into consideration, the constrained maximization apparatus of neoclassical theory is in trouble. Salvage attempts are feasible if the problems in knowledge can be expressed in probabilistic terms, that is if they are risky in Knightian terms. It is when situations are characterized by genuine Knightian uncertainty that constrained maximization techniques break down and bounded rationality constitutes a severe problem for neoclassical theory.

Thus, bounded rationality/Knightian uncertainty represents the starting point for the newer theories of industrial organization discussed here. Traditional mainstream theorists tend to have great difficulty in accepting the legitimacy of these concepts. They associate them with states of disorder or even anarchy. The inappropriateness of the constrained maximization apparatus in these circumstances reinforces their belief that theory building in such cases is likely to be unfruitful and misdirected. They are wrong on at least three counts.

Firstly, even if maximizing behaviour is not possible because of Knightian uncertainty, this does not mean that alternative theorizing is impossible. For example, even if a specific environment is surprise-ridden and highly uncertain, this does not necessarily mean that nothing can be said about human behaviour in that context (Earl and Kay, 1985). Many devices and strategies, such as multiple sourcing, diversification,short-term contracting and modular system design, can be analyzed as rational attempts to deal with surprising and uncertain environments. Indeed, it is only in a Keynesian or Knightian world that these phenomena begin to make sense; they would generally be redundant or inefficient in a neoclassical world.

Secondly, there is a hint of intellectual arrogance – or defensiveness – in the belief that a problem only has significance if it can be expressed in the terms and concepts of a particular framework. This is of special significance for traditional theorists given the highly restricted and specific nature of the neoclassical question. If your framework only permits you to see a world characterized by static technology, optimality, products, markets and prices, a high degree of myopia is guaranteed. In fact, what neoclassical theory would treat (or ignore) as a problem or embarrassment is frequently regarded as an opportunity or starting point for alternative perspectives; thus Knightian uncertainty only represents an insuperable difficulty for theorizing if you are incorruptably wedded to the concept of optimality, and technological competition is easier to analyze if you are not an incorrigible price theorist. The alternative perspectives tend to introduce concepts and terms more appropriate to the analysis of bounded rationality than are the components of the neoclassical question they leave behind.

Thirdly, and related to the last point, neoclassical theorizing spills over into a tendency to regard the economic world as analyzable, either in terms of a component/consequence of the neoclassical question, or its converse or negation. Thus, the world is either rational or irrational, optimal or non-optimal, in equilibrium or in disequilibrium; we have aggregation or we have an aggregation problem. In fact, the influence of the neoclassical question is pervasive in economics; the theorist who reacts against the tradition by adopting the apparent opposite may still be far more influenced by the tradition than they realize. Thus, rather than choosing between 'A or not-A' it may be appropriate to go one step further back in the process and ask whether the question is a useful one in the first place.

For example, Hodgson (1985) points out that many acts are influenced by considerations other than rational, conscious, articulable decision processes; habits, reflexes and instincts are examples. It could be argued that applying the test of rationality to these phenomena would not be appropriate. It might be more suitable to describe them as arational rather than rational/irrational.[3]

Similarly, the aggregation problem has been debated with great heat by neoclassicalists and post-Keynesians. From a neoclassical vantage point, Samuelson commented:

Until the laws of thermodynamics are repealed, I shall continue to relate outputs to inputs – i.e., to believe in (aggregate) production functions. (Samuelson 1966(a), quoted in Chase 1983, p. 153)

But why did Samuelson appeal to the laws of thermodynamics and not to those of chemistry and biology? Why was it not pointed out that economics is the only social science that uses aggregation as its dominant technique (Kay 1982)?[4] An obvious answer is that the neoclassical economists had set the agenda and consequently the battle was fought on their terms. However, for those accustomed to systemic and structuralist[5] concepts in disciplines such as chemistry, biology, anthropology and psycholinguistics it would surely appear a curious debate. Quite simply, aggregation is not the only means of describing higher level systems, and, in fact, is only legitimate if systems are decomposable. Anyone who doubts this should first try to describe water as the aggregate of its constituents, hydrogen and oxygen.

To return to a theme introduced above, while problems of aggregation may present a severe difficulty for neoclassical theory, they may also signal opportunities for theory development. Preoccupation with aggregation may be a symptom of the 'A or not-A' problem and may also be indicative of a need to model behaviour in systemic or structuralist terms. Though it may be surprising to neoclassical theorists, it is possible to develop empirically testable theories without invoking aggregation. (Kay, 1979, 1982).

CONNECTIONS BETWEEN THE NEW INDUSTRIAL ECONOMICS AND POST-KEYNESIAN ECONOMICS

In the next three sections, we shall use Davidson's (1981) three propositions[6] summarizing the characteristics of post-Keynesian models as coat-hangers on which to attach discussions of the newer theories of industrial organization following Simon's work.[7] It is hoped this may help to signpost common ground or interest between post-Keynesians and those of us working in those areas of industrial organization.

It should also be noted that sympathetic connections between the spirit of behavioural theory following on Simon, and post-Keynesian approaches (particularly that of Shackle) have already been remarked upon by Garner (1982). As Garner points out, 'the behavioural approach is consistent . . . with the post-Keynesian view that the moment of decision matters in economics, and that ahistorical methods are fundamentally inadequate' (p. 421). We explore these potential linkages in more depth below.

Proposition 1: In a world where uncertainty and surprises are unavoidable, expectations have an unavoidable and significant effect on economic outcomes (Davidson, 1981, p. 159)

Davidson argues: 'In an uncertain world, economic decisions are continually affected by the decision makers' expectations, and these expectations are shaped by the "inherited stocks" possessed by economic actors – the accumulated results of past guesses, both correct and incorrect. In other words, economic decisions are rarely made on anything like a clean slate. As different individuals or groups approach the same economic circumstances with different "slates" so their expectations and hence their decisions may also differ' (p. 159).

The newer theories of industrial organization can be interpreted as being in broad agreement with Davidson on these counts, though expectations tend not to have such a central role in these theories. In fact, ironically, expectations may themselves involve too strong or precise assumptions concerning knowledge conditions in certain environments, unless one removes expectations to the more abstract realm postulated by Boulding (1968) when he advocated that we should often 'expect the unexpected'. The newer theories of industrial organization frequently avoid the need to identify specific expectations; substituting 'experience' for 'expectations' in the above quotes from Davidson would represent a fair description of the consensus in these areas.

It might seem that avoiding expectations would be a strange path for theory building in this area to take. However there are two main reasons why this might be justified; it might be difficult or impossible to identify expectations in practice, and it might be unnecessary to do so in any case.

First, it might be difficult or impossible to track expectations, because the world being analyzed here is too complex. It is true that eventually all events may impinge on prices, quantities and/or profits, but frequently action must be taken before they do so. Decisions must be taken with respect to a wide variety of phenomena, not just market variables such as expected prices and quantities.

Secondly, and most importantly, theory building may avoid the need for explicit hypotheses concerning expectations. For example, actions may be reactive, contingent on the appearance of a specific problem or surprise, as in Cyert and March's (1963) concept of problemistic search. Corporate action may also be regarded as determined by organizational routines which may also incorporate search elements as part of the set of routines (Nelson and Winter, 1981).[8] Behaviour is then determined largely by corporate experience and history (possibly with stochastic elements influencing action) in conjunction with an environmental selection mechanism. A further possibility is provided by Williamson's (1975, 1985) argument that opportunism (self-interest-seeking with guile) is a fundamental determinant of the form economic activity takes. Williamson's analysis of transaction costs presumes that active or potential opportunistic behaviour may pose general problems for economic efficiency. It is not necessary to identify expectations as to the form opportunistic behaviour could take, it is sufficient to identify certain transactions as being vulnerable to severe transaction costs in the face of opportunism. If internalization then appears as a potentially more efficient method of economic organization through its ability to monitor and control the effects of opportunism, it is possible to use transaction costs to explain a wide variety of phenomena in industrial organization, such as vertical integration and internal capital markets (Williamson, 1975), diversification (Kay 1982) and multinational enterprise (Galbraith and Kay, 1986). If expectations are relevant in these contexts, it is the mild form of the 'expect the unexpected' type with some environments expected to be more turbulent than others.

Thus, behaviour in these approaches may be characterized as reactive, routine or, in Williamson's analysis, an attempt to pre-empt, avoid or mitigate 'surprises'. There is no need to make strong inferences about expectations, whether historically determined, adaptive or rational. Those who wish to identify expectations might argue that Nelson and Winter's routine driven decision-making implies historically determined expectations. However if we can draw an analogy between organizational routines and habits, there is no more need to argue that routines imply expectations than to argue habits imply explicitly rational decision processes.

Thus, expectations are not an important element of these new theories, though bounded rationality and environmental uncertainty are. The firm is characterized as a combination of assets, routines or procedures operating in an uncertain environment.

Proposition 2: The economy is a process in historical time (Davidson, 1981, p. 158)

Davidson argues that the historical process is associated with irreversibilities. As Joan Robinson points out: 'The purpose of "malleable capital" is to overcome the difference between the future and the past' (Robinson, 1975, p. XII) and neoclassical theory builds on this ahistorical assumption. Post-Keynesians bring the historical process into account by emphasizing irreversibilities and non-malleabilities and some have usefully extended the argument into analysis of other resources; 'human capital is just as nonfungible (clay not putty) as physical capital' (Wiles, 1983, p. 75).

Irreversibilities also play a central role in the new theories of industrial organization; for example, asset specificity and task idiosyncracies in Williamson's transaction cost economics, and organizational routines in Nelson and Winter's evolutionary theory. The role of bounded rationality/uncertainty is still critical however, since the absence of bounded rationality problems means that irreversibilities would not pose a serious problem for decision-makers. As Williamson points out (1985, pp. 30–1), unrestricted cognitive competences means that all relevant issues of contract can be established and settled *ex ante*. Irreversibilities only have significance in a world of uncertainty and surprise. The role of time is also reflected in the general presumption that the particular history and experience of individual firms and their associated resources determine the form asset specificity and organizational routines take in given circumstances. Firms are heterogenous in those respects.

A contrasting perspective is provided by the contestable markets literature in industrial organization.[9] A standard assumption in this approach is that resources can be costlessly and quickly redeployed in and out of alternative uses. This may be regarded as being in the neoclassical tradition in so far as reversibilities are emphasized and asset specificity downplayed. Thus, interestingly, the reversibility/irreversibility issue is one which serves to partition theories in industrial organization just as in macroeconomics.

While the orientation of the Simon-influenced theories obviously leans towards emphasis on system specific assets and routines, it is fair to say there has been some tension between the desire to capture the richness, variety and complexity of the structures and processes described in these approaches, and the desire to formally model the behaviour of firms. It is not impossible to model a world characterized by history, heterogeneity and uncertainty, but to the extent the tension between descriptive richness and formal modelling has existed, compromises have had to bc made, and may continue to be necessary in the future. At the moment it is probably fair to say that it is unclear whether future development will tend more towards formal modelling or case study/historical analyses. A critical consideration will be the ability of the new theories to identify systemic features and consistent patterns underlying the varieties of behaviour being analyzed.

Proposition 3: Economic and political institutions are not negligible, and, in fact play an extremely important role in determining real-world economic outcomes (Davidson, 1981, p. 162)

Davidson (1982, pp. 13–14) further analyzes the nature of institutions and cites the banking and monetary sytems, time orientated markets for goods and resources, and money contracts including money wage contracts.

As far as the new theories of industrial organizations are concerned, Nelson and Winter's concept of routine has institutional features such as a degree of stability and continuity that contributes towards ordering and direction in an uncertain environment. In principle, Williamson's analysis of hierarchy introduces further elements of an institutional routine in so far as corporate organization is identified as an alternative system of economic organization to market exchange. There are some difficulties with Williamson's approach such as the tendency to interpret hierarchy in contractual terms (Kay, 1987). This tends to bias analysis towards internal markets versus external markets and downplays the organizational properties of genuinely hierarchial systems.

This emphasis on markets is understandable, particularly given the central role accorded market exchange in the economics tradition. However, as implied earlier, such emphasis may represent an overly mild reaction to the tradition; the appropriate question may not be: 'are markets external or not?' but 'do alternatives to market organization exist?'.

One line of development with respect to this latter question is represented by Kay (1979, 1982, 1984) in which the firm is regarded as a structured entity possessing hierarchial and organizational properties which may require it to be analyzed as a non-decomposable system. Hierarchies are analyzed as alternatives to markets, not merely as another expression of markets. Hierarchy may be regarded as another contribution of an institutional nature, and indeed Williamson regards his development of the concept as following in a neo-institutionalist tradition.

The role of bounded rationality is also central here. Not only is the behaviour of institutions influenced by bounded rationality, their very existence is generally attributable to such considerations. An argument along these lines was developed in Kay (1984). Starting off with a functionally organized hierarchical corporation, the question was then raised as to what would happen to the firm if bounded rationality was not an issue and all parties had unlimited cognitive competences. First, since marketing, finance, and R & D functions were essentially concerned with generation of information to consumers and/or managers, these functions would become redundant since all relevant information would already be in the possession of the relevant actors. Production would remain if it was concerned with physical goods or services. Secondly, hierarchy would disappear. since superior-subordinate delegation is a consequence of cognitive limitations on the part of decision-makers. However, managers would themselves disappear since owners have no need to delegate to such agents if they do not face effective cognitive limits on their decision-making ability. If bounded rationality is not a problem, functions (save production), hierarchies and managers disappear. The firm re-emerges as the owner-driven profit maximizing production unit of neoclassical theory. This *reductio ad absurdum* approach helped demonstrate the pervasive and fundamental effect of bounded rationality in determining real world phenomena. It is the existence of bounded rationality that creates the need for institutions like hierarchy. If bounded rationality is not a problem we can analyze the economy in terms of the traditional pictures of general equilibrium models. In the next section we shall analyze how one approach in industrial organization attempts to analyze the corporation as a complex system operating in a world of bounded rationality.

AN APPROACH TO PROBLEMS IN INDUSTRIAL ORGANIZATION

It is not possible in the space of this paper to give more than a brief indication of possible connections between the newer approaches to industrial economics and post-Keynesian economics. It would also be misleading to overemphasize the similarities between the newer theories of industrial economics discussed here; even though there is a high degree of agreement between them as to what constitute the important concepts and issues, theoretical development within each approach tends to be fairly idiosyncratic. Consequently in this section we shall concentrate on one particular approach for illustrative purposes, building on the work of Kay (1982).

Rather than take individual product markets as basic building blocks for analytical purposes, this approach maps the strategy of the corporation by analyzing resource linkages and commonalities between the firm's respective product markets. We can illustrate the basic logic of the approach by showing how it would develop, and analyze a stylized representation of the company BIC's strategy of diversification.

In Figure 9.1, M and T represent marketing and technological links between respective product markets in the form of common resources. For example, on the market side these may be common advertizing, marketing staff, distribution channels, plant and equipment, materials and R & D. BIC's development of lightweight disposable consumer products

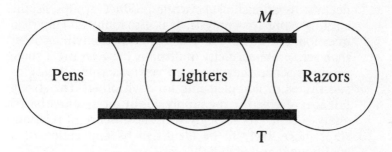

Key:
M = Marketing link
T = Technological link

Figure 9.1   BIC's diversification strategy

(pens, lighters, razors) guarantees strong links and potential synergies on the marketing side (e.g., point-of-sale marketing techniques; common retail outlets and distribution) and on the technological side (e.g., similar materials and production techniques; R & D spillover effects). These links and commonalities are represented by M and T respectively in Figure 9.1. Not all resources or assets will be shared, some will be specific to individual product markets; however those that are shared may generate cost savings in the form of synergies (Ansoff, 1965) or economies of scope (Baumol *et al.*, 1982) between product markets.

By identifying linkages in this fashion, systematic maps of the strategy of the corporation can be built up.[10] They can be used in a variety of ways which suggest interesting possibilities for economic analysis.[11] There are a number of issues and perspectives raised by analysis of this type which contrast with traditional neoclassical analysis and its applied derivative, the structure-conduct-performance (SCP) approach. We discuss some of these below.

(a) The identification of resource linkages between products differs from the traditional market-oriented SCP approach which is first of all concerned with identifying demand relationships between product groups as the starting point for analysis. It is essentially an empirical question, but we have no reason to expect anything other than zero cross-elasticity of demand between BIC's three products since they have no obvious role to play as substitutes or complements for each other. The strong linkages revealed on the supply side by our resource based analysis contrasts strongly with the absence of relationships more likely to be identified by application of a traditional approach in this case.

(b) Economies or synergies are not a free good, and the mapping technique helps illustrate issues in competition, diversification and merger activity. Although the products operate in distinctive market arenas, the same resource linkages that provide internal economies may also create vulnerability to external competitive threats. For example, if a competitor in disposable consumer products managed to secure exclusive supplier status for a major chain of supermarket and displace BIC, then BIC would be attacked along its marketing linkage right across the board. Similarly, if a competitor makes a technological breakthough in the design of disposable consumer products, all BIC's products may face the threat of technological obsolescence simultaneously, the technological link being the focus of attack from outside. Thus, the resource link that provides strengths in the form of internal economies may also provide weaknesses in the form of vulnerability to external threats. In an uncertain world, how firms react to this is a strategic question. If firms face a turbulent environment characterized by unexpected developments and technological surprises, then the price of a richly linked product strategy may be regular vulnerability to the possible decline of all the firms businesses, and the firm with it.[12] Diversification away from costly links, and a merger/acquisition strategy associated with this objective is one response to such a situation. In Kay (1982) such considerations were also seen as contributing towards the development of many conglomerate strategies, particularly in science-based firms in US industry. In the same work, such a perspective also proved useful in analyzing patterns of diversification, merger and changes in overall concentration.

(c) The system described in Figure 9.1 is non-decomposable. BIC cannot be treated as if it could be broken down into separable, constituent product-markets without the nature of the system being described undergoing a transformation. A corollary is that BIC cannot be treated as the simple aggregate of its component products since this would ignore systematic linkages across product boundaries. This is not a problem but instead reflects the different orientation of the analysis compared to the SCP approach. Just as analyzing bonds and links between atoms illuminates different molecular properties for a chemist, so it helps analysis of corporate behaviour in industrial behaviour. As we argued earlier, it may not be only the laws of thermodynamics that economists should turn to as scientific yardsticks for economic analysis, and indeed thermodynamics may be the most inappropriate for these purposes.

(d) The analysis can be used to analyze specificities and irreversibilities in firm and industrial growth. For example, it is possible to chart the growth of firms around their resource characteristics, for example BIC's development of cheap disposable consumer products from early marketing and technological skills developed in ballpoint pens, or Boeing's postwar growth around marketing and technological skills developed in manufacturing and selling military aircraft.[13] Such analysis is also likely to illuminate firm specific distinctive competences and skills developed through the historical process of corporate evolution and development. In this respect, the firm is not seen as a static bundle of product markets, but a combination of resources evolving through time, a picture much more in sympathy with Penrose's (1959) characterization of the firm than the traditional neoclassical one. It also may help chart the logic of technological innovation relative to the firm's resource base. It would have been surprising if BIC had developed the 757 and Boeing the disposable lighter, rather than the other way around; more sophisticated analysis may facilitate analysis of patterns of innovative activity obscured by traditional economic frameworks.

(e) The analysis also may serve as a starting point for analysis of institutional behaviour. For example, Nelson's and Winter's routines are likely to be central, defining characteristics of the resource complexes composing firms. Also, in Kay (1982, 1984), analysis of strategy as in Figure 9.1 led naturally to analysis of the form of hierarchy or internal organization likely to be associated with respective strategies. In an aggregative decentralized world, hierarchy will be minimalized or redundant; it is the non-decomposable world of boundedly rational corporate actors which requires the co-ordinating function that hierarchy provides. If, as has been often remarked, there is no 'firm' in the traditional theory of the firm, it is equally true there is no 'organization' in traditional industrial organization.

Our analysis has far more in common with the alternative perspectives charted in Table 9.1. than it has with the neoclassical agenda. The core concepts revolve around resources, decision-making under uncertainty, hierarchies and technological change. As such the mapping of strategy provides a useful organizing approach that facilitates theoretical development along the lines of the alternative perspective discussed earlier. It is hoped that such noises strike agreeable noises also in post-Keynesian ears.

CONCLUSION

It is remarkable that there is so much tacit consensus as to what constitutes important concepts and issues between the different approaches discussed in this paper. We have been able to give only a superficial indication of possible areas of agreement between these different frameworks, but it is clear that certain basic conceptions and principles recur regularly. The tendency towards Balkanization in economic analysis may have impeded communication between analysts working alternative analytical lodes to the original neoclassical workings. However, ironically, such Balkanization may also be regarded as generally reinforcing the claims made in the respective approaches. Continual and independent rediscovery of the central importance of issues like uncertainty, irreversibilities, history, institutional characteristics and technological change should lend credence to arguments that these phenomena are fundamental driving forces in economic behaviour. It is noteworthy that movement away from neoclassical theory has often led to identification of similar types of pattern and order in the way the economic world works.

It is possible to overstate the parallels and points of convergence between the new approaches in industrial organization; for example, technological change is central to Nelson and Winter's analysis, but is peripheral in Williamson's. Nevertheless, there does exist a high degree of correspondence between alternative approaches in industrial organization and post-Keynesian economics, and it is hoped that these connections can be developed further. The divisiveness that is attendant upon Balkanization weakens the ability to develop a coherent alternative agenda to replace the traditional one. Deficiencies in consistency and coherence in this respect buttress the status quo.

If Keynes represents the major starting point in post-Keynesian economics, then Herbert Simon frequently occupies such a role in the new industrial economics. While other prior authorities receive differential emphasis depending on the approach (e.g., Coase is frequently cited by Williamson; Schumpeter by Nelson and Winter), Simon's analysis of the role of bounded rationality in decision-making is a fairly consistent theme in the new industrial economics. It is from such roots in the analysis of decision-making under uncertainty that the promising developments in the new industrial economics really derive. It is to be hoped that such perspectives may also suggest possible insights and interpretations for those economists starting from a post-Keynesian vantage point.

NOTES

1. I am grateful to participants at the Great Malvern conference for helpful comments, and to an anonymous referee. The latter was especially helpful in drawing my attention to Garner's prior work.
2. Though constrained maximization does not itself guarantee that optimizing behaviour may take place from the point of view of society, e.g., allocative inefficiency in monopoly.
3. However this does presume we are interpreting rationality as involving conscious, articulable decision-making.
4. It should also be noted that in the same year, Samuelson effectively conceded defeat over the reswitching debate (see Samuelson, 1966(b)).
5. Structuralist in this context refers to the group of frameworks adopted by social scientists such as Piaget, Chomsky and Levi Strauss.
6. Davidson (1982) does extend the three propositions, but the truncated list is sufficient for our purpose.
7. Other theories of industrial organization not discussed here include managerial theory, principal-agent theory and the theory of contestable markets. These approaches are close cousins to neoclassical theory especially in their use of constrained optimization techniques.
8. Cyert and March's theory also incorporated routines and standard operating procedures as part of the determinants of search, the difference with Nelson and Winter is more one of emphasis.
9. Baumol *et al.* (1982) represents a summary of major work in this area.
10. See Kay (1982) for further discussion and elaboration.
11. Kay (1982, 1984), Galbraith and Kay (1986) and Kay and Clarke (1986) conduct analysis using this technique.
12. This is a managerial interpretation. Owners are more easily able to diversify risk by spreading portfolio ownership. It is management whose role is closely tied to the survival of the firm, and they are the relevant decision-makers in this context.
13. See Kay and Clarke (1986) for further discussion.

10. The Composition of Government Expenditures and the Effectiveness of Fiscal Policy

John N. Smithin[1]

INTRODUCTION

What is meant in this essay by the composition of government expenditure is not a detailed breakdown by expenditure category, but the more elementary distinction between investment or capital spending on the one hand, and consumption or current spending on the other. This distinction seems to have been important to Keynes when he gave policy advice, but was apparently regarded as not very important at all in the mainstream or orthodox macroeconomics which developed after Keynes's death. For this reason, at least at the outset of the discussion, it is necessary to go back to what Keynes actually said on the matter, and this is one of the concerns of this paper.

In recent years, a number of economists from differing schools of thought, including Kregel (1985), Meltzer (1981, 1983), Pheby (1987), and Pressman (1987), have returned to a discussion of what Kregel (1985, pp. 32–8) calls 'Keynes's long-term policy proposals'. A key reference seems to be the wartime Treasury memoranda of 1943–4, which are now reprinted in volume XXVII of the *Collected Writings* (Keynes, 1980, pp. 264–419).

In the memoranda, involving explicit discussions of the

plans for postwar employment policy, Keynes showed a clear preference for government policies which would encourage investment spending rather than consumption spending; including both a relatively larger direct contribution by the state to fixed capital formation and also a broader set of initiatives by which the authorities would be able to 'influence' a substantial proportion of total investment spending. On the other hand, there is little or no advocacy of the policy of fiscal fine-tuning which later came to be regarded as characteristically Keynesian. Contrary to what continues to be the popular belief, this pattern is not inconsistent with the *General Theory*, as really the only major policy proposal which emerges from that work is the so-called 'socialization of investment' (*CW*, vol. VII, p. 378).[2]

The purpose of this paper is to inquire whether or not there are any lessons for contemporary economic analysis in the apparent dissonance between 'Keynesian policy and the policy of Keynes'. It will not be suggested that very much can be learnt directly about current policy problems from a textual exegesis of Keynes's writings of more than 40 years ago, and it goes without saying that the 'socialization of investment' does not impress as a very attractive political slogan in the modern era of privatization. However, the determination of the appropriate composition of state expenditure as between consumption and investment clearly does raise substantive questions of macroeconomic policy. Most obviously these concern the topical issue of budget deficits and the national debt, but they also involve both our theoretical understanding of the channels by which government policy may be expected to affect macroeconomic variables and the choice of empirical criteria by which policy should be evaluated.

Dow (1985, pp. 228, 238) suggests that post-Keynesian policy proposals actually do centre around a capital spending programme, but even a casual reading of any standard textbook will confirm that the distinction between state investment spending and consumption spending has not been regarded as a central issue by the majority of the profession. R. Eisner's (1986) recent and influential re-evaluation of the effectiveness of fiscal policy does attempt to deal with this question, and devotes a complete chapter (ch. 3, pp. 26–32) to 'Capital Budgeting or Its Lack'.[3] However, even in this work, a closer examination reveals that the relevant chapter is not well integrated with the empirical and theoretical work which makes up the rest of the book. This main channel through which fiscal policy is expected to affect output and employment is a wealth effect of changes in the real value of outstanding government debt on private sector consumption spending (pp. 61–8). For the latter mechanism, the issue of the composition of the excess of government expenditure over revenues is essentially irrelevant.

THE SOCIALIZATION OF INVESTMENT

Apart from the Treasury memoranda, mentioned above, the major sources in the reconstruction of what were the general principles of Keynes's policy of the 'socialization of investment' are Chapter 24 of the *General Theory* (*CW*, vol. VII, pp. 372–84), and, interestingly enough, Keynes's 1926 contribution, 'The End of Laissez-Faire' (*CW*, vol. IX, pp. 272–94). The latter was published 17 years before the Treasury memoranda were written, and ten years before the *General Theory*, but as pointed out by both Kregel (1985, pp. 36–7) and Pressman (1987), in some respects it shows a remarkable degree of continuity with the later proposals.[4]

Clearly the starting point must be that, if left to its own devices, the free market or private enterprise system will tend to generate a level of investment which is in some sense inadequate. Establishing this point rigorously, of course, is what ultimately required the theoretical innovation leading to the *General Theory*, because such a suggestion was theoretically inadmissable in the orthodox economics of Keynes's time, as indeed it is again in our own era. Granted the possibility, however, the remedy is then some form of social control of investment, the state either accepting responsibility to undertake investment directly or to provide incentives or the 'right climate' for the private sector to do the job.

Keynes made two main types of proposal to achieve this goal, only the more narrowly focused of which would come under the heading of fiscal policy or public finance *per se*. In this connection, remarkably, we find Keynes generally adverse to deficit financing.[5] He advocates a sharp distinction between the 'ordinary' (or current) budget and a capital budget, with the ordinary budget balanced or even in surplus (*CW*, vol. XXVII, pp. 277–80). The capital budget could be unbalanced in the short-term, but even in this case one of the advantages of state capital spending is that it is 'capable of paying for itself' and 'does not involve the progressive increase of budgetary difficulties' (*CW*, vol. XXVII, p. 320).[6] The broader set of initiatives goes far beyond the confines of narrowly defined public finance, and as Keynes put it in the title of Chapter 24 of the *General Theory* (*CW*, vol. VII, p. 372), amount to a change in 'social philosophy'. Ultimately a situation is envisaged in which 'two-thirds or three-quarters of total investment is carried out or can be influenced by public or semi-public bodies' (*CW*, vol. XXVII, p. 322). Both types of investment policy, in another striking feature from the modern point of view, are conceived of as part of a 'stable long-term pro-gramme' (*CW*, vol. XXVII, p. 322), and not primarily as counter-cyclical policy devices.

Although the inclination of the technically minded econ-omist might be to concentrate on the implications of the more narrowly defined fiscal policy issues, none the less some brief remarks on Keynes's broader social vision are also in place. One extremely important point, which is noted by a number of recent authors including Kregel (1985, p. 30), Skidelsky (1988) and Durbin (1988), is that the term 'socialization' is something of a misnomer, and that Keynes certainly did not advocate socialism in the technical sense of public ownership of the means of production.[7] Apart from the element of direct state spending via the separate capital budget, the broader vision of social control of investment could hardly be further removed from the usual notion of the 'command' economy. In fact, the characteristics of the 'public' or 'semi-public' bodies which would control the bulk of investment actually seem to be drawn from a reassuring model of traditional English society. This is made clear in a number of places,[8] including the following quotation from 'The End of Laissez-Faire' (*CW*, vol. IX, pp. 288-9), which is also cited by Kregel (1985, pp. 36-7):

progress lies in the growth and recognition of semi-autonomous bodies within the State–bodies whose criterion of action within their own field is solely the public good as they understand it, and from whose deliberations motives of private advantage are excluded. . . . I propose a return, it may be said, to mediaeval conceptions of separate autonomies. But . . . in England . . . corporations are a mode of government which has never ceased to be important and is sympathetic to our institutions. It is easy to give examples . . . the Universities, the Bank of England, the Port of London Authority . . . more interesting than these is the trend of Joint Stock Institutions, when they have reached a certain size, to approximate to the status of public corporations. . . . A point arrives . . . [at which] . . . the general stability and reputation of the institution are more considered . . . than the maximum of profit . . . The extreme instance . . . of this . . . is the Bank of England . . . [b]ut the same thing is partly true of many other big institutions . . . [t]hey are, as time goes on, socializing themselves.

The example of the large private sector companies 'socializing themselves' seems to be of particular significance here in indicating the (small c) conservative nature of the proposals. And indeed, so far from the 'corporatist' state being an implausible dream, one can of course recognize many elements of Keynes's vision in the type of society which did emerge, not only in England, but in many of the Western industrialized countries after the Second World War and is now under attack from the populist right. In this sense, Keynes's ideas were and remain central to the ongoing debate about the economic and social evolution of the industrialized democracies, but one would learn very little about this from the standardized discussions of 'Keynesian economics' in the current textbooks.

THE POLITICAL ECONOMY OF THE CAPITAL BUDGET

Returning now to the narrower topic of the capital budget, it can immediately be seen that deficit financing of state capital spending is much easier to defend politically than deficit financing of undifferentiated expenditure. Keynes was aware of this and gave the political argument as one of the reasons (not the only one) for a bias in favour of investment spending (*CW*, vol. XXVII, pp. 319–20).

Consider, for example, Coddington's view (1983, pp. 1–5) that a distinguishing feature of Keynesian economics is that it takes a 'utilitarian' view of the public finances as opposed to a position which would judge the state of the public finances by internal criteria such as concepts of sound finance or financial propriety. According to this characterization of the debate, the proponents of sound finance base their case on straightforward analogies to the position of an invididual household, arguing that both households and governments must 'live within their means', whereas their Keynesian opponents have the more difficult task of explaining to a sceptical public both why the analogy to the individual case is invalid and also the indirect macroeconomic benefits of deviating from the various internal criteria. The concept of a separate capital budget, however, turns the analogy to an individual household on its head. For although we might agree that it may not be sensible for a household to go into debt to support extravagant consumption expenditure, we would surely not raise the same objection to household deficit financing of its investment or capital spending, taking out a mortgage on a home being the obvious example. On the contrary, we would regard a household which delayed the purchase of a home until it could afford the full purchase price as eccentric in the extreme. As far as the capital budget is concerned the analogy to the household case works in the opposite direction.

A potentially more controversial point is that productive state investment spending may be less vulnerable to the standard 'crowding out' charge which might be legitimately applied (Dow, 1985, p. 228) to deficit financed current spending. According to the argument of Chapter 24 of the *General Theory*, Keynes's socialization of investment would reduce interest rates (admittedly over a different time horizon than that assumed in the crowding out literature) via capital saturation (*CW*, vol. VII, p. 374–77). As the latter takes place there is supposedly no diminution of incentives for profit-seeking private firms and entrepreneurs to undertake physical investment. It is only the position of the owners of financial capital which is adversely affected, Keynes's famous 'euthanasia of the rentier' (*CW*, vol. VII, p. 376). Even allowing for the fact that this is a long-run proposition, it leaves a substantially different impression than that which might be gained from an IS/LM type analysis in which Keynesian expansionary fiscal policy seems inevitably to increase interest rates.

WHICH MACROECONOMIC PROBLEM?

As is well known, Keynes maintained that his policy proposals derived directly from his theory, and that this sharply differentiated his work from that of his contemporaries. If we can take Keynes at his word, then one of the most important tasks which arise from a reconsideration of these proposals is to work backwards, as it were, and inquire what kind of theory is implied by them. In more practical terms, this might be expressed as inquiring exactly what was the macroeconomic problem which Keynes thought was being solved by the socialization of investment.

This is a question which is very closely related to the issues raised in a recent paper by Harcourt and O'Shaughnessy (1985) in which they document the revival of the view that Keynes was providing an equilibrium rather than a disequilibrium theory, and also comment on recent attempts to extend Keynes's theory of effective demand to the 'long period'.[9] Hamouda and Harcourt (1989, see Chapter 1) also refer to the debates touched off by the latter developments within the post Keynesian camp. In this context, obviously, the concept of an 'equilibrium theory' does not necessarily mean market-clearing equilibrium (in the sense in which modern 'New Classical' theorists exclusively use this term) but has a broader connotation of 'no tendency to change'.[10]

The idea that Keynes was providing an equilibrium rather than a disequilibrium theory, which Harcourt and O'Shaughnessy (1985, p. 4) attribute to authors as diverse as Meltzer

(1981), Patinkin (1982), and Eatwell and Milgate (1983), ties in with our observation here that his policy proposals seemed to be mainly concerned with promoting a stable investment programme rather than with confronting the problems of the business cycle. The implication is that the actual macroeconomic problem under discussion was that of improving the *average* performance of the economy in regard to such variables as output growth and employment, rather than modifying fluctuations around the average level.

Bixley (1988) complains (with some justice) that in an earlier generation an equilibrium interpretation of Keynes was standard,[11] and, in effect, suggests that the more recent writers are guilty of the economic equivalent of reinventing the wheel. This misses the point, however, that at least from around 1968 onwards (the publication date of Friedman's Presidential Address to the American Economic Association) almost all discussions of macroeconomic policy have been carried on in terms of fluctuations around a Friedmanian 'natural rate'. Acceptance of this framework was a fatal trap for self-styled Keynesians, as Keynesian economics was reduced to a series of assertions about speed of adjustment of the economy to the 'natural' rate, relying on such devices as adaptive expectations and nominal rigidities in the argument that disequilibrium adjustment was likely to be slow. There was also inevitably a tendency to interpret the *General Theory* retrospectively in these terms. These concepts then provided an easy target for the economists of the 'New Classical' school, who were essentially playing on their home field and by the late 1970s were proclaiming victory over a Keynesian economics which owed more to the econometricians, Phillips and even Friedman himself, than to Keynes.[12] In these circumstances, the recent writers who are insisting on an interpretation of Keynesian theory as equilibrium theory and Keynesian policy as concerned with improving average economic performance rather than with smoothing the cycle, are contributing to an important refocusing of the debate.

If we single out investment spending for particular concern, it is also impossible to avoid the second issue raised in the Harcourt and O'Shaughnessy contribution. Investment spending, obviously enough, has two aspects. In the short run, changes in the volume of investment spending will have implications for the level of capacity utilization, but not in a way that is fundamentally different from consumption spending. On a longer-term view, however, net investment spending adds to productive capacity, and as Harcourt and O'Shaughnessy insist (1985, p. 24), a theory of investment (or an account of the forces determining investment) necessarily takes on the aspect of a theory of accumulation. The question then arises as to which of these two facets of capital spending is the more important. The older equilibrium interpretations of Keynes, alluded to in Bixley's paper, seemed to focus on the former (for example, in variants of the 'Keynesian cross'), as do the more recent treatments by Patinkin (1982) and Kohn (1986). Of the authors cited by Harcourt and O'Shaughnessy, however, both Meltzer (1981) and Eatwell and Milgate (1983), though arriving at this position by very different routes, concentrate on the latter. Meltzer's interpretation, which, as the author indicates, is deliberately couched in a fairly conventional neoclassical framework (1981, p. 52; 1983, p. 74) is essentially to emphasize Keynes's view that the major defect of capitalism is both the volatility and inadequate average volume of private investment expenditures due (crucially) to pervasive uncertainty. This leads not only to deficient aggregate demand in the short run, but also (as Meltzer would express it) a sub-optimal level of the capital stock over a longer time horizon. Hence the policy proposal for the socialization of investment. Meltzer would also like to redefine the concepts of full employment and involuntary unemployment in these terms (1981, p. 36):

Keynes's involuntary unemployment is the difference between maximum employment and equilibrium employment. Keynes believed that private decisions produce an equilibrium rate of investment lower, and an equilibrium capital stock smaller, than the social optima. Because investment is lower than the rate required for maximum output, aggregate demand is deficient – that is, less than the amount required to *maintain* full (maximum) employment. Nothing in the market economy adjusts. The equilibrium position is stable; everyone expects the equilibrium to persist. The problem is

not that people do not know and cannot learn the equilibrium values
of the money wage, the rate of interest, and the level of investment.
The problem is that they know these values and cannot change them.
(Original emphasis)

Harcourt and O'Shaughnessy (1985, pp. 15–21) and Smithin
(1985) point out the difficulties in a strict textual interpretation of the *General Theory* itself in these terms. As these
authors read the *General Theory*, most of Keynes's analysis,
certainly up to chapter 18, 'The General Theory Re-stated'
(*CW*, vol. VII, pp. 245–54), is conducted in terms of the short
period. The discussion of the longer-term consequences of
insufficient investment really only comes in at the end in
Chapter 24.

But it can also be argued that this is precisely the point at
which detailed textual exegesis of the *General Theory* is
unhelpful in pushing the debate any further, and at which we
should become impatient with the continuing discussions
about what Keynes 'really meant'. Obviously the short-period
and long-period aspects are not mutually exclusive, and an
insufficiency of investment spending is going to have implications both for capacity utilization in the short-term and for
the accumulation of physical capital on a longer view. Both in
the *General Theory* and elsewhere it would be possible to make
the case that Keynes himself generally kept both things in
mind,[13] but, in any event, our contemporary interest in Keynes's policy proposals should not really hinge on the way he
happened to express himself in his various theoretical contributions, or on whether or not he was able to keep both the
short-run and long-run aspects of the proposals consistently in
view. From the contemporary analytical perspective there are
really only two important points to establish. First, is it true
(was it true in Keynes's day and is it still true) that the unaided
market system will typically not generate an adequate level of
investment and, if so, how can this be explained? Secondly,
will the proposed policy of the socialization of investment be
able to remedy the situation without damaging side effects?

Given the former task, it is rather a surprising development,
which is noted by Harcourt and O'Shaughnessy (1985, p. 8–9),

that one of the concerns of the other main group of writers who favour a long-period interpretation of the theory of employment has been to downplay the importance of expectations and uncertainty (Eatwell and Milgate, 1983, pp. 12–14). These writers clearly have a different agenda than Meltzer, which is to link up Keynes's theory of employment with the post-Sraffa theory of value and distribution. In this context the argument seems to be that the characteristics of the accumulation process depend in a general way on the nature of the economic society and historical period within which it takes place (the mode of production one might say), and that investment cannot be reduced to the status of a behavioural function (1983, p. 14).

For our present purposes, however, one of the ways in which it is possible to interpret the task which Keynes apparently set himself is to inquire why, specifically, one of the characteristics of the economic society in which he was living (a particular historical phase of market oriented capitalism) was that the volume of investment was persistently less than seemed to be required for full employment. For this, an account of expectations formation and uncertainty (using the latter term in the sense of the 1937 *Quarterly Journal of Economics* article, as opposed to mathematical risk), would definitely seem to be required. It would also be required in our own historical epoch, if contemporary conditions continue to resemble in important respects those which Keynes was observing.

Harcourt and O'Shaughnessy (1985, pp. 7–8) indicate that in order to explain why the volume of investment is persistently less than it otherwise might be, they would lay stress on a persistent or pervasive state of uncertainty, which would dampen the 'animal spirits' of investors. We should note, however, that this is not inconsistent with the idea stressed by other writers[14] that the volatility of expectations under uncertainty can also lead to structural breaks and crisis situations. The possibility of the latter, evidently, would simply contribute to the general reluctance of investors to commit themselves.

Keynes's proposals for the social control of investment

would do two things to remedy this perceived state of affairs. First, it would actually fill the gap left by reluctant private investors. Secondly, it would also encourage more private investment itself (crowding in rather than crowding out) by promoting a more stable environment and lowering uncertainty.

One point that is noteworthy in reviewing the literature discussing the longer-term consequences of investment spending, is that none of the writers concerned, whatever their other differences, have any difficulty in continuing to use the concept of 'effective demand', even though in discussing the accumulation of physical capital and so on, one might argue that 'supply side' elements must obviously be involved. The point seems to be that whether one looks at it from a long-run or short-run perspective the fundamental problem is a lack of *demand* for investment goods, which in turn stems ultimately from the producer's concern about a lack of future demand for consumption goods due to uncertainty. Increasing the current demand for investment goods is supposed to break this circle, and via the incomes created increase the future demand for consumption goods also. It might be argued, in fact, that the appropriate definition of a true supply-side theory would be one in which savings, in the classical fashion, always brings forward the correct amount of investment rather than vice versa. This is not true in Keynes either in the short run or the long run, investment always determines savings, not the other way round (Meade, 1975, p. 82).

OPEN ECONOMY CONSIDERATIONS

The major practical objection to Keynes's long-term policy proposals (as opposed to philosophical or political objections) involves the question of whether they would be a feasible option for an individual country which is part of an integrated international trading system. In other words, as Tarshis (1987) has recently put it, whether 'Keynesianism a Single Country' is possible. Tarshis's paper concentrates on the current-account consequences of a demand-based expansion, but in the present context there is a question of whether there might not also be serious capital-account consequences. As indicated above, Keynes predicted that the socialization of investment would quickly lead to (physical) capital saturation and a falling money or financial rate of interest as well as an increased supply of goods. The mechanism by which this is supposed to occur is not fully spelled out, but it must involve one variation or another on the theme of the 'Keynes effect' of falling goods prices on the real money stock. Whatever the mechanism, Keynes was confident (*CW*, vol. VII, p. 575) that 'the rate of interest is likely to fall steadily' and 'it would not be difficult to increase the stock of capital up to a point where its marginal efficiency had fallen to a very low figure'.

This is all very well in a closed economy context as in the *General Theory*, but there must be some doubt as to how far the euthanasia of the rentier could realistically be pushed in a small open economy with (financial) capital mobility. Meltzer (1981, pp. 62–3), for example, stresses this issue and is answered by Crotty (1983) who suggests that Keynes envisaged strict capital controls to deal with the situation. Crotty's argument implies a more far-reaching 'socialization' than was suggested above, but this is none the less a position which would be consistent with the general objective of bringing investment under state control.

An alternative way to escape from the dilemma is to take seriously Sir John Hicks's suggestion (1985, p. 22) that the *General Theory* was not intended to apply to a small closed economy but to the world economy as a whole, and what is envisaged is an expansion in a number of the most important countries in concert. In this regard Keynes's interest in the reform of the international monetary system, and in the setting up of the international monetary organizations after the Second World War, might be seen in the light of creating an environment in which such a co-ordinated expansion would be possible.

Finally, since in practice not all economies are the small open economy of the textbooks, the policy advice may be construed to apply to a major player, a country which is an 'interest rate maker' rather than an 'interest rate taker' on the world scene. Capital outflow from such a country might be sufficiently large to stimulate wide-scale investment spending overseas and ultimately bring down interest rates in other countries also. The policy advice, in other words, may be supposed to apply to a country which is strong enough to play the role of the engine of world economic growth. One thinks obviously of the Britain of the nineteenth century as a model for such a country, and the United States at various times in the twentieth century. On the other hand, the Treasury memoranda were addressed to plans for the post Second World War British economy, which was not going to be in anything like this situation.

THE HISTORICAL RECORD

Naturally enough there has been some interest recently in establishing empirical evidence about the extent to which Keynes's policy proposals were actually implemented in the years between the Second World War and the present. For example, Pressman (1987) investigates the situation in the United States and Kregel (1985) examines evidence from a number of industrialized countries including the USA, Japan, Austria, France, Germany, Italy, the Netherlands and the UK. Broadly speaking, their evidence shows that for several of these countries government investment spending as a percentage of GNP or GDP, and also relative to private investment spending, was at a peak during the early 1960s and has declined since. According to Kregel (1985, p. 42) 'even those countries that initially carried out Keynesian policies have not continued to do so'. In addition, particularly for more recent periods, there has been little evidence that state investment spending has been consciously employed as a stabilizing factor. One example given by Kregel is the decline in US government investment spending after the supply shocks of the 1970s (1985, p. 40). What is also interesting, in the light of our discussion of open economy issues, is that similar patterns occur in many of the countries at the same historical time period. This tends to validate the point that Keynes's policies are best pursued if the individual countries act in concert.

There would clearly be problems with attempts to quantify

precisely the *broader* concept of the socialization of investment as this was described above. It is easy enough in most jurisdictions to find evidence on government fixed capital formation and so on, and compare this to GNP or private investment spending. But the more far-reaching aspects of the programme, with government 'influence' being felt via Keynes's 'public or semi-public bodies' evidently does not readily lend itself to exact measurement. Even keeping to a narrower fiscal policy focus, we would presumably want a broader definition of state investment than simply fixed capital formation. For example, to include at least some part of non-capital expenditure on health and education as being investment, on the grounds that a healthier and better educated population would be more productive and that this expenditure can indeed 'pay for itself' in future tax collections. Even spending on items like defence and law and order spending might conceivably be justified on similar grounds.

In spite of the difficulties of quantification, however, and as suggested earlier, it is reasonable to argue that the world which emerged in the immediate postwar years did actually possess many of the aspects of Keynes's overall vision of the 'corporate state'. It is also fair to point out that the period in which these developments were taking place, say in the 25 years or so before 1973, are now looked back on in the favoured industrialized nations as a period of enviable growth and stability.

Of course, contrary to this apparent historical evidence, it is clear that in today's era of privatization the idea of the corporate state is unpopular politically (particularly in Britain); that today's governments have little intention of pursuing the macroeconomic policies that Keynes intended, and that contemporary electorates at least acquiesce. It is debatable, however, whether this change in attitude really reflects a conscious rejection of Keynes's long-term policy proposals (as these have been identified here), or rather disenchantment with the standard 'deficit-financing' interpretation of Keynesianism, combined with frustration at the perceived microeconomic inefficiencies of current examples of public enterprise. This is a fundamental issue of contemporary political economy which is worthy of further research.

We should be careful to note that the mere transfer of ownership from the state to private shareholders entailed in privatization does not in itself signify much about investment policy, particularly if the state enterprise was previously operating on a set of rules laid down by a government which was not committed to Keynesian principles in the first place. What is important is what happens after privatization. If, for example, the privatized company is a utility whose policies thereafter are influenced by the state via regulation the position is no different. Keynes's insistence that the socialization of investment was not state ownership seems important here.

This distinction seems to be significant also in interpreting the microeconomic dimension of the current political hostility to state enterprise. What seems to be genuinely unpopular is what J.K. Galbraith, in a telling phrase, called 'post office socialism', in other words the inefficiency and high cost of services in enterprises awarded a state monopoly. To this one might also add the apparent propensity of public funds to be spent or wasted in propping up the so-called 'lame ducks': industries which are in irreversible decline. But it is hard to read a defence of post office socialism into Keynes's version of the socialization of investment. There is no suggestion that standard criteria of economic efficiency in project choice are to be abandoned. What Keynes is actually saying is that numerous desirable projects were not undertaken in a pure *laissez-faire* system because of uncertainty. The objective is not to crowd out productive private projects with inefficient state projects,[15] but to ensure a larger aggregate volume of desirable projects. The basic assumption in today's drive for privatization is that private enterprise will inevitably be more efficient than state enterprise. There may be some justification for this in terms of actual examples of inefficiency of bureaucratic state enterprises in recent years, but Keynes's socialization of investment was clearly intended to be something different. In a renewed contemporary debate it should be possible to try to make this point clear, and hopefully also to focus attention on the direction and productivity of investment as well as sheer volume.[16]

The foregoing remarks are mainly concerned with Keynes's overall social vision, but similar sentiments would apply to the pure fiscal policy aspects also. Contemporary governments apparently have less and less intention of directly funding desirable investment projects via the capital budget, and when government expenditure has increased it has been in terms of what Keynes called the 'ordinary' budget. Yet the arguments both for and against the capital budgeting idea are very different from the usual discussion of Keynesian policy in terms of the ordinary budget, and a revitalized current debate would also be useful in making this distinction.

CONCLUSION

Nothing in the above discussion could reasonably be interpreted as providing direct support for the application of Keynes's policy proposals of the 1940s to the modern world 45 years later. This would require a concrete analysis of contemporary conditions in individual countries, which this paper does not pretend to provide.

What has been established, however, is that the distinction between government policies which encourage investment and those which encourage consumption is important both from a theoretical and a practical point of view; that Keynes was well aware of the distinction, and that, on the other hand, it has not played a major part in macroeconomic debates ever since.

Recently some economists[17] have noticed a revival of 'Keynesian' opinion, if not in government, at least among certain sections of the economics profession. But this can hardly be complete if the issue of the composition of government expenditures continues to be neglected.

NOTES

1. I should like to thank Lorie Tarshis for a very helpful discussion of some issues related to this topic; and Geoff Harcourt, Tony Lawson, John Pheby, Steve Pressman and other participants at the 1987 Malvern Conference for a stimulating debate on that occasion. The

author, however, must bear the final responsibility for the particular interpretation presented here.

2. The *General Theory*, though (according to Keynes himself), was not primarily concerned with policy issues (*CW*, vol. VII, p. vii), hence the Treasury memoranda, written post-*General Theory* and when Keynes was in a position of some official influence, take on a special significance. They presumably also supersede a number of policy proposals, seemingly more obviously 'Keynesian' in the usual sense, which were made in journalistic contributions in the depths of the Great Depression and pre-*General Theory* in the early 1930s. As an example of the latter, consider the following statement in an article for the American magazine *Redbook* (*CW*, vol. XXI, p. 337): 'I have been advocating government expenditure without much reference to the purpose to which the money is devoted. The predominant issue, as I look at the matter, is to get the money spent'. But even then Keynes immediately goes on to say, '[b]ut productive and socially useful expenditure is naturally to be preferred to unproductive expenditure'.

3. Eisner's work has been described by at least one reviewer (James Galbraith, 1986, p. 62) as providing 'material . . . for a full-fledged renaissance of Keynesian opinion'.

4. Kregel (1985, pp. 36–7) points out the congruence between the 'semi-autonomous bodies' mentioned in the 'End of Laissez-Faire' and the 'public or semi-public bodies' in the Treasury memoranda.

5. As noted by Pheby (1987). Pheby also identifies 'an embryonic form of Friedman's Permanent Income Hypothesis' (1987, p. 18) in remarks made by Keynes which cast doubt on the macroeconomic effectiveness of transitory tax cuts. This is equally remarkable in the light of the usual textbook treatment of the 'Keynesian consumption function'.

6. Keynes actually distinguished between four different types of capital budget, the Exchequer Capital Budget, the Public Capital Budget, the Investment Budget and the Remanet Budget (*CW*, vol. XXVII, pp. 405–6). The difference between the first two is that the Exchequer Budget only recognizes funds under the direct control of the Exchequer (Treasury), whereas the Public Capital Budget deals with total spending under public control (e.g., including local authorities). The Investment Budget would be a forecast of capital spending for the economy as a whole, including the private sector, and the Remanet Budget would simply be a transitional device in the immediate postwar period to take account of discrepancies arising from wartime spending. From the point of view of analyzing the effect of changes in the public finances on the economy, the Public Capital Budget would seem to be the most important of these concepts.

7. Cf. the explicit statement to this effect in Chapter 24 of the *General Theory* (*CW*, vol. VII, p. 378).

8. Skidelsky (1988) quotes from a letter that Keynes wrote to *The Times*

on 25 March 1925, and from a 'Reply to Shaw' in the *New Statesman* on 10 November 1934, which echo the themes in the 'End to Laissez-Faire'.

9. The reference (1985, p. 4) is to 'a position developed by John Eatwell and Murray Milgate, drawing on the work of Pierangelo Garegnani'. The volume edited by Eatwell and Milgate (1983) contains a number of the key contributions.

10. See the discussion in Smithin (1985, p. 222).

11. Bixley refers to the work of Klein (1947), Dillard (1948), Hansen (1953) and Kurihara (1956).

12. For example, in Lucas and Sargent's 'After Keynesian Macroeconomics' (1981).

13. For example, by simply pointing to the structure of the *General Theory* itself, which contains both a summary of the short period theory in Chapter 18, and a discussion of the longer-term consequences of investment spending in the 'Concluding Notes' in Chapter 24. Also relevant is the letter to Josiah Wedgwood of 7 July 1943 (*CW*, vol. XXVII, pp. 350-1).

14. More detailed references to the relevant literature can be found in recent papers by Hamouda and Smithin (1988a, 1988b).

15. Both Kregel (1985, p. 37) and Skidelsky (1988), quote Keynes's remarks about the distinction between services which are 'technically social' and 'technically individual' (from the 'End of Laissez-Faire') which seem to make this point.

16. Kilpatrick and Lawson (1980) point out that the productivity of state investment will also depend on the efficiency of the labour process, and argue for reforms of the latter in the case of contemporary Britain.

17. Cf. P. Howitt's recent Innis Lecture (1986).

Bibliography

Addison, J. T., J. Burton and T. S. Torrance (1984), 'Causation, social science and Sir John Hicks', *Oxford Economic Papers*, vol. 36, no. 1, pp. 1-11.

Adorno, T. W., *et al.* (1976), *The Positivist Dispute in German Sociology*, trans, G. Adey and D. Frisby, introd. D. Frisby (London: Heinemann; New York: Harper and Row).

Alchian, A. A. (1950) 'Uncertainty, evolution and economic theory', *Journal of Political Economy*, vol. 58, pp. 211-22.

Allaoua, H. A. (1986), 'Ricardo's Theory of Growth and Distribution: A Natural Equilibrium Interpretation', Cambridge University, Research Paper series, no. 33, mimeo.

Amedeo, E. J. and A. K. Dutt (1986), 'The Neo-Ricardian Keynesians and the Post-Keynesians', Rio de Janerio and Miami, mimeo.

Anderson, W. T., E. P. Cox and C. Berenson (1976), 'Bank selection decisions and market segmentation', *Journal of Marketing*, 40 (January) pp. 40-5.

Andrews, P. W. S. (1949), *Manufacturing Business* (London: Macmillan).

Ansoff, H. I., (1965), *Corporate Strategy* (London, Penguin).

Archer, S. H. and C. A. D'Ambrosio (1983), *The Theory of Business Finance: a Book of Readings*, 3rd edn (London: Macmillan 1983).

Arestis, P. and T. Skouras (1985), *Post-Keynesian Economic Theory* (Brighton: Wheatsheaf Books).

Arestis, P. (1987), 'Post-Keynesian Theory of Money, Credit and Finance', *Thames Papers in Political Economy*

(Spring).

Asimakopulos, A. (1969, 1970), 'A Robinsonian growth model in one-sector notation', *Australian Economic Papers*, vol. 8, pp. 41, 58; 'An amendment', vol. 9, pp. 171-6.

Asimakopulos, A. (1975), 'A Kaleckian theory of income distribution', *Canadian Journal of Economics*, vol. 8, pp. 313-33.

Asimakopulos, A. (1977), 'Profits and investment: a Kaleckian approach', in G. C. Harcourt (ed.), *The Microeconomic Foundations of Macroeconomics* (London: Macmillan), pp. 328-42.

Asimakopulos, A. (1980-1), 'Themes in a post-Keynesian theory of income distribution', *Journal of Post-Keynesian Economics*, vol. 3 (Winter) pp. 158-69.

Asimakopulos, A. (1982), 'Keynes' theory of effective demand revisited', *Australian Economic Papers*, vol. 21, pp. 18-36.

Asimakopulos, A. (1983), 'The Role of the Short Period', in Kregel (ed.) (1983a), pp. 28-34.

Azariadis, C. and Stiglitz, J. (1983), 'Implicit contracts and fixed price equilibria', *Quarterly Journal of Economics*, vol. 93, pp. 1-22.

Baird, C. W. (1987), '*The economics of time and ignorance:* a review', in *Review of Austrian Economics*, M. N. Rothbard (ed.) (Mass: Lexington Books), vol. 1, pp. 189-206.

Ball, R. J. (1964), *Inflation and the Theory of Money* (London: Allen and Unwin).

Baranzini, M. and R. Scazzieri (eds.) (1986), *Foundations of Economics* (Oxford: Basil Blackwell).

Barro, R. J. (1979), 'Second thoughts on Keynesian economics', *American Economic Review, Papers and Proceedings,* vol. 69, pp. 54-68.

Bateman, B. W. (1987), 'Keynes's changing conception of probability', *Economics and Philosophy*, vol. 3, no. 1, pp. 97-120.

Baumol, W. J.; J. C. Panzaar and R. D. Willig (1982), *Contestable Markets and the Theory of Industry Structure* (San Diego: Harcourt Brace Jovanovich).

230   Bibliography

Bell, D. and I. Kristol (eds) (1981), *The Crisis in Economic Theory* (New York: Basic Books).

Bhaduri, A. and J. Robinson (1980), 'Accumulation and exploitation: an analysis in the tradition of Marx, Sraffa and Kalecki', *Cambridge Journal of Economics,* vol. 4, no. 2 (June), pp. 103–15.

Bhaduri, A. (1986), *Macroeconomics: the Dynamics of Commodity Production* (London: Macmillan).

Bharadwaj, K. (1978a), *Classical Political Economy and the Rise to Dominance of Supply and Demand Theories* (Calcutta: Orient Longman).

Bharadwaj, K. (1978b), 'The subversion of classical analysis: Alfred Marshall's early writing on value', *Cambridge Journal of Economics,* vol. 2, pp. 253–71.

Bharadwaj, K. (1983), 'On effective demand: certain recent critiques', in J. A. Kregel (ed.) (1983a), pp. 3–27.

Bixley, B. (1988), 'Keynesian economics or plus ça change', in O. F. Hamouda and J. N. Smithin (eds), *Keynes and Public Policy After Fifty Years* (Upleadon: Edward Elgar).

Blatt, J. (1979) 'The utility of being hanged on the gallows', *Journal of Post-Keynesian Economics,* vol. 2 (Winter) pp. 231–9.

Blatt, J. (1983), *Dynamic Economic Systems: a Post-Keynesian Approach* (Armonk, New York, M. E. Sharpe).

Blinder, A. S. and R. M. Solow (1973), 'Does fiscal policy matter?', *Journal of Public Economics,* vol. 2, pp. 319–37.

Blinder, A. S. and R. M. Solow (1974), 'Analytical foundations of fiscal policy', in Blinder, A. S., *et al.*, *The Economics of Public Finance* (Washington, DC, Brookings Institution).

Blinder, A. S. and R. M. Solow (1976a) 'Does fiscal policy matter? A correction', *Journal of Public Economics,* vol. 15, pp. 183–4.

Blinder, A. S. and R. M. Solow (1976b), 'Does fiscal policy still matter? A reply', *Journal of Monetary Economics,* vol. 2, pp. 501–10.

Block, W. (1988), 'On Yeager's "Why subjectivism?" ', in *Review of Austrian Economics,* ed. M. N. Rothbard and W. Block, vol. 2, pp. 199–208.

Böhm, S. (1982), 'The ambiguous notion of subjectivism: comment on Lachmann', in Kirzner (ed.) (1982), pp. 41-52.

Boland, L. A. (1979), 'Knowledge and the role of institutions in economic theory', *Journal of Economic Issues*, vol. 13, no. 4 (December) pp. 957-72.

Boland, L. A. (1986), *Methodology for a New Microeconomics* (Boston, Mass.: Allen and Unwin).

Bootle, R. (1984), 'Origins of the monetarist fallacy: the legacy of gold', *Lloyds Bank Review*, no. 153 (July), pp. 16-37.

Bortis, H. (1986), *An Essay on Post-Keynesian Economics'* (Fribourg, Switzerland: mimeo).

Boulding, K. E. (1975), *Beyond Economics* (Michigan, University of Michigan Press).

Boulding, K. E. (1981), *Evolutionary Economics* (London: Sage Publications).

Broome, J. (1983), *The Microeconomics of Capitalism* (New York, Academic Press).

Brothwell, J. F. (1987), 'On the nature and use of the MPP concept in post-Keynesian economics', *Journal of Post-Keynesian Economics*, vol. 9 (Summer) pp. 496-502.

Brown-Collier, E. K. (1985), 'Keynes' view of an organic universe: the implications', *Review of Social Economy*, vol. 43, no. 1, pp. 14-23.

Bruner, J. (1986), *Actual Minds, Possible Worlds* (Boston, Mass.: Harvard University Press).

Caldwell, B. J. (1982), *Beyond Positivism: Economic Methodology in the Twentieth Century* (London: Allen & Unwin).

Carabelli, A. (1985), 'Keynes on cause, chance and possibility', in Lawson and Pesaran (eds) (1985), pp. 151-80.

Carew, E. (1985), *Fast Money 2. The Money Market in Australia* (Sydney: Allen and Unwin).

Carvalho, F. (1983-4) 'On the concept of time in Shacklean and Sraffian economics', *Journal of Post-Keynesian Economics*, vol. 6, no. 2 (Winter), pp. 265-80.

Carvalho, F. (1984-5) 'Alternative analyses of short and long run in post-Keynesian economics', *Journal of Post-Keynesian Economics*, vol. 7, no. 2 (Winter) pp. 214-34.

232   *Bibliography*

Chakravarty, S. (1986), 'Some remarks on "Production of Commodities by Means of Commodities' ", Cambridge University, mimeo.

Champernowne, D. G. (1963), 'Expectations and the links between the economic future and the present', in Lekachman (1964), pp. 174–202.

Chase, R. X. (1983), 'The development of contemporary mainstream macroeconomics: vision, ideology and theory', in Eichner (1983).

Chick, V. (1978), 'The Nature of the Keynesian revolution: a reassessment', *Australian Economic Papers*, vol. 17, pp. 1–20.

Chick, V. (1983), *Macroeconomics After Keynes: A Reconsideration of the General Theory* (Oxford: Philip Allen 1983).

Chick, V. (1986), 'The evolution of the banking system and the theory of savings, investment and finance', *Économies et sociétés*, vol. 20, Monnair et production 3.

Chick, V. (1987), 'Sources of finance, recent changes in bank behaviour and the theory of investment and interest', (London: University College) mimeo.

Clark, C. M. A. (1987–8), 'Equilibrium, market process, and historical time', *Journal of Post-Keynesian Economics*, vol. 10, no. 2, pp. 270–81.

Clark, L. H. (ed.) (1954), *Consumer Behavior,* vol. I: *The Dynamics of Consumer Reaction* (New York: New York University Press).

Clark, L. H. (ed.) (1955) *Consumer Behavior*, vol. II, *The Life Cycle of Consumer Behavior* (New York: New York University Press).

Clark, N. and C. Juma (1987), *Long Run Economics: An Evolutionary Approach to Economic Change* (London: Pinter).

Clower, R. W. (1967), 'A Reconsideration of the microfoundations of monetary theory', *Western Economic Journal*, vol. 6, pp. 1–9; reprinted in Clower (1969).

Clower, R. W. (ed.) (1969), *Monetary Theory* (Harmondsworth: Penguin).

Coddington, A. (1975), 'Creaking semaphore and beyond: a

consideration of Shackle's *Epistemics and Economics'*, *British Journal for the Philosophy of Science*, vol. 26, pp. 151–63.

Coddington, A. (1976), 'Keynesian economics: the search for first principles', *Journal of Economic Literature*, vol. 14, no. 4, pp. 1258–73.

Coddington, A. (1982), 'Deficient foresight: a troublesome theme in Keynesian economics', *American Economic Review*, vol. 72, no. 3, pp. 480–7.

Coddington, A. (1983), *Keynesian Economics: The Search for First Principles* (London: Allen and Unwin).

Cohen, A. J. and J. S. Cohen (1983), 'Classical and neoclassical theories of general equilibrium', *Australian Economic Papers*, vol. 22, pp. 180–200.

Colander, David A. (1987), *Selected Economic Writings of Abba P. Lerner* (New York: New York University Press).

Coombs, R., P. Saviotti and V. Walsh (1987), *Economics and Technological Change* (London: Macmillan).

Cornwall, J. (1972), *Growth and Stability in a Mature Economy* (London: Martin Robertson).

Cornwall, J. (1977), *Modern Capitalism: Its Growth and Transformation* (London: Martin Robertson).

Cornwall, J. (1983), *The Conditions for Economic Recovery: A Post-Keynesian Analysis* (Armonk, New York: M. E. Sharpe).

Cottrell, A. (1986), 'The endogeneity of money and money-income causality', *Scottish Journal of Political Economy*, vol. 33, pp. 2–27.

Coutts, K., W. A. H. Godley and W. Nordhaus (1978), *Industrial Pricing in the United Kingdom* (Cambridge: Cambridge University Press).

Cowling, K. (1981), 'Oligopoly, distribution and the rate of profit', *European Economic Review*, vol. 15, pp. 195–224.

Cowling, K. (1982), *Monopoly Capitalism* (London: Macmillan).

Crapp, H. and M. T. Skully (1985), *Credit Unions for Australians* (Sydney, Allen and Unwin).

Cripps, F. and W. A. H. Godley (1976), 'A formal analysis of the Cambridge Economic Policy Group model',

Economica, vol. 43, pp. 335–48.

Crotty, J. R. (1980), 'Post-Keynesian theory: an overview and evaluation', *American Economic Review*, vol. 70, pp. 20–25.

Crotty, J. R. (1983), 'On Keynes and Capital Flight', *Journal of Economic Literature*, vol. 21 (March), pp. 59–65.

Cyert, R. M. and J. O. March (1963), *A Behavioural Theory of the Firm* (Englewood Cliffs, NJ, Prentice Hall).

Darity, W. Jr. (1986), 'Did the commercial banks push loans on the LDCs?', in *World Debt Crisis: International Lending on Trial* M. P. Claudon (ed.), (Cambridge, Mass.: Ballinger).

Dasgupta, P. (1980), 'Decentralization and rights', *Economica*, vol. 47 (May) pp. 107–24.

Davidson, P. and E. Smolensky (1964), *Aggregate Supply and Demand Analysis* (New York: Harper and Row).

Davidson, P. (1965), 'Keynes' finance motive', *Oxford Economic Papers*, vol. 17, pp. 47–65.

Davidson, P. (1967), 'The importance of the demand for finance', *Oxford Economic Papers*, vol. 19, pp. 245–53.

Davidson, P. (1972, 1978), *Money and the Real World*, 2nd ed (London: Macmillan).

Davidson, P. and S. Weintraub (1973), 'Money as cause and effect', *Economic Journal*, vol. 83.

Davidson, P. (1980a), 'Post-Keynesian economics', *The Public Interest* (special issue).

Davidson, P. (1980b), 'The dual-faceted nature of the Keynesian revolution', *Journal of Post-Keynesian Economics*, vol. 2 (Spring), pp. 291–307.

Davidson, P. (1981), 'Post-Keynesian Economics', in D. Bell and I. Kristol (eds), *The Crisis in Economic Theory* (New York: Basic Books).

Davidson, P. and J. A. Kregel (1980), 'Keynes's paradigm: a theoretical framework for monetary analysis', in Nell (ed.) (1980) ch. 8.

Davidson, P. (1982), *International Money and the Real World* (London: Macmillan).

Davidson, P. (1988), 'Finance, funding, saving, and investment', *Journal of Post-Keynesian Economics*, vol. 9,

no. 4 (FAU) pp. 101–110.
Davies, G. and J. Davies (1984), 'The revolution in monopoly theory', *Lloyds Bank Review*, no. 153 (July) pp. 38–52.
Dillard, D. (1948), *The Economics of John Maynard Keynes* (Englewood Cliffs, NJ: Prentice-Hall).
Dillard, D. (1980), 'A monetary theory of production: Keynes and the institutionalists', *Journal of Economic Issues*, vol. 14, no. 2 (June) pp. 255–73.
Dixon, R. (1986), 'Uncertainty, unobstructedness and power', *Journal of Post-Keynesian Economics*, vol. 8, no. 4 (Summer) pp. 585–90.
Dobb, M. H. (1970), 'The Sraffa system and critique of the neo-classical theory of distribution'. *De economist*, no. 118, pp. 347–62.
Dobb, M. H. (1973), *Theories of Value and Distribution since Adam Smith* (Cambridge: Cambridge University Press).
Douglas, M. (ed.) (1973), *Rules and Meanings* (Harmondsworth: Penguin).
Dow, A. C. and S. C. Dow (1985), 'Animal spirits and rationality', in T. Lawson and H. Pesaran (eds) *Keynes' Economics* (London: Croom Helm).
Dow, S. C. (1985), *Macroeconomic Thought: A Methodological Approach* (Oxford: Basil Blackwell).
Dow, S. C. (1986), 'Speculation and the monetary circuit: with particular attention to the Euro-currency market', *economies et sociétés*, vol. 20, *Monnaie et production*, 3.
Dow, S. C. (1986–7), 'Post-Keynesian monetary theory for an open economy', *Journal of Post-Keynesian Economics*, vol. 9.
Dow, S. C. (1987), 'Beyond dualism', University of Stirling Discussion Papers in Economics, Finance and Investment, no. 137.
Dow, S. C. and P. E. Earl (1982), *Money Matters: A Keynesian Approach to Monetary Economics*, (Oxford, Martin Robertson).
Dow, A. C. and S. C. Dow (1987), 'Idle balances in Keynesian theory', University of Stirling Discussion Papers in Economics, Finance and Investment, no. 134.
Duesenberry, J. (1949), *Income, Saving and the Theory of*

Consumer Behaviour (Cambridge, Mass.: Harvard University Press).

Dumenil, G. and D. Levy (1987), 'The dynamics of competition: a restoration of the classical analysis', *Cambridge Journal of Economics*, vol. 11, no. 2 (June) pp. 133-64.

Dunlop, J. T. (1958), *Industrial Relations Systems* (New York: Holt, Rinehart & Winston).

Durbin, E. (1988), 'Keynes, the British Labour Party and the economics of democratic socialism', in O. F. Hamouda and J. N. Smithin (eds), *Keynes and Public Policy After Fifty Years* (Upleadon: Edward Elgar).

Dutt, A. K. (1986), 'On the classical dichotomy; the theory of prices with given output and distribution', Department of Economics, Florida International University, Discussion Paper no. 47.

Dyer, A. W. (1984), 'The habit of work: a theoretical exploration', *Journal of Economic Issues*, vol. 18, no. 2 (June) pp. 557-64.

Earl, P. E. (1983), *The Economic Imagination: Towards a Behavioural Analysis of Choice* (Brighton: Wheatsheaf).

Earl, P. E. and N. M. Kay (1985), How economists can accept Shackle's critique of economic doctrines without arguing themselves out of their jobs, *Journal of Economic Studies*, vol. 12, pp. 34-68.

Earl, P. E. (1986), *Lifestyle Economics: Consumer Behaviour in a Turbulent World* (Brighton: Wheatsheaf; New York: St Martin's Press).

Eatwell, J. (1979), *Theories of Value, Output and Employment*, Thames Papers in Political Economy (Summer); reprinted in Eatwell and Milgate (eds) (1983).

Eatwell, J. (1983), 'The long-period theory of employment', *Cambridge Journal of Economics*, vol. 7, pp. 269-85.

Eatwell, J. and M. Milgate, (eds) (1983), *Keynes's Economics and the Theory of Value and Distribution* (London: Duckworth).

Eichner, A. S. (1973), 'A theory of the determination of the mark-up under oligopoly', *Economic Journal*, vol. 83, pp. 1184-1200.

Eichner, A. S. and J. A. Kregel, (1975), 'An essay on post-Keynesian theory: a new paradigm in economics', *Journal of Economic Literature*, vol. 13, pp. 1293–1314.

Eichner, A. S. (1976), *The Megacorp and Oligopoly* (Cambridge: Cambridge University Press).

Eichner, A. S. (1979), 'A Post-Keynesian short-period model', *Journal of Post-Keynesian Economics*, vol. 1.

Eichner, A. S. (ed.) (1979), *A Guide to Post-Keynesian Economics* (White Plains: M. E. Sharpe).

Eichner, A. S. (ed.) (1983), *Why Economics is Not Yet a Science* (New York: M. E. Sharpe).

Eichner, A. S. (1985), *Towards a New Economics: Essays in Post-Keynesian and Institutionalist Theory* (Armonk, NY: M. E. Sharpe).

Eisner, R. (1986), *How Real is the Federal Deficit?* (New York: The Free Press).

Eldredge, N. (1985), *Time Frames: The Rethinking of Darwinian Evolution and the Theory of Punctuated Equilibria* (New York: Simon and Schuster).

Evans, D. (1975, 1976), 'Unequal exchange and economic policies: some implications of the neo-Ricardian critique of the theory of comparative advantage', *IDS Bulletin, no. 4*, pp. 28–52; reprinted (with revisions) in *Economic and Political Weekly*, vol. II, pp.143–58.

Evans, D. (1984), 'A critical assessment of neo-Marxian trade theories', *Journal of Development Studies*, special issue on Industrialisation (October).

Evans, D. (1986), *A Political Economy of Trade and Development*, vol. I, *Comparative Advantage and Growth* (Brighton: Wheatsheaf).

Feinstein, C. H. (ed.) (1967), *Socialism, Capitalism and Economic Growth,* (Cambridge: Cambridge University Press).

Ferber, R. (1955), 'Factors influencing durable goods purchases', in Clark (1955) pp. 75–112.

Foreman, L., M. Groves and A. S. Eichner (1984), 'The demand curve for money further considered', in M. Jarsulic (ed.), *Money and Macro Policy* (Boston, Mass.: Kluwer-Nijhoff).

Foster, J. (1987), *Evolutionary Macroeconomics* (London: Allen and Unwin).

Frey, B. S. (1986), 'Economists favour the price system – who else does?' *Kyklos*, vol. 39, fasc. 4, pp. 537–63.

Friedman, M. (1953), 'The methodology of positive economics', in his *Essays in Positive Economics* (Chicago: University of Chicago Press), pp. 3–43.

Friedman, M. (1968), 'The role of monetary policy', *American Economic Review*, vol. 58 (March) pp. 1–17.

Galbraith, C. and N. M. Kay (1986), 'Towards a theory of multinational enterprise', *Journal of Economic Behaviour and Organisation*, vol. 7, pp. 3–19.

Galbraith, James K. (1986), Review of *How Real is the Federal Deficit?* by R. Eisner, *Challenge*, vol. 29 (September–October) pp. 61–3.

Garegnani, P. (1959), 'A problem in the theory of distribution from Ricardo to Wicksell', unpublished PhD dissertation, University of Cambridge.

Garegnani, P. (1970), 'Heterogeneous capital, the production function and the theory of distribution', *Review of Economic Studies*, vol. 37, pp. 407–436.

Garegnani, P. (1976), 'On a change in the notion of equilibrium in recent work on value and distribution', in M. Brown, K. Sato and P. Zarembka (eds), *Essays in Modern Capital Theory* (Amsterdam: North Holland; reprinted in Eatwell and Milgate (eds) (1983).

Garegnani, P. (1978), 'Notes on consumption, investment and effective demand, Part I', *Cambridge Journal of Economics*, vol. 2, pp. 335–53; reprinted in Eatwell and Milgate (eds) (1983).

Garegnani, P. (1979a), 'Notes on consumption, investment and effective demand, Part II', *Cambridge Journal of Economics*, vol. 3, pp. 63–82; reprinted in Eatwell and Milgate (eds) (1983).

Garegnani, P. (1979b), 'Notes on consumption, investment and effective demand: a reply to Joan Robinson, *Cambridge Journal of Economics*, vol. 3, no. 2 (June) pp. 181–7; reprinted in Eatwell and Milgate (1983).

Garegnani, P. (1983a), 'The classical theory of wages and the role of demand schedules in the determination of relative prices', *American Economic Review* (Supplement), vol. 73, pp. 309–18.

Garegnani, P. (1983b), 'Two routes to effective demand', in Kregel (ed.) (1983a) pp. 69–80.

Garegnani, P. (1984), 'Value and distribution in the classical economists and Marx', *Oxford Economic Papers*, vol. 36, pp. 291–325.

Garegnani, P. (1985), Sraffa: classical versus marginalist analysis' (paper for conference on Sraffa's *Production of Commodities* after 25 years), University of Florence, mimeo.

Garegnani, P. (1986), 'Professor Hahn and the neoclassical Hoss-Shay', Cambridge University, mimeo.

Garner, C. A. (1982), 'Uncertainty, human judgement, and economic decisions', *Journal of Post-Keynesian Economics*, vol. 4, no. 3 (Spring) pp. 413–24.

Garrison, R. W. (1982), 'Austrian economics as the middle ground: comment on Loasby', in Kirzner (ed.) (1982) pp. 131–8.

Garrison, R. W. (1984), 'Time and money: the universals of macro-economic theorizing', *Journal of Macroeconomics*, vol. 6, no. 2, pp. 197–213.

Garrison, R. W. (1985), 'Intertemporal coordination and the invisible hand: an Austrian perspective on the Keynesian vision', *History of Political Economy*, vol. 17, no. 2, pp. 309–21.

Garrison, R. W. (1986), 'From Lachmann to Lucas: on institutions, expectations and equilibrating tendencies', in Kirzner (ed.) (1986) pp. 87–101.

Garrison, R. W. (1987a), 'Full employment and intertemporal coordination: a rejoinder', *History of Political Economy*, vol. 19, no. 2, pp. 335–41.

Garrison, R. W. (1987b), 'The kaleidic world of Ludwig Lachmann', *Critical Review*, vol. 1, no. 3, pp. 77–89.

Gedeon, S. J. (1985), 'A comment and extension of Lavoie's "The Endogenous Flow of Credit and the Post-Keynesian Theory of Money" ', *Journal of Economic Issues*, vol. 19, pp. 837–42.

240   Bibliography

Giddens, A. (1979), *Central Problems in Social Theory: Action, Structure and Contradiction in Social Analysis* (London: Macmillan).
Giddens, A. (1982), *Profiles and Critiques in Social Theory* (London, Macmillan).
Giddens, A. (1984), *The Constitution of Society: Outline of the Theory of Structuration* (Cambridge: Polity Press).
Godley, W. A. H. (1983), 'Keynes and the management of real national income and expenditure', in Worswick and Trevithick (1983), pp. 135-56.
Godley, W. A. H. and F. C. Cripps (1983), *Macroeconomics* (Oxford: Oxford University Press).
Godley, W. A. H. and W. D. Nordhaus (1972), 'Pricing in the trade cycle', *Economic Journal*, vol. 82, pp. 853-82.
Goodhart, C. A. E. (1984), *Monetary Theory and Practice: The UK Experience* (London: Macmillan).
Goodwin, R. M. (1967), 'A growth cycle', in Feinstein (ed.) (1967) and reprinted in Goodwin (1982).
Goodwin, R. M. (1982), *Essays in Economic Dynamics* (London: Macmillan).
Goodwin, R. M. (1983), *Essays in Linear Economic Structures* (London: Macmillan).
Goodwin, R. M. (1986), 'The M-K-S system: the functioning and evolution of capitalism', in H. J. Wagener and J. W. Drukker (eds), *The Economic Laws of Modern Society* (Cambridge: Cambridge University Press).
Goodwin, R. M. and L. F. Punzo (1987), *The Dynamics of a Capitalist Economy* (Oxford: Polity Press, Basil Blackwell).
Gram, H. and V. Walsh (1983), 'Joan Robinson's economics in retrospect', *Journal of Economic Literature*, vol. 21, pp. 518-50.
Gray, J. (1986), *Hayek on Liberty*, 2nd edn (Oxford: Basil Blackwell).
Groenewegen, P. D. (1986), 'In defence of post-Keynesian economics', (the 1986 Newcastle Lecture in Political Economy) (University of Newcastle, NSW).
Groenewegen, P. D. and J. Halevi, (eds) (1983), *Altro Polo: Italian Economics Past and Present* (Sydney: University of

Sydney).

Gruchy, A. G. (1948), 'The philosophical basis of the new Keynesian economics', *Ethics,* vol.58, no. 4 (July), pp. 235–44.

Gruchy, A. G. (1949), 'J. M. Keynes' concept of economic science', *Southern Economic Journal,* vol. 15, no. 3 (January), pp. 249–66.

Hahn, F. H. (1981) 'General equilibrium theory' in Bell and Kristol (1981) pp. 123–38.

Hahn, F. H. (1982), 'The neo-Ricardians', *Cambridge Journal of Economics,* vol. 6, pp. 353–74; reprinted in Frank Hahn (1984), *Equilibrium and Macroeconomics,* (Oxford: Basil Blackwell).

Hamouda, O. F. (1984), 'On the notion of short-run and long-run: Marshall, Ricardo and equilibrium theories', *British Review of Economic Issues,* vol. 6, (Spring), pp. 55–82.

Hamouda, O. F. (1988), 'Time, choice and dynamics', in S. F. Frowen and D. Reisman (eds) Essays in Honour of G. L. S. Shackle (London: Macmillan).

Hamouda, O. F. and G. C. Harcourt (1989), 'Post-Keynesianism: from criticism to coherence?' (chapter 1 in this volume).

Hamouda, O. F. and J. N. Smithin (1988a), 'Some remarks on uncertainty and economic analysis', *Economic Journal,* vol. 98 March, pp. 159–64.

Hamouda, O. F. and J. N. Smithin (1988b), 'Rational behaviour with deficient foresight', *Eastern Economic Journal,* vol. 14.

Hands, D. W. (1985), 'Karl Popper and economic methodology: a new look', *Economics and Philosophy,* vol. 1, no. 1, pp. 83–99.

Hansen, A.H. (1953), *A Guide to Keynes* (New York: McGraw Hill).

Harcourt, G. C. (1969), 'Some Cambridge controversies in the theory of capital', *Journal of Economic Literature,* vol. 7, pp. 369–405; reprinted in Harcourt (1986) pp. 145–206.

Harcourt, G. C. and N. F. Laing (eds) (1971), *Capital and Growth: Selected Readings* (Harmondsworth, Penguin).

Harcourt, G. C. (1972), *Some Cambridge Controversies in the*

Theory of Capital (Cambridge, Cambridge University Press).

Harcourt, G. C. and Peter Kenyon (1976), 'Pricing and the investment decision', *Kyklos*, vol. 29, fasc. 3, pp. 449-77; reprinted in Harcourt (1982b), pp. 104-26.

Harcourt, G. C. (1979), 'Review of Ian Steedman, *Marx after Sraffa*, 1977', *Journal of Economic Literature*, vol. 17, pp. 534-6.

Harcourt, G. C. (1980), 'Appraisal of post-Keynesian economics: discussion', *American Economic Review, Papers and Proceedings*, vol. 7, pp. 27-8.

Harcourt, G. C. (1981a), 'Marshall, Sraffa and Keynes: incompatible bedfellows?' *Eastern Economic Journal*, vol. 5, pp. 39-50; reprinted in Harcourt (1982b), pp. 205-21.

Harcourt, G. C. (1981b), 'Notes on an economic querist: G. L. S. Shackle', *Journal of Post-Keynesian Economics*, vol. 4, (Fall) pp. 136-44.

Harcourt, G. C. (1982a), The Sraffian contribution: an evaluation', in Ian Bradley and Michael Howard (eds), *Classical and Marxian Political Economy: Essays in Honour of Ronald L. Meek,* (London: Macmillan) pp. 255-75.

Harcourt, G. C. (1982b), *The Social Science Imperialists*, ed. Prue Kerr (London: Routledge and Kegan Paul).

Harcourt, G. C. (1982c), 'Post-Keynesianism: quite wrong and/or nothing new?' *Thames Papers in Political Economy* (Summer); reprinted in Arestis, P. and Skouras, T. (eds) (1985).

Harcourt, G. C. (1983), 'On Piero Sraffa's contributions to economic theory', in Groenewegen and Halevi (eds); reprinted in Harcourt (1986).

Harcourt, G. C. (1985a), 'On the influence of Piero Sraffa on the contributions of Joan Robinson to economic theory', *Economic Journal* (Conference Papers), vol. 96, pp. 96-108.

Harcourt, G. C. (ed.) (1985b), *Keynes and his Contemporaries. The Sixth and Centennial Keynes Seminar held at the University of Kent at Canterbury, 1983* (London: Macmillan).

Harcourt,G. C. and T. J. O'Shaughnessy (1985c), 'Keynes's unemployment equilibrium: some insights from Joan Robinson, Piero Sraffa and Richard Kahn', in Harcourt (ed.) (1985a) pp. 3–41.

Harcourt, G. C. (1986a), *Controversies in Political Economy*, ed. O. F. Hamouda (Brighton, Wheatsheaf Books).

Harcourt, G. C. (1986b), 'The legacy of Keynes: theoretical methods and unfinished business', Nobel Conference, St Peter, Minnesota.

Hargreaves Heap, S. P. (1986–7), 'Risk and culture: a missing link in the post-Keynesian tradition', *Journal of Post-Keynesian Economics*, vol. 9, no. 2 (Winter) pp. 267–78.

Harris, D.J. (1974), 'The price policy of firms, the level of employment and distribution of income in the short run', *Australian Economic Papers*, vol. 13, pp. 144–57.

Harris, D.J. (1975), 'The theory of economic growth: a critique and reformulation', *American Economic Review*, vol. 65, pp. 329–37.

Harris, D.J. (1978), *Capital Accumulation and Income Distribution* (Stanford, Stanford University Press).

Harris, D.J. (1982), 'Structural change and economic growth: a review article', *Contributions to Political Economy*, vol. 1, pp. 25–46.

Harrod, R.F. (1936), *The Trade Cycle: An Essay* (Oxford, Clarendon Press).

Harrod, R.F. (1939), 'An Essay in Dynamic Theory', *Economic Journal*, vol. 49, pp. 14–33.

Harrod, R.F. (1948), *Towards a Dynamic Economics* (New York: Macmillan).

Harrod, R.F. (1972 (1951)), *The Life of John Maynard Keynes* (Harmondsworth: Penguin).

Hart, A.G. (1945), ' "Model building" and fiscal policy', *American Economic Review*, vol. 35 (September) pp. 531–58.

Hart, A.G. (1947) 'Keynes' analysis of expectations and uncertainty', in S.E. Harris (ed.). (1947), *The New Economics: Keynes' Influence on Theory and Public Policy* (New York: Knopf).

Hayek, F.A. (1937), 'Economics and knowledge',

Economica, n.s., vol. 4 (February) pp. 33–54; reprinted in his *Individualism and Economic Order* (London: Routledge & Kegan Paul, 1949; Chicago: University of Chicago Press, 1948).

Hayek, F.A. (1948) *Individualism and Economic Order* (Chicago: University of Chicago Press).

Hayek, F.A. (1967), *Studies in Philosophy, Politics and Economics* (London: Routledge & Kegan Paul; Chicago: University of Chicago Press).

Hayek, F.A. (1973), *Law, Legislation and Liberty. A new statement of the liberal principles of justice and political economy*, vol. I: *Rules and Order* (London: Routledge & Kegan Paul; Chicago University of Chicago Press).

Hayek, F.A. (1979 (1952)), *The Counter-revolution of Science: Studies on the Abuse of Reason*, 2nd edn (Indianapolis: Liberty Press).

Hayek, F.A. (1982) *Law, Legislation and Liberty*, 3 vols combined edn (London: Routledge and Kegan Paul).

Hayek, F.A. (1984), 'The origins and effects of our morals: a problem for science', in C. Nishiyama and K.R. Leube (eds), *The Essence of Hayek* (Stanford: Hoover Institution Press) pp. 318–30.

Heiner, R.A. (1983), 'The origin of predictable behaviour', *American Economic Review*, vol. 73 (September) pp. 560–95.

Hempel, C.G. and P. Oppenheim (1948), 'Studies in the logic of explanation', *Philosophy of Science*, vol. 15, pp. 135–75.

Hicks, John (1976), *The Crisis in Keynesian Economics* (Oxford: Clarendon Press).

Hicks, John (1977), *Economic Perspectives: Further Essays on Money and Growth* (Oxford, Clarendon Press).

Hicks, J. (1978), 'Capital, expectations and the market process' (review note), *South African Journal of Economics*, vol. 46, no. 4, pp. 400–2.

Hicks, John (1979a), *Causality in Economics* (New York: Basic Books).

Hicks, J. (1979b), 'Is interest the price of a factor of production?', in Rizzo (ed.) (1979), pp. 51–63.

Hicks, J. (1985a) 'Keynes and the world economy', in F.

Vicarelli (ed.), *Keynes's Relevance Today* (London: Macmillan).

Hicks, John (1985b), *Methods of Dynamic Economics* (Oxford: Clarendon Press).

Hines, A.G. (1971), *On the Reappraisal of Keynesian Economics* (London: Martin Robertson).

Hodgson, G.M. (1981), 'Money and the Sraffa System', *Australian Economic Papers*, vol. 20 (June) pp. 83–95.

Hodgson, G.M. (1982) *Capitalism, Value and Exploitation* (Oxford: Martin Robertson).

Hodgson, G.M. (1985a) 'Persuasion, expectations and the limits to Keynes', in Lawson and Pesaran (1985) pp. 10–45.

Hodgson, G.M. (1985b) 'The rationalist conception of Action', *Journal of Economic Issues*, vol. 19, no. 4 (December) pp. 825–51.

Hodgson, G.M. (1986) 'Behind methodological individualism', *Cambridge Journal of Economics*, vol. 10, no. 3 (September) pp. 211–24.

Hodgson, G.M. (1988) *Economics and Institutions: A Manifesto for a Modern Institutional Economics* (Oxford: Polity Press).

Hodgson, G.M. (1989) 'Post-Keynesianism and Institutionalism: the missing link', Chapter 5 in this volume.

Hollis, M. and E.J. Nell (1975), *Rational Economic Man: A Philosophical Critique of Neo-Classical Economics* (Cambridge: Cambridge University Press).

Howitt, P. (1986), 'The Keynesian recovery', *Canadian Journal of Economics*, vol. 19 (November) pp. 626–41.

Jarsulic, M. (ed.) (1984), *Money and Macro Policy* (Boston, Mass.: Kluwer-Nijhoff).

Jarsulic, M. (1987), *Effective Demand and Income Distribution. A Critical Exposition of Post-Keynesian and Surplus Economics* (Oxford: Polity Press, Basil Blackwell).

Kahn, R.F. (1972), *Selected Essays on Employment and Growth* (Cambridge: Cambridge University Press).

Kahn, R.F. (1984), *The Making of Keynes' General Theory* (Cambridge: Cambridge University Press).

Kahneman, D., J. Knetsch and R. Thaler (1986), 'Fairness as a constraint on profit seeking: entitlements in the market', *American Economic Review*, vol. 76 no. 4 (September) pp. 728-41.

Kahneman, D., P. Slovic and A. Tversky (eds) (1982), *Judgement Under Uncertainty: Heuristics and Biases* (Cambridge: Cambridge University Press).

Kaish, S. (1986), 'Behavioral economics in the theory of the business cycle', in B. Gilad and S. Kaish (eds) (1986), *Handbook of Behavioral Economics*, volume B: *Behavioral Macroeconomics* (Greenwich, Conn.: JAI Press).

Kaldor, N. (1939), 'Speculation and Economic Stability', *Review of Economic Studies*, vol. 7, pp. 1-27.

Kaldor, N. (1956), 'Alternative theories of distribution', *Review of Economic Studies*, vol. 23, pp. 83-100.

Kaldor, N. (1957), 'A model of economic growth', *Economic Journal*, vol. 67, pp. 591-624.

Kaldor, N. (1959), 'Economic growth and the problem of inflation', Parts I and II, *Economica*, vol. 26, pp. 212-26; 287-98.

Kaldor, N. (1960), *Essays on Economic Stability and Growth* (London: Duckworth).

Kaldor, N. (1961a), 'Capital accumulation and economic growth', in F.A. Lutz and D.C. Hague (eds), *The Theory of Capital* (London: Macmillan).

Kaldor, N. (1961b), *Essays on Value and Distribution* (London: Duckworth).

Kaldor, N. (1966), 'Marginal productivity and the macro-economic theories of distribution', *Review of Economic Studies*, vol. 33, pp. 309-19.

Kaldor, N. (1970) 'The new monetarism', *Lloyds Bank Review*.

Kaldor, N. (1972), 'The irrelevance of equilibrium economics', *Economic Journal*, vol. 82, pp. 1237-55.

Kaldor, N. (1978), *Further Essays on Economic Theory* (London: Duckworth).

Kaldor, N. and J. Trevithick (1981a), 'A Keynesian perspective on money', *Lloyds Bank Review* no. 139 (January) pp. 1-19.

Kaldor, N. (1981b), *Origins of the New Monetarism* (Cardiff:

University College of Cardiff Press).

Kaldor, N. (1982) *The Scourge of Monetarism* (Oxford: Oxford University Press).

Kaldor, N. (1985), *Economics Without Equilibrium* (Armonk, NY: M.E. Sharpe).

Kalecki, M. (1938), 'The determinants of distribution of national income', *Econometrica*, vol. 6, pp. 67–112.

Kalecki, M. (1943), 'Political aspects of full employment', *Political Quarterly*, vol. 14, pp. 322–31.

Kalecki, M. (1954), *Theory of Economic Dynamics* (London: Allen & Unwin).

Kalecki, M. (1971), *Selected Essays on the Dynamics of the Capitalist Economy*, (1933–1970) (Cambridge: Cambridge University Press).

Karacaoglu, G. (1984), 'Absence of gross substitution in portfolios and demand for finance: some macroeconomic implications', *Journal of Post-Keynesian Economics*, vol. 6 (Summer) pp. 576–89.

Katona, G. and E. Mueller (1954), 'A study of purchase decisions', in Clark (1954).

Katona, G. (1975), *Psychological Economics* (New York: Elsevier).

Kay, N.M. (1979), *The Innovating Firm: A Behavioural Theory of Corporate R & D* (London: Macmillan).

Kay, N.M. (1982), *The Evolving Firm: Strategy and Structure in Industrial Organisation* (London: Macmillan).

Kay, N.M (1984), *The Emergent Firm: Knowledge, Ignorance and Surprise in Economic Organisation* (London: Macmillan).

Kay, N.M. and P. Clarke (1986), Boeing corporate strategy and technological change, *Heriot-Watt University Working Paper*.

Kay, N.M. (1987) 'Markets and false hierarchies: some problems in transaction cost economics', *European University Institute Working Paper* no. 87/282.

Kay, N.M. (1989), 'Post-Keynesian economics and new approaches to industrial economics', Chapter 9 in this volume.

Kenyon, Peter (1980), 'Appraisal of post-Keynesian

economics: discussion', *American Economic Review, Papers and Proceedings*, vol. 70, pp. 26–7.

Kern, S. (1983), *The Culture of Time and Space, 1880–1918* (London: Weidenfeld and Nicolson).

Keynes, J.M. (1936) *The General Theory of Employment, Interest and Money* (London: Macmillan).

Keynes, J.M. (1937) 'The General Theory of Employment', *Quarterly Journal of Economics*, vol. 51.

Keynes, J.M. (1971a) *A Treatise on Money: The Pure Theory of Money, Collected Writings*, vol. V (London: Macmillan, for the Royal Economic Society).

Keynes, J.M. (1971b) *A Treatise on Money: The Applied Theory of Money, Collected Writings*, vol. VI (London: Macmillan for the Royal Economic Society).

Keynes, J.M. (1973), *The General Theory and After. Part II: Defence and Development, Collected Writings*, vol. XIV (London: Macmillan for the Royal Economic Society).

Keynes, J.M. (1973(a) (1921), *A Treatise on Probability, Collected Writings*, vol. VIII, (London: Macmillan).

Keynes, J.M. (1973b), *Collected Writings*, vol. VII, *The General Theory of Employment, Interest and Money*, (London: Macmillan).

Keynes, J.M. (1972a), *Essays in Persuasion, Collected Writings*, vol. IX, (London: Macmillan).

Keynes, J.M. (1972b), *Collected Writings*, vol. X (London: Macmillan).

Keynes, J.M. (1982), *Collected Writings*, vol. XXI (London: Macmillan).

Keynes, J.M. (1979), *The General Theory and After: A Supplement, Collected Writings*, vol. XXIX (London: Macmillan).

Keynes, J.M. (1980) *Activities, 1940–46: Shaping the Post-War World: Employment, Collected Writings, vol. XXVII* (London: Macmillan).

Kilpatrick, A. and T. Lawson (1980) 'On the nature of industrial decline in the UK', *Cambridge Journal of Economics*, vol. 4 (March) pp. 85–102.

Kirzner, I.M. (1973), *Competition and Entrepreneurship* (Chicago: University of Chicago Press).

Kirzner, I.M. (1979), *Perception, Opportunity and Profit: Studies in the Theory of Entrepreneurship* (Chicago: University of Chicago Press).

Kirzner, I.M. (ed.) (1982), *Method, Process, and Austrian Economics: Essays in Honor of Ludwig von Mises* (Lexington, Mass.: D.C. Heath, Aldershot: Gower).

Kirzner, I.M. (1985a), *Discovery and the Capitalist Process* (Chicago: University of Chicago Press).

Kirzner, I.M. (1985b), 'Review of *The Economics of Time and Ignorance*', *Market Process*, vol. 3, no. 2.

Kirzner, I.M. (1986a), 'Ludwig von Mises and Friedrich von Hayek: the modern extension of Austrian subjectivism', in N. Leser (ed.), *Die Wiener Schule der Nationalökonomie* (Vienna: Böhlau), pp. 133–55.

Kirzner, I.M. (ed.) (1986b), *Subjectivism, Intelligibility and Economic Understanding: Essays in Honor of Ludwig M. Lachmann on his Eightieth Birthday* (London: Macmillan; New York: New York University Press).

Kirzner, I.M. (1987), 'Austrian School of Economics', in *The New Palgrave: A Dictionary of Economics*, ed. J. Eatwell, M. Milgate and P. Newman, vol. 1, pp. 145–51.

Klamer, Arjo (1984), *The New Classical Macroeconomics*, (Brighton: Wheatsheaf).

Klein, L.R. (1947), *The Keynesian Revolution* (New York: Macmillan).

Knight, F.H. (1947), *Freedom and Reform: Essays in Economic and Social Philosophy* (New York: Harper; reprinted 1982 with a foreword by J.M. Buchanan (Indianapolis).

Knight, F.H. and T.W. Merriam (1948), *The Economic Order and Religion* (London: Kegan Paul, Trench Trubner).

Kohn, M. (1986), 'Monetary analysis, the equilibrium method and Keynes's General Theory', *Journal of Political Economy*, vol. 94 (December) pp. 1191–224.

Kornai, J. (1982), *Growth, Shortage and Efficiency* (Oxford: Basil Blackwell).

Kregel, J.A. (1973), *The Reconstruction of Political Economy: An Introduction to Post-Keynesian Economics* (New York, Wiley, Halsted Press).

Kregel, J.A. (1976), 'Economic Methodology in the face of uncertainty', *Economic Journal*, vol. 86, pp. 209–25.

Kregel, J.A. (1980), 'Markets and institutions as features of a capitalistic production system', *Journal of Post-Keynesian Economics*, vol. 3, no. 1 (Fall), pp. 32–48.

Kregel, J.A. (1982), 'Money, expectations and relative prices in Keynes' monetary equilibrium', *Economie Appliquée*, vol. 35, no. 4, 449–65.

Kregel, J.A. (ed.) (1983a), *Distribution, Effective Demand and International Economic Relations* (London: Macmillan).

Kregel, J.A. (1983b), 'The microfoundations of the 'Generalisation of *The General Theory*' and 'Bastard Keynesianism': Keynes's theory of employment in the long and the short period', *Cambridge Journal of Economics*, vol. 7, pp. 343–61.

Kregel, J.A. (1983c), 'Effective demand: origins and development of the notion', in Kregel, J.A. (ed.) (1983a) pp. 50–68.

Kregel, J. A. (ed.) (1983d), *Distribution, Effective Demand and International Economic Relations* (London: Macmillan).

Kregel, J. A. (1984–5), 'Constraints on the expansion of output and employment: real or monetary?' *Journal of Post-Keynesian Economics*, vol. 7.

Kregel, J. A. (1985a), 'Hamlet without the prince: Cambridge macroeconomics without money', *American Economic Review (Papers and Proceedings)*, vol. 75, pp. 133–9.

Kregel, J. A. (1985b), 'Sidney Weintraub's macrofoundations of microeconomics and the theory of distribution', *Journal of Post-Keynesian Economics*, vol. 7 (Summer), pp. 540–58.

Kregel, J. A. (1985c), 'Budget deficits, stabilisation policy and liquidity preference: Keynes's post-war policy proposals', in F. Vicarelli (ed.), *Keynes's Relevance Today* (London: Macmillan) pp. 28–50.

Kregel, J. A. (1986a), 'A note on finance, liquidity, saving and investment', *Journal of Post-Keynesian Economics*, vol. 9.

Kregel, J. A. (1986b), 'Conceptions of equilibrium: the logic of choice and the logic of production', in Kirzner (ed.) (1986), pp. 157–70.

Kriesler, P. (1987a), *Keynes and Kalecki on Method* (University of Cambridge) mimeo.

Kriesler, P. (1987b), *Kalecki's Microanalysis: The Development of Kalecki's Analysis of Pricing and Distribution* (Cambridge, Cambridge University Press).

Kropotkin, P. (1902), *Mutual Aid: A Factor in Evolution* (New York: Doubleday).

Kurihara, K. K. (1956), *Introduction to Keynesian Dynamics* (London: George Allen & Unwin).

Kurz, H. D. (1985), 'Sraffa's contribution to the debate on capital theory', *Contributions to Political Economy*, vol. 4, pp. 3–24.

Lachmann, L. M. (1973), *Macro-economic Thinking and the Market Economy* (London: Institute of Economic Affairs).

Lachmann, L. M., (1976), 'From Mises to Shackle: an essay on Austrian economics and the kaleidic society', *Journal of Economic Literature*, vol. 14, no. 1, pp. 54–62.

Lachmann, L. M. (1978 (1956)), *Capital and Its Structure*, 2nd edn (Kansas City: Sheed Andrews & McMeel).

Lachmann, L. M. (1983), 'John Maynard Keynes: a view from an Austrian window', *South African Journal of Economics*, vol. 51, no. 3, pp. 368–79.

Lachmann, L. M. (1985), 'Review of *The Economics of Time and Ignorance*', *Market Process*, vol. 3, no. 2.

Lachmann, L. M. (1986a), *The Market as an Economic Process* (Oxford: Basil Blackwell).

Lachmann, L. M. (1986b), 'Austrian economics as a hermeneutic approach', unpublished manuscript.

Lancaster, K. J. (1966), 'A new approach to consumer theory', *Journal of Political Economy*, vol. 74 (April) pp. 132–57.

Lancaster, K. J. (1971), *Consumer Demand: A New Approach* (New York: Columbia University Press).

Langlois, R. N. (1985), 'Knowledge and rationality in the Austrian school: an analytical survey', *Eastern Economic Journal*, vol. 11, no. 4, pp. 309–30.

Langlois, R. N. (1986a), 'Rationality, institutions and

explanation', in Langlois (1986b, pp. 225–55).

Langlois, R. N. (ed.) (1986b), *Economics as a Process: Essays in the New Institutional Economics* (Cambridge: Cambridge University Press).

Latsis, S. J. (ed.) (1976), *Method and Appraisal in Economics* (Cambridge: Cambridge University Press).

Lavoie, M. (1984a), 'The endogenous flow of credit and the post-Keynesian theory of money', *Journal of Economic Issues*, vol. 18, pp. 771–98.

Lavoie, M. (1984b), 'Credit and money: the dynamic circuit, overdraft economics and post-Keynesian economics', in M. Jarsulic (ed.), *Money and Macro Policy* (Boston, Mass.: Kluwer-Nijhoff).

Lavoie, M. (1985), 'The post-Keynesian theory of endogenous money: a reply', *Journal of Economic Issues*, vol. 19, pp. 843–8.

Lawson, T. (1985a), 'Uncertainty and economic analysis', *Economic Journal*, vol. 95 (December) pp. 909–27.

Lawson, T. (1985b), 'Keynes, prediction and econometrics', in Lawson and Pesaran (eds) (1985c) pp. 116–33.

Lawson, T. and H. Pesaran (eds) (1985c), *Keynes' Economics. Methodological Issues* (London: Croom Helm).

Lawson, T. (1987), 'The relative/absolute nature of knowledge and economic analysis', *Economic Journal*, vol. 97 (December) pp. 951–70.

Leibenstein, H. (1976), *Beyond Economic Man: A New Foundation for Microeconomics* (Cambridge, Mass.: Harvard University Press).

Leibenstein, H. (1983), 'Property rights and X-efficiency: comment', *American Economic Review*, vol. 73, no. 4 (September) pp. 831–42.

Leijonhufvud, A. (1968), *On Keynesian Economics and the Economics of Keynes: A Study in Monetary Theory* (Oxford: Oxford University Press).

Lekachman, R. (1964), *Keynes' General Theory: Reports of Three Decades* (London: Macmillan).

Lerner, Abba P. and D. C. Colander (1979), 'MAP: a cure for inflation', in David C. Colander (ed.), *Solutions to*

Inflation (New York, Harcourt Brace Jovanovich); reprinted in Colander (ed.) (1987).

Levine, D. P. (1981), *Economic Theory*, vol.2: *The System of Economic Relations as a Whole* (London, Routledge and Kegan Paul).

Levine, D. P. (1986), 'Reconceptualizing Classical Economics', in P. Mirowski (ed.) (1986), pp. 13–40.

Lichtenstein, M. (1983), *An Introduction to Post-Keynesian and Marxian Theories of Value and Price* (Armonk, N.Y., M. E. Sharpe).

Littlechild, S. C. (1979), 'Comment: radical subjectivism or radical subversion?', in Rizzo (ed.) (1979) pp. 32–49.

Loasby, B. J. (1976), *Choice, Complexity and Ignorance: An Enquiry into Economic Theory and the Practice of Decision-making* (Cambridge: Cambridge University Press).

Lucas, R. E. Jr, and T. J. Sargent (1981), 'After Keynesian macroeconomics', in R. E. Lucas and T. J. Sargent (eds), *Rational Expectations and Econometric Practice* (London: George Allen & Unwin) pp. 295–319.

Lutz, F. A. and D. C. Hague (eds) (1961), *The Theory of Capital* (London: Macmillan).

Machlup, F. (1982), 'Austrian economics', in *Encyclopedia of Economics*, ed. D. Greenwald (NewYork: McGraw-Hill), pp. 38–43.

Magnani, M. (1983), ' "Keynesian Fundamentalism": a critique', in J. Eatwell and M. Milgate (eds), *Keynes's Economics and the Theory of Value and Distribution* (London: Duckworth) pp. 247–59.

Mainwaring, L. (1979), 'Monopoly power, income distribution and price determination', *Kyklos*, vol. 30, pp. 674–90.

Mainwaring, L. (1984), *Value and Distribution in Capitalist Economies: An Introduction to Sraffian Economics* (Cambridge: Cambridge University Press).

Maital, S. (1982), *Minds, Markets and Money* (New York: Basic Books).

Marglin, S. A. (1984a), 'Growth, distribution and inflation: a centennial synthesis', *Cambridge Journal of Economics*,

254 *Bibliography*

vol. 8, pp. 115–44.

Marglin, S. A. (1984b), *Growth, Distribution and Prices* (Cambridge, Mass.: Harvard University Press).

Marsden, D. (1986), *The End of Economic Man? Custom and Competition in Labour Markets* (Brighton: Wheatsheaf Books).

Marshall, A. (1920/1959), *Principles of Economics* (London: Macmillan).

Marx, K. (1973), *Grundrisse: Foundations of the Critique of Political Economy* , trans M. Nicolaus (Harmondsworth: Pelican).

Meade, J. (1975), 'The Keynesian Revolution', in M. Keynes (ed.), *Essays on John Maynard Keynes* (Cambridge: Cambridge University Press) pp. 82–8.

Medio, A. (1978), 'A mathematical note on equilibrium in value and distribution, *Economic Notes*, vol. 7.

Meek, R. L. (1961), 'Mr Sraffa's rehabilitation of classical economics', in R. L. Meek (1967), *Economics and Ideology and Other Essays: Studies in the Development of Economic Thought* (London, Chapman and Hall).

Meek, R. L. (1973), *Studies in the Labour Theory of Value*, 2nd edn (London: Lawrence and Wishart).

Meek, R. L. (1977), *Smith, Marx and After* (London: Chapman and Hall).

Meltzer, A. H. (1981), 'Keynes's General Theory: a different perspective', *Journal of Economic Literature*, vol. 19 (March) pp. 34–64.

Meltzer, A. H. (1983), 'Interpreting Keynes', *Journal of Economic Literature*, vol. 21 (March) pp. 66–78.

Metcalfe, S. (1987), 'The diffusion of innovation: an interpretive survey', paper prepared for IFIAS conference, University of Maastrict (May).

Mill, J. (1821), *Elements of Political Economy* (London; Reprinted 1965 (New York: Augustus Kelley).

Minsky, H. P. (1974), 'The modelling of financial instability: an introduction', in W. G. Vogt and M. H. Mickle (eds), *Modelling and Simulation*, vol. 5, Proceedings of the Fifth Annual Pittsburgh Conference (School of Engineering, University of Pittsburgh).

Minsky, H. P. (1975), *John Maynard Keynes* (New York: Columbia University Press).

Minsky, H. P. (1977), 'A theory of systemic fragility', in E. Altman and A. N. Sametz, (eds), *Financial Crises* (New York: Wiley Interscience).

Minsky, H. P. (1978), 'The financial instability hypothesis: a restatement', in *Thames Papers in Political Economy* (Autumn); reprinted in Arestis and Skouras (eds) (1985).

Minsky, H. P. (1982a), 'Can it happen again? A reprise', *Challenge*, vol. 25, pp. 5–13.

Minsky, H. P. (1982b), *Can 'it' Happen Again?* (Armonk, N.Y.: M. E. Sharpe).

Minsky, H. P. (1982c), *Inflation, Recession and Economic Policy* (Brighton: Wheatsheaf).

Minsky, H. P. (1986), *Stabilizing an Unstable Economy* (New Haven, Conn.: Yale University Press).

Mirowski, P. (ed.) (1986), *The Reconstruction of Economic Theory*, (Boston, Dordrecht, Lancaster: Kluwer-Nijhoff).

Mises, L. v. (1949/1966), *Human Action: A Treatise on Economics*, 3rd rev. edn (Chicago: Henry Regnery).

Modigliani, F. and M. H. Miller (1958), 'The cost of capital corporation finance, and the theory of investment', *American Economic Review*, vol. 48.

Moggridge, D. E. (1976), *Keynes* (London: Macmillan).

Moore, B. J. (1979), 'The endogenous money stock', *Journal of Post-Keynesian Economics,* vol. 2, (Fall) pp. 49–70.

Moore, B. J. (1983), 'Unpacking the Post-Keynesian black box: bank lending and the money supply', *Journal of Post-Keynesian Economics,* vol. 5 (Summer) pp. 537–56.

Moore, B. J. (1984), 'Wages, bank lending, and the endogeneity of credit money', in M. Jarsulic (ed.), *Money and Macro Policy* (Boston, Mass.: Kluwer-Nijhoff).

Myrdal, G. (1958), *Value in Social Theory* (New York: Harper).

Neild, R. R. (1963), 'Pricing and employment in the trade cycle', *NIES Occasional Paper*, no. 21 (Cambridge: Cambridge University Press).

Nell, E. J. (1967), 'Theories of growth and theories of value', *Economic Development and Cultural Change,* vol. 16, pp.

15–26; reprinted in Harcourt and Laing (eds) (1971) pp. 196–210.

Nell, E. J. (ed.) (1980) *Growth, Profits and Property* (New York: Cambridge University Press).

Nell, E. J. (1983), 'Keynes after Sraffa. The essential properties of Keynes's theory of interest and money: comment on Kregel', in Kregel (ed.) (1983).

Nelson, R. R. and S. G. Winter (1982), *An Evolutionary Theory of Economic Change* (Cambridge, Mass.: Harvard University Press).

Newman, G. (1976), 'An institutional perspective on information', *International Social Science Journal*, vol. 28, pp. 466–92.

Newman, J. W. and R. Staelin (1972), 'Prepurchase information seeking for new cars and major household appliances', *Journal of Marketing Research*, vol. 9, pp. 249–57.

Nisbett, R. E. and L. Ross (1980), *Human Inference: Strategies and Shortcomings of Social Judgement* (Englewood Cliffs, N.J.: Prentice-Hall).

Oakeshott, M. (1962), *Rationalism in Politics and Other Essays* (London: Methuen).

O'Driscoll, G. P. and M. Rizzo (1985), *The Economics of Time and Ignorance* (Oxford: Basil Blackwell).

Olshansky, R. W. and D. H. Granbois (1979), 'Consumer decision making: fact or fiction?', *Journal of Consumer Research*, vol. 6 (September) pp. 93–100.

O'Sullivan, P. J. (1987), *Economic Methodology and Freedom to Choose* (London: Allen & Unwin).

Panico, C. (1980), 'Marx's analysis of the relationship between the rate of interest and the rate of profits', *Cambridge Journal of Economics*, vol. 4, no. 4 (December) pp. 363–78; reprinted in Eatwell and Milgate (1983).

Parrinello, S. (1980), 'The price level implicit in Keynes' effective demand', *Journal of Post-Keynesian Economics*, vol. 3, (Fall) pp. 63–78.

Pasinetti, L. L. (1962), 'Rate of profit and income distribution in relation to the rate of economic growth', *Review of Economic Studies*, vol. 29, pp. 267–79; reprinted in

Pasinetti (1974).

Pasinetti, L. L. (1966), 'New results in an old framework: comment on Samuelson and Modigliani', *Review of Economic Studies*, vol. 33, pp. 303-6; reprinted in Pasinetti (1974).

Pasinetti, L. L. (1974), *Growth and Income Distribution: Essays in Economic Theory* (Cambridge: Cambridge University Press).

Pasinetti, L. L. (ed.) (1980), *Essays on the Theory of Joint Production* (London: Macmillan).

Pasinetti, L. L. (1981), *Structural Change and Economic Growth, A Theoretical Essay on the Dynamics of the Wealth of Nations* (Cambridge: Cambridge University Press).

Pasinetti, L. L. (1986), 'Theory of value – a source of alternative paradigms in economic analysis', in M. Baranzini and R. Scazzieri (eds) (1986), pp. 409-31.

Patinkin, D. (1982), *Anticipations of the General Theory? and Other Essays on Keynes* (Chicago: University of Chicago Press).

Penrose, E. T. (1959), *The Theory of the Growth of the Firm* (Oxford: Blackwell).

Peterson, W. C. (1977), 'Institutionalism, Keynes and the real world', *Journal of Economic Issues*, vol. 11, no. 2 (June) pp. 201-21.

Pheby, J. (1985), 'Are Popperian criticisms of Keynes justified?', in Lawson and Pesaran (eds) (1985) pp. 99-115.

Pheby, J. (1987), 'A new perspective on Shackle's Keynesian fundamentalism', *Journal of Economic Studies*, vol. 14, no. 4. pp. 24-35.

Popper, K. R. (1976), 'The logic of the social sciences', in Adorno *et al.* (1976) pp. 87-104.

Prendergast, C. (1986), 'Alfred Schutz and the Austrian school of economics', *American Journal of Sociology*, vol. 92, no. 1, pp. 1-26.

Pressman, S. (1987), The policy relevance of the General Theory' *Journal of Economic Studies*, vol. 14, no. 4, pp. 13-23.

Radcliffe Report (1959), *The Committee on the Working of the*

Monetary System, Report, Cmnd. 827 (London: HMSO).

Richardson, G. B. (1959), 'Equilibrium, expectations and information', *Economic Journal*, vol. 69, pp. 223–37.

Richardson, G. B. (1960), *Information and Investment* (Oxford: Oxford University Press).

Rizzo, M. J. (ed.) (1979) *Time, Uncertainty, and Disequilibrium: Exploration of Austrian Themes* (Lexington, Mass.: D.C. Heath).

Robinson, Joan (1959–79), *Collected Economic Papers*, 5 vols. (Oxford: Basil Blackwell).

Robinson, Joan (1960), *Exercises in Economic Analysis* (London: Macmillan).

Robinson, Joan (1962a), 'Review of H. G. Johnson, *Money, Trade and Economic Growth 1962*', *Economic Journal*, vol. 72, pp. 690–2.

Robinson, Joan (1962b), *Essays in the Theory of Economic Growth* (London: Macmillan).

Robinson, Joan (1971), *Economic Heresies* (London: Macmillan).

Robinson, Joan (1973), 'Ideology and analysis', in *Sozialismus Geschichte und Wirtschaft. Festschrift für Eduard Marz* (Vienna: Europaverlags); reprinted in Robinson (1979a).

Robinson, Joan (1974), *History versus Equilibrium* (London: Thames Papers in Political Economy).

Robinson, Joan (1975), foreword to J. A. Kregel, *The Reconstruction of Political Economy* 2nd edn (London: Macmillan) pp. ix–xiii.

Robinson, Joan (1978), *The Generalisation of the General Theory and Other Essays* (London: Macmillan).

Robinson, Jean (1979a), *Collected Economic Papers,* vol. 5 (Oxford: Basil Blackwell).

Robinson, Joan (1979b), 'Garegnani on effective demand', *Cambridge Journal of Economics*, vol. 3, no. 2 (June) pp. 179–80; reprinted in Eatwell and Milgate (1983).

Robinson, Joan (1980), *Further Contributions to Modern Economics*,Oxford, Basil Blackwell.

Roncaglia, A. (1978), *Sraffa and the Theory of Prices* (Chichester: Wiley).

Rotheim, R. J. (1981), 'Keynes' monetary theory of value (1933)', *Journal of Post-Keynesian Economics*, vol. 3.

Rousseas, S. (1985), 'Financial innovation and control of the money supply: the Radcliffe Report revisited' in M. Jarsulic (ed.), *Money and Macro Policy* (Boston: Kluwer-Nijhoff).

Rousseas, S. (1986), *Post-Keynesian Monetary Theory* (London: Macmillan).

Rowthorn, R. (1974), 'Neo-Classicism, neo-Ricardianism, and Marxism', *New Left Review*, no. 86; reprinted in R. Rowthorn (1980), *Capitalism, Conflict and Inflation* (London: Lawrence and Wishart).

Rowthorn, R. (1981), 'Demand, real wages and economic growth', *Thames papers in Political Economy* (Autumn).

Rutherford, M. (1984), 'Rational expectations and Keynesian uncertainty: a critique', *Journal of Post-Keynesian Economics*, vol. 6, no. 3, pp. 377–87.

Rymes, T. K. (1987), 'Review of *The Economics of Time and Ignorance*' *Canadian Journal of Economics*, vol. 20 (February) pp. 190–2.

Salter, W. E. G. (1960, 1966), *Productivity and Technical Change* (Cambridge: Cambridge University Press; 2nd edn with addendum by W. B. Reddaway, 1966).

Samuels, W. J. (1986), 'What aspects of Keynes's economic theories merit continued or renewed interest? One interpretation", *Journal of Post-Keynesian Economics*, vol. 9, pp. 3–16.

Samuelson, P. A. (1946), 'The General Theory', *Econometrica* vol. 14 (July).

Samuelson, P. A. 1966(a), 'Rejoinder, agreements, disagreements, doubts and the case of the induced Harrod-neutral technical change', *Review of Economics and Statistics*, vol. 48, pp. 444–8.

Samuelson, P. A. 1966(b), 'A Summing up', *Quarterly Journal of Economics*, vol. 80, pp. 568–83.

Sardoni, C. (1984), 'Some ties of Kalecki to the 1926 "Sraffian Manifesto" '. *Journal of Post-Keynesian Economics* (Spring), vol. 6, pp. 458–65.

Sardoni, C. (1986), 'Marx and Keynes on effective demand and unemployment', *History of Political Economy*, vol. 18, pp. 419–41.

Sardoni, C. (1987), *Marx and Keynes on Economic Depression* (Brighton: Wheatsheaf).

Sargan, N. (1977), 'Economic indicators and country risk appraisal', *Federal Reserve Bank of San Francisco Economic Review*.

Sawyer,M. C. (1982), *Macro-Economics in Question: The Keynesian-Monetarist Orthodoxies and the Kaleckian Alternative* (Brighton: Wheatsheaf).

Sawyer, M. C. (1985), *The Economics of Michal Kalecki* (London: Macmillan).

Schefold, B. (1971), *Mr Sraffa on Joint Production*, Ph.D. dissertation, University of Basle.

Schefold, B. (1976), 'Different forms of technical progress', *Economic Journal*, vol. 86, pp. 806–19.

Schefold, B. (1985), 'Cambridge price theory: special model or general theory of value?', *American Economic Review*, vol. 75, pp. 140–5.

Schotter, A. (1981), *The Economic Theory of Social Institutions* (Cambridge: Cambridge University Press).

Schumpeter, J. A. (1942), *Capitalism, Socialism and Democracy* (New York: Harper & Row).

Schumpeter, J. A. (1974), *History of Economic Analysis* (London: Allen & Unwin).

Schutz, A. (1953), 'Common-sense and scientific interpretation of human action', *Philosophy and Phenomenological Research*, vol. 14, no. 1, pp. 1–38.

Schutz, A. (1954), 'Concept and theory formation in the social sciences', *Journal of Philosophy*, vol. 51, no. 9, pp. 257–73; page reference refers to reprint in *Collected Papers*, vol. I: *The Problem of Social Reality*, ed. M. Natanson (The Hague: Nijhoff), pp. 48–66.

Selgin, G. A. (1988), 'Praxeology and understanding: an analysis of the controversy in Austrian economics', in M. N. Rothbard and W. Block (eds), *Review of Austrian Economics* (Mass.: Lexington Books), vol. 2, pp. 19–58.

Semmler, W. (1984), 'On the classical theory of competition, value and prices of production', *Australian Economic Papers*, vol. 23, pp. 130–50.

Shackle, G. L. S. (1955), *Uncertainty in Economics* (Cambridge: Cambridge University Press).

Shackle, G. L. S. (1969), *Decision, Order and Time*, 2nd edn (Cambridge: Cambridge University Press).

Shackle, G. L. S. (1972), *Epistemics and Economics* (Cambridge: Cambridge University Press).

Shackle, G. L. S. (1973), 'Keynes and today's establishment in economic theory', *Journal of Economic Literature*, vol. 11 (June) pp. 516–19.

Shackle, G. L. S. (1974) *Keynesian Kaleidics* (Edinburgh: Edinburgh University Press).

Shackle, G. L. S. (1976), 'Time and choice' (Keynes Lecture in Economics), *Proceedings of the British Academy*, vol. 62, pp. 309–29.

Shackle, G. L. S. (1979), *Imagination and the Nature of Choice* (Edinburgh: Edinburgh University Press).

Shackle, G. L. S. (1981), 'F. A. Hayek', in D. P. O'Brien and J. R. Presley (eds), *Pioneers of Modern Economics in Britain* (London: Macmillan), pp. 234–60.

Shackle, G. L. S. (1983–4), 'The romantic mountain and the classic lake: Alan Coddington's *Keynesian Economics*', *Journal of Post Keynesian Economics*, vol. 6, no. 3, pp. 241–51.

Shackle, G. L. S. (1989), 'What did the *General Theory* do?', ch. 3 of present volume.

Shackleton, J. R. and G. Locksley (eds) (1981), *Twelve Contemporary Economists* (London: Macmillan).

Shapiro, N. (1977), 'The revolutionary character of post-Keynesian economics', *Journal of Economic Issues*, vol. 11, pp. 541–60.

Simon, H. A. (1957), *Models of Man: Social and Rational* (New York: Wiley).

Simon, H. A. (1959), 'Theories of decision-making in economic and behavioral sciences', *American Economic Review*, vol. 49 (June) pp. 253–83.

Simon, H. A. (1968), *The Sciences of the Artificial* (Cambridge, Mass.: MIT Press).

Simon, H. A. (1976), 'From substantive to procedural rationality', in S. Latsis (1976), pp. 129–48.

Simon, H. A. (1983), *Reason in Human Affairs* (Oxford: Basil Blackwell).

Simon, H. A. (1984), 'On the behavioural and rational foundations of economic dynamics', *Journal of Economic Behaviour and Organisation*, vol. 5, pp. 35–55.

Skidelsky, R. (1988), 'Keynes's political legacy', in O. F. Hamouda and J. N. Smithin (eds), *Keynes and Public Policy After Fifty Years* (Upleadon: Edward Elgar).

Skouras, T. (1981) 'The economics of Joan Robinson', in Shackleton and Locksley (1981), pp. 199–218.

Smithin, J. N. (1985), 'On the definition of involuntary unemployment in Keynes's General Theory: a note', *History of Political Economy*, vol. 17 (Summer) pp. 219–22.

Snippe, J. (1985), 'On the scope of hydraulic macroeconomics: some reflections on Alan Coddington's *Keynesian Economics*', *De Economist*, vol. 133, no. 4, pp. 467–83.

Snippe, J. (1987a), 'Intertemporal coordination and the economics of Keynes: comment on Garrison', *History of Political Economy*, vol. 19, no. 2, pp. 329–34.

Snippe, J. (1987b), 'Momentary equilibrium versus the Wicksell connection', *Banca Nazionale del Lavoro Quarterly Review*, no. 161 (June) pp. 197–212.

Solow, R. M. (1984), 'Robert M. Solow', in Klamer (1984) pp. 137–8.

Sraffa, Piero (1925), 'Sulle relazione fra costo e quantita prodotta,' *Annali i Economica*, vol. III, no. 1, pp. 277–328.

Sraffa, Piero (1926), 'The laws of returns under competitive conditions', *Economic Journal*, vol. 36, pp. 535–50.

Sraffa, Piero (1930), 'A criticism and 'A rejoinder', *Economic Journal*, vol. 60, pp. 89–92 and 93.

Sraffa, Piero (1960), *Production of Commodities by Means of Commodities. Prelude to a Critique of Economic Theory* (Cambridge, Cambridge University Press).

Sraffa, Piero (1961), 'Comment', in Lutz and Hague (eds) (1961), pp. 305–6.

Sraffa, Piero (1962), 'Production of commodities: a comment', *Economic Journal*, vol. 72, pp. 477–9.

Sraffa, Piero, Maurice Dobb (eds) (1951–5, 1973), *Works and Correspondence of David Ricardo*, 11 vols (Cambridge, Cambridge University Press).

Steedman, I. (1977), *Marx after Sraffa* (London: New Left Books).

Steedman, I. (ed.) (1979), *Fundamental Issues in Trade Theory* (London: Macmillan).

Steedman, I. (1984), 'Natural prices, differential profit rates and the classical competitive process', *The Manchester School of Economic and Social Studies*, vol. 52, pp. 123–40.

Stein, J. L. (1982), *Monetarist, Keynesian and New Classical Economics* (Oxford: Basil Blackwell).

Steindl, J. (1952), *Maturity and Stagnation in American Capitalism* (Oxford: Basil Blackwell).

Steindl, J. (1981), 'Ideas and concepts of long run growth', *BNL Quarterly Review*, vol. 136, 35–48.

Strange, S. (1986), *Casino Capitalism* (Oxford: Basil Blackwell).

Sylos-Labini, P. (1962), *Oligopoly and Technical Progress*, (Cambridge, Mass.: Harvard University Press).

Sylos-Labini, P. (1974), *Trade Unions, Inflation and Productivity* (Lexington, Mass.: Lexington Books).

Sylos-Labini, P. (1979), 'Prices and income distribution in manufacturing industry', *Journal of Post-Keynesian Economics*, vol. 11 (Fall) pp. 3–25.

Sylos-Labini, P. (1984), *The Forces of Economic Growth and Decline* (Cambridge, Mass.: MIT Press).

Targetti, F. and B. Kinda-Hass (1982), 'Kalecki's review of Keynes' *General Theory*', *Australian Economic Papers*, vol. 21, pp. 244–60.

Tarshis, L. (1939), 'The determination of labour income', unpublished Ph.D. dissertation, Cambridge University.

Tarshis, L. (1947), *The Elements of Economics: An Introduction to the Theory of Price and Employment* (Boston, Mass.: Houghton Mifflin).

Tarshis, L. (1948), 'An Exposition of Keynesian Economics', *American Economic Review*, vol. 38, pp. 261–91.

Tarshis, L. (1979a), 'The aggregate supply function in Keynes's *General Theory*' in Michael J. Boskin (ed.),

Economics and Human Welfare: Essays in Honour of Tibor Scitovsky (New York, Academic Press) pp. 361-92.

Tarshis, L. (1979b), 'The macroeconomic effects of OPEC's price hikes', *Ontario Economic Council*, Proceedings of a conference on energy policies.

Tarshis, L. (1980), 'Post-Keynesian economics: a promise that bounced?', *American Economic Review. Papers and Proceedings*, vol. 70, pp. 10-15.

Tarshis,L. (1981), 'A macroeconomic analysis of stagflation', *Ontario Economic Council* Conference on Stagflation: Focus on Supply.

Tarshis, L. (1984), *World Economy in Crisis, Unemployment, Inflation and International Debt*, Canadian Institute for Economic Policy (Toronto: James Lorimer).

Tarshis,L. (1989a), 'Keynes' co-operative economy and his aggregate supply function', ch. 2 in this volume.

Tarshis, L. (1989b), Keynesianism in a single country: can it work?', *New Political Perspectives*, forthcoming.

Taylor, L. (1983), *Structuralist macroeconomics* (New York: Basic Books).

Thaler, R. and H. M. Shefrin (1981), An economic theory of self control', *Journal of Political Economy*, vol. 89 (April) pp. 396-406.

Thirlwall, A. P. *et al* (1983), 'Symposium: Kaldor's Growth Laws', *Journal of Post-Keynesian Economics*, vol. 5 (Spring) pp. 341-79.

Thirlwall, A. P. (1986), 'A general model of growth and development on Kaldorian lines', *Oxford Economic Papers*, vol. 38, pp. 199-219.

Tobin, J. (1978), 'Government deficits and capital accumulation', in D. A. Currie and W. Peters (eds), *Contemporary Economic Analysis*, vol. 2 (London: Croom Helm).

Tobin, J. (1980), *Asset Accumulation and Economic Activity* (Oxford: Basil Blackwell).

Torr, C. S. W. (1980), 'The distinction between an entrepreneur economy and a co-operative economy' (review note), *South African Journal of Economics*,vol. 48, no. 4, pp. 429-34.

Torr, C. S. W. *(1981), 'The role of the entrepreneur' (review note), South African Journal of Economics*, vol. 49, no. 3, pp. 283-8.

Townshend, H. (1937), 'Liquidity-premium and the theory of value, *Economic Journal*, vol. 47, no. 1 (March), pp. 157-69.

Veblen, T. B. (1899), *The Theory of the Leisure Class: An Economic Study of Institutions* (New York: Macmillan).

Veblen, T. B. (1909), 'The limitations of marginal utility', *Journal of Political Economy*, vol. 17, pp. 235-45, reprinted in Veblen (1936).

Veblen, T. B. (1919) *The Place of Science in Modern Civilisation, and Other Essays* (New York: Huebsch).

Veblen, T. B. (1936), *What Veblen Taught*, ed. W. C. Mitchell (New York: Augustus Kelley).

Veblen, T. B. (1964) *The Instinct of Workmanship* (New York: Augustus Kelly).

Vines, D. (1984), 'Review of Godley and Cripps (1983)', *Economic Journal*, vol. 94, pp. 397-9.

Walsh, V. and H. Gram (1980), *Classical and Neoclassical Theories of General Equilibrium* (Oxford: Oxford University Press).

Weber, M. (1922/1962), *Basic Concepts in Sociology*, trans. and introd. H. P. Secher (London: P. Owen).

Weintraub, S. (1958), *An Approach to the Theory of Income Distribution* (Philadelphia: Chilton).

Weintraub, S. (1961), *Classical Keynesianism, Monetary Theory and the Price Level* (Philadelphia: Chilton).

Weintraub, S. (1977a), 'The price level in the open economy', *Kyklos*, vol. 30, pp. 22-37.

Weintraub, S. (1977b), 'Hicksian Keynesianism: dominance and decline', in S. Weintraub (ed.), *Modern Economic Thought* (Philadelphia: University of Pennsylvania Press).

Weintraub, S. (1978a), *Capitalism's Inflation and Unemployment Crisis* (Boston, Mass.: Addison-Wesley).

Weintraub, S. (1978b), *Keynes, Keynesians and Monetarists* (Philadelphia, University of Pennsylvania Press).

Weintraub, S. (1980), 'Money supply and demand interdependence', *Journal of Post-Keynesian Economics*, vol. 2 (Summer) pp. 566–75.

Weintraub, S. (1980–1), 'Keynesian demand serendipity in supply-side economics', *Journal of Post-Keynesian Economics*, vol. 3 (Winter), pp. 181–91.

Weintraub, S. (1981), 'An eclectic theory of income shares', *Journal of Post-Keynesian Economics*, vol. 4 (Fall), pp. 10–24.

Weitzman, Martin (1984), *The Share Economy* (Cambridge, Mass.: Harvard University Press).

Wells, P. (1983), ' A post-Keynesian view of liquidity preference and the demand for money', *Journal of Post-Keynesian Economics*, vol. 5, pp. 523–36.

Wiles, P. (1983), 'Ideology, methodology and neoclassical economics', in Eichner (1983), pp. 61–89.

Williamson, O. E. (1975), *Markets and Hierarchies: Analysis and Antitrust Implications* (New York: Free Press).

Williamson, O. E. (1985), *The Economic Institutions of Capitalism: Firms, Markets, Relational Contracting* (London: Macmillan).

Winter, S. G. Jr (1964), 'Economic "natural selection" and the theory of the firm', *Yale Economic Essays*, vol. 4 (Spring), pp. 224–72.

Wiseman, J. (ed.) (1983), *Beyond Positive Economics?* (London: Macmillan).

Wood, A. (1975), A Theory of Profits (Cambridge: Cambridge University Press).

Wood, A. (1978), *A Theory of Pay* (Cambridge: Cambridge University Press).

Worswick, David and James Trevithick, (eds) (1983), *Keynes and the Modern World* (Cambridge: Cambridge University Press).

Yeager, L. B. (1987), 'Why subjectivism?' in M. N. Rothbard (ed.), *Review of Austrian Economics*, vol. 1, pp. 5–31.

Yeager, L. B. (1988), 'Reply to comment by Walter Block', in M. N. Rothbard and W. Block (eds), *Review of Austrian Economics* (Mass.: Lexington Books), vol. 2, pp. 209–10.

Yellen, Janet, L. (1980), 'On Keynesian economics and the economics of post-Keynesians', *American Economic Review, Papers and Proceedings*, vol. 70, pp. 15–19.

Name Index

267

Subject Index

273